Bulbs

How to Select, Grow and Enjoy

by George Harmon Scott

Published by HPBooks
P.O. Box 5367
Tucson, AZ 85703   602/888-2150
ISBN: 0-89586-146-1
Library of Congress Catalog Card Number: 81-84156
©1982 Fisher Publishing Inc.
Printed in U.S.A.

HPBooks

Publishers
Bill and Helen Fisher

Executive Editor
Rick Bailey

Editorial Director
Randy Summerlin

Editor
Scott Millard

Art Director
Don Burton

Book Design
Kathleen Koopman

For Horticultural Publishing Co.

Executive Producer
Richard M. Ray

Editor
Michael MacCaskey

Associate Editors
Susan Chamberlin,
Lance Walheim

Production Editor
Kathleen S. Parker

Technical Editor
James Bauml, Botanist,
Huntington Botanical Gardens,
San Marino, CA

Illustrations
Roy Jones

Major Photography
Michael Landis and William Aplin

Additional Photography
James Bauml, Karen Ecker,
Derek Fell, Alice Gans,
Pamela Harper

About the Author
George Harmon Scott has been growing bulbs for more than 30 years. He is one of the most respected horticulturists of his native southern California. In addition to his gardening expertise, Scott has been a garden writer for 20 years, including 10 years with the *Los Angeles Times Home Magazine.* Scott keeps informed of new trends in bulb gardening by visiting Holland frequently.

About the Cover
Darwin hybrid tulip 'Dover.' Photo by Derek Fell.

Acknowledgments
Polly Anderson, La Canada, CA
Bota Gardens, Richmond, British Columbia, Canada
John Catlin, La Canada, CA
Francis Ching, Department of Arborea and Botanic Gardens, Arcadia, CA
Robert Cowden, Horticulturist, Walnut Creek, CA
Davids & Royston Bulb Co., Inc., Gardena, CA
Mrs Elizabeth DeForest, Santa Barbara, CA
Addie Farrell, Napa, Ca
Joe Ghisletta Jr., Napa, CA
Irma Giacomini, St. Helena, CA
Charles Hardman, Temple City, CA
William Hawkinson, Department of Arborea and Botanic Gardens, Arcadia, CA
Theodore Kalil, Santa Barbara, CA
Dr. Harold Koopawatz, Director, University of California, Irvine Botanical Garden, Irvine, CA
Mary Landis, Napa, CA
John MacGregor, Botanist, Huntington Botanical Gardens, San Marino, CA
Fred Meyer, Rancho Vista Del Mundo, Santa Barbara, CA
Erwin Mojonnier, Mojonnier Flowers, Encinitas, CA
Robert Shufeldt, Pasadena, CA
A. Cort Sinnes, Napa, CA
Ray Sodomka, Turk Hesselund Nursery, Santa Barbara, CA
Robert and Evelyn Weidner, Encinitas, CA

Contents

Garden Magic

Mention the word bulbs to someone, and what images come to mind? *Color* is often mentioned, usually in the form of tulip beds, blended together like a brilliant rainbow. *Spring,* with its spirit of renewal, is also associated with bulbs. For many gardeners, the brilliant sun-gold yellow of a daffodil, more than any other flower, announces that spring has arrived.

This book is intended to introduce you to the magical group of plants known as *bulbs.* It is fascinating to plant a bulb, enjoy its bloom and have it disappear, knowing it will reappear. Most bulbs live for years, and it is fun to anticipate their annual return.

Bulbs are easy to grow and care for. For best results, you should know which ones are best suited to your tastes and climate, and details of their culture. Use the Encyclopedia of Bulbs, beginning on page 55, to guide you in your selections. It pictures and describes 250 bulbs. Favorites, such as tulips, hyacinths and daffodils, are included, along with many unusual kinds.

Adventurous gardeners are in for many exciting surprises when they experiment with some of the lesser-known bulbs. Although such experimentation is not always successful, I have had a great deal of fun growing out-of-the-ordinary bulbs. I encourage you to grow them too.

BULBS IN THE PAST
Before written history, about 1500 B.C., fresco paintings of *Crocus,* lilies and *Iris* were used to decorate the walls of the palace of Knossos, Crete. Garden designs that include bulbs have been found among the hieroglyphics of ancient Egypt. Persian sultans of the 15th and 16th centuries sent emissaries throughout the Near East to scout for tulips and other bulbs. In 1593, the Austrian ambassador to Turkey brought the first tulips to Europe. "Tulipmania" soon followed. During this period, speculation by the Dutch sent bulb prices to astronomical heights. It wasn't unusual for a single bulb of a new tulip variety to cost more than $5,000!

Since that time, Holland has been commonly associated with bulbs. The Dutch, more than any other people, have elevated bulb growing to an art. By seeking out new species and through extensive hybridizing, they have enhanced the vigor and beauty of bulbs.

BULBS ARE ADAPTABLE
Most bulbs are adapted to regions that have cold winters or seasonally dry conditions when dormancy is required. The majority of bulbs prefer dry, well-drained soil during dormancy. This often occurs shortly after flowering. Some, such as *Lilium* species, never become completely dormant. They should not be allowed to dry out completely.

Many variations exist among the different kinds of bulbs. This diversity is what makes bulbs such fascinating garden subjects. This book will help you learn the "personalities" of the different kinds of bulbs, common and unusual, helping to ensure successful bulb culture year after year.

Left: Fresh spring blooms of 'Big Chief' tulips brighten this garden scene. Above: 'Spellbinder' daffodils, aglow with afternoon sun, cast their spell on a young admirer.

Bulbs are Bold

Most bulbs appear above ground only when conditions are favorable to their growth. As a result, they may spend half to three-quarters of their life beneath the ground. Because their above-ground life is often short, they compensate by producing brilliant displays of colorful or fragrant flowers. These unique characteristics have made bulbs popular throughout the world.

The Dutch Bulb Growers Association sponsors Keukenhof, a 60-acre park devoted exclusively to the display of spring bulbs. Open only six weeks each year during April, May or June, depending on the weather, it is a spellbinding sight. Lawns, lakes, trees, fountains and sculptures are featured with the bulb plantings. Areas of the park are informal, with paths wandering among trees. Other sections are spectacular, with expansive plantings of bulbs in full bloom. After the brilliant spring show, the park is closed and plans are made for the following year.

Above: Colorful tulips welcome spring at Old Westbury Gardens, Long Island, New York.

Right: 'King Alfred' was introduced in the early 1900s, and quickly became the premier daffodil. As with all daffodils, it is a superb bulb for containers.

Above Left: 'Professor Einstein' is one of many popular daffodils. A gallery of daffodil varieties can be seen on pages 132 and 133.

Left: Keukenhof Gardens, Holland, is open to the public only six weeks out of the year. During this time, thousands visit the gardens daily, awed by the spectacular displays of spring-blooming bulbs.

Bulbs and Their Origins

Bulbs can be found all over the world. Probably the greatest number come from South Africa. The long, dry, summer weather has forced plants to retreat into life-preserving bulb forms. *Gladiolus* is the most widely grown, but *Freesia, Sparaxis, Tritonia, Ixia, Babiana, Lachenalia, Amaryllis, Clivia, Agapanthus* and many others are from there.

In Asia Minor, winters are exceedingly cold and summers are hot. Tulips have adapted to these conditions. Without cold, top growth begins before roots are able to develop sufficiently to support the plant. During the heat of summer, the bud is formed. *Tulipa clusiana* and *T. saxatilis* are among the few species that can thrive in mild-winter areas. Hyacinths prefer areas with similar conditions, but their close relative, *Muscari*, grape hyacinth, is well adapted to a wide range of climates.

From the western Mediterranean, Portugal, Spain and North Africa, come most of the *Narcissus* species. A few are native to England. Poeticus *Narcissus* come from the mountains of southern Europe. The Tazettas, a special group that produces foliage in the fall, grow in mild-winter areas that extend as far east as Japan.

Crocus also hails from around the Mediterranean. Certain species have adapted to other locales. *C. vernus,* from the Alps, requires cold to do well. *C. goulimyi* from Sparta and *C. imperati* from Naples have adapted to milder climates.

In most parts of the Northern Hemisphere, some species of *Iris* are native. Surprisingly, none are native to the Southern Hemisphere. The largest number come from the Mediterranean and from Asia Minor. *Iris x germanica* var. *florentina* became the symbol of the city of Florence. *I. pseudacorus,* the yellow water iris, was the emblem of Louis VII. It was stylized into the *Fleur-De-Lis,* the armorial emblem of the French royal family. *Iris germanica,* the bearded iris and its many hybrids, is probably the most widely grown.

Several *Irises* are natives of North America, such as the Louisiana iris and the Pacific Coast iris. *Irises* are also found in the Orient and Siberia. The tall, bulbous iris comes from North Africa, Spain and France. The early blooming dwarfs are from the eastern Mediterranean and Asia Minor.

The biggest contribution of bulbs from Asia are the many superb lilies. *Lilium auratum,* the gold-banded lily, *L. speciosum rubrum* with its pink shades and dots and *L. longiflorum,* the Easter lily, are from Japan. *L. regale,* the regal lily, is from Tibet. Many fine lilies also come from North America, Europe and Asia Minor.

Lycoris, from the mild areas of the Orient, is the counterpart to *Nerine* of South Africa. Both have similar, handsome flowers and are often confused with each other.

North and South America have all classes of bulbs: *true bulbs, corms, rhizomes, tubers* and *tuberous roots.* Rhizomes, tubers and tuberous roots are most numerous. They include favorites such as *Cannas, Dahlias,* tuberous begonias and *Caladiums.*

Hippeastrum are from South America. Botanists have separated them from the *Amaryllis* of South Africa. Dutch amaryllis were developed from *Hippeastrum,* and have managed to keep their now-incorrect name.

One genus, the legendary *Paramongaia* of Peru, is rare and seen only in a few botanical gardens. It resembles a large, fragrant, oversize daffodil.

According to modern-day bulb explorers, many bulbs remain to be discovered, especially in regions of South America and Russia.

Trillium grandiflorum, commonly known as *wake robin,* is native to North America. It requires moist, forestlike conditions.

Alstroemeria species and hybrids are tuberous-rooted plants native to South America. They make unusually long-lasting cut flowers, and come in a range of bright colors.

Tigridia pavonia is a summer-blooming bulb from Mexico. Large, showy flowers last only one day, but many flowers are produced over a long period.

Bulbous oxalis are found throughout the world, but the best garden kinds come from South America and South Africa. Most are deciduous and reliable plants in mild climates. In cold-climate areas, they make attractive house plants.

Narcissus, common daffodil, is planted more than any other bulb. Most are native to Portugal, Spain and England. Some are native to areas around the Mediterranean. The family is large—daffodils are adapted to almost every climate.

Anthericum is a fine bulb for Eastern gardens. Native to European Alps, it is a distant relative of the common house plant known as *spider plant, Chlorophytum comosum.*

Tulipa clusiana, the lady tulip, is a charming, informal species tulip. A Mediterranean native, it is one of the few tulips that grows well in southern California. It spreads by *droopers,* small bulbs that form at the root tip.

Crocus is native to the Mediterranean region. Flowers truly announce the beginning of spring: Without sufficient warmth from the sun, flowers cannot open.

Muscari is native to the Mediterranean region. It is a rampant naturalizer, sometimes to the extent that it becomes a weed. Its flowers are rich, deep blue—the best to combine with yellow daffodils.

Gladiolus is a large group of corms from South Africa. The most common hybrid comes in a wide range of sizes and colors.

Zantedeschia, the well-known calla lily, is native to South Africa. It is easy to grow in mild climates and is an adaptable house plant.

Amaryllis belladonna is a South-African native. Rainfall is usually sufficient to provide water needs, making it one of the easiest bulbs to naturalize in dry-summer areas.

Bulb Basics

Bulbs are ideal beginner's plants. Most contain enough stored food to provide for a season's growth, needing only moisture, warmth and light to grow. With minimum care, bulbs will succeed almost anywhere.

Even though bulbs are forgiving, it makes sense to learn their cultural requirements. The following section on bulb basics will acquaint you with the fundamentals of bulb growth and care. Understanding them will increase your pleasure of gardening with bulbs.

BUYING BULBS
One of the best places to purchase bulbs is at your nursery or garden center. You can inspect the bulbs, purchasing only the best ones. Nursery personnel can be a big help, providing information on bulb selection and care.

In the store, each bin of bulbs usually has a picture of the bulb in flower. The pictures are fairly accurate. If an exact picture is not available, a substitute of a similar bulb might be used. When the name of the variety is *printed* on the picture, it is most often accurate. If the name is *pasted* or *written* on the picture, it is likely to be a similar substitute.

Bulbs labeled as *mixed* are sometimes available at a discount. Pictures of mixed bulbs may have little relation to what is actually in the mix. Mixed bulbs may be made up of varieties that the supplier has in excess, or varieties that have lost their labels. If you are particular about the bulbs you want to grow, the savings may not be worthwhile.

LOOK BEFORE YOU BUY
Bulbs vary in size and quality, so examine them before you buy. Generally, the larger the bulb, the better the results at bloom time. Choose firm bulbs. With a few exceptions, soft, mushy bulbs indicate damage from rot fungus or insects. Bulbs missing their *tunics*—thin, outer coverings— may be dried out and will not bloom. They are usually lighter in weight than fresh bulbs. Avoid lily bulbs that are wilted and soft. This probably means they are dehydrated. Choose firm, moist bulbs. Do not buy any bulbs infested with insects.

All bulb types do not become available at the same time, so it may be necessary to make several trips to the nursery to get the freshest stock. For example, madonna lilies may arrive at the end of August, and tulips at the beginning of October. Oregon-grown daffodils do not arrive at the store the same time as those grown in Holland.

When bulbs go "on sale," it usually signals the end of the planting season, and retailers want to close out their stocks. Bulbs purchased at this time should be examined closely.

MAIL-ORDER SUPPLIERS
In addition to local sources, you can order bulbs from mail-order catalogs. A listing of several companies is provided on page 16. These suppliers

---

Left: Many kinds of bulbs are available from local nurseries or mail-order suppliers. Most bulbs should be stored in a cool, dry place until planting time. Some, such as lilies, should be kept moist until they are planted. Above: Bulb planting tool makes it easy to dig individual planting holes.

generally have a larger selection than retail nurseries. If you want to specialize in growing lilies, daffodils or *Iris*, for example, ordering by mail is a must. Many varieties are available only in these catalogs. Specialty catalogs that feature one group of bulbs usually contain the newest bulbs and novelties.

Mail-order bulbs are usually mailed so they will arrive at the proper planting time for your area. This is a big advantage when purchasing lilies, which should not be out of the ground any longer than necessary.

When you receive bulbs in the mail, open and examine packages immediately. Check for signs of damage. If the bulbs are injured, contact the company.

HORTICULTURAL SOCIETIES

An excellent way of acquiring bulbs is to go to sales sponsored by local horticultural societies. Members often donate their extra bulbs to the society to raise money. Many of these bulbs are not available from commercial sources, giving you an opportunity to grow out-of-the-ordinary bulbs. Check for such sales listed in your newspaper, in garden publications and on nursery bulletin boards.

MISTAKEN IDENTITY

Gardeners may buy the same type of bulb two years in a row and discover at bloom time that they have two different bulbs. This is an exasperating experience that seems to occur most often with tulips. One reason for this mix-up is the complicated distribution network of certain bulbs. A grower in Holland sells bulbs to a wholesaler in Holland, who sells them to a distributor in the United States. This person in turn sells them to a nursery, which finally sells them to you. In passing through so many hands, the labels can be switched.

If you order bulbs from a mail-order source that specializes in a certain type of bulb, you can be almost certain that you will receive what you ordered.

Sometimes the bulb in the garden does not resemble the emerald-green daffodil or cobalt-blue *Gladiolus* shown in the catalog. Occasionally, it is the photograph or printed matter that is inaccurate. In addition, various cultural conditions affect flower color. For example, a green flower can fade to yellow in full sun.

Tips for Buying Bulbs

Bulb	Comments
Achimenes	Small and brittle. Handle roots carefully.
Alstroemeria	Sometimes available growing in 1-gallon cans. Takes 3 to 4 years before flowers are produced from plants grown from seeds.
Amaryllis belladonna	Plant in fall when in bloom so growth cycle is not interrupted. If dug or planted any other time, bloom cycle can be set back for years.
Anemone	Bulbs vary greatly in shape. European bulbs look like dried raisins. United States bulbs are shaped like cones. With European bulbs, it is difficult to determine which end goes up or down. Plant sideways to be safe. Large bulbs are not necessarily the best. Select smaller, younger bulbs.
Canna	Usually tough. They are reliable performers unless they dry out.
Colchicum	Avoid soft spots, an indication of damage or rot.
Cyclamen	Check for small bumps from the tuber—new growth appears from these. These bumps are easily broken off. Without them, it takes bulb a year to recover.
Dahlia	Tubers should be firm and connected to a stem bud. If not, the tuberous root is worthless.
Endymion	Soft, fleshy bulb, unlike other bulbs.
Freesia	Bulbs have netted tunic, which should be held close to the corm.
Gladiolus	Quality determined by depth of bulb, not width. A small, thick bulb is superior to a large, flat bulb.
Hippeastrum	Large bulbs produce two or more spikes of flowers.
Hyacinthus	Carefully graded by size. The larger the bulb, the larger the flower spike. The largest, called *exhibition*, are often grown to be used in pots and hyacinth jars, but second-size bulbs make a respectable showing. They are usually grown in large beds. Handling bulbs may cause skin irritation. Keep away from eyes.
Hemerocallis	Daylily roots do not last long out of the ground, so plant or replant as soon as possible. Often available blooming in 1-gallon cans.
Iris	Large rhizomes accept a lot of abuse. For bulbous iris, look for firm, unwrinkled bulbs. Wrinkling can be a sign of drying out.
Lilium	Bulbs should be firm and moist, not shriveled. Bulbs should have roots intact. Lilies never go completely dormant, so plant bulbs as soon as possible.
Narcissus	Daffodils can be judged by the size of the bulb within their own group. Depending on species, bulbs can range from 1/2 inch to 5 inches wide. Avoid bulbs with soft, mushy spots, especially if near the basal plate. Lightweight bulbs are dried out and should be discarded.
Polianthes	With tuberose, it is commonly advised to buy them when green shoots begin to show. I believe green shoots are unnecessary.
Ranunculus	Bulb size does not determine size or quality of flower, but definitely influences the number of blooms.
Tulipa	Bulb should have brown, protective coating. Bulb without coating tends to dry out. Avoid tulips showing green shoots. They have probably been in the store a long time and are sending up what should be spring growth, but roots are not developed.
Zantedeschia	Select firm bulbs. Avoid those with soft spots, whether bulbs are common white, pink, or yellow.

Bulb Types

When selecting bulbs, you must be aware of the difference between the botanical definition and the everyday usage of the word *bulb.* To the botanist, only tulips, hyacinths, daffodils and a few others are considered *true bulbs.* But in common usage, crocus and gladiolus *corms,* dahlia *tubers* and iris *rhizomes* are referred to as *bulbs.* All of these store food that supports life until climatic conditions are right to renew growth.

Tubers are the swollen part of an underground stem. Like true bulbs and corms, they have leaf scales that can be almost invisible. The main body of a tuber is solid. Often, it is rounded or knobby, with the roots usually coming from the lower half. *Cyclamen, Anemones* and dog-tooth violets are typical tubers.

Rhizomes are underground stems that grow horizontally along the surface of the soil. Roots grow from the bottom of the rhizome. Leaves grow from the sides or top. Rhizomes grow horizontally, so it is possible for plantings to cover great distances. The bearded iris is a common rhizome.

True bulbs are the bases of stems enlarged and surrounded by fleshy, food-storing scales, which are actually rudimentary leaves. They usually have an oval or pear shape and a growing point at the central base. Bulbs live from year to year, adding layers of growth in *scales.* They have a *basal plate,* a disklike plate on the bottom of the bulb, from which roots develop. Daffodils and tulips have a hard shell that helps protect the bulb and retains moisture. Lilies lack this covering and are easily damaged by rough handling.

Tuberous roots are different from tubers in that the storage area is not part of the stem. Rather, the root holds the storage area, often separated from the stem. It is important that tuberous roots be connected to a stem with a bud. Without a bud, they are unable to grow. *Dahlia* and *Ranuculus* are tuberous roots.

Corms are composed of solid stem tissue with a growing tip at the apex. Roots emerge from the sides. The corm becomes depleted by the end of the growing season. A new corm forms to replace the depleted one to continue growth the following year. *Gladiolus* is a typical corm.

Growth Cycles of Bulbs

Most bulbs have cyclic periods of *growth, bloom* and *dormancy*. These cycles enable the bulb to survive periods of drought, cold or otherwise inhospitable weather. Bulbs that bloom in spring are dormant in winter, and have adapted to survive cold. Others such as *Colchicum* and *Gladiolus* are dormant during the dry season. The following illustrations show the growth cycles of popular bulbs—both above and below ground. Timing of the cycles will vary with climate and time of planting.

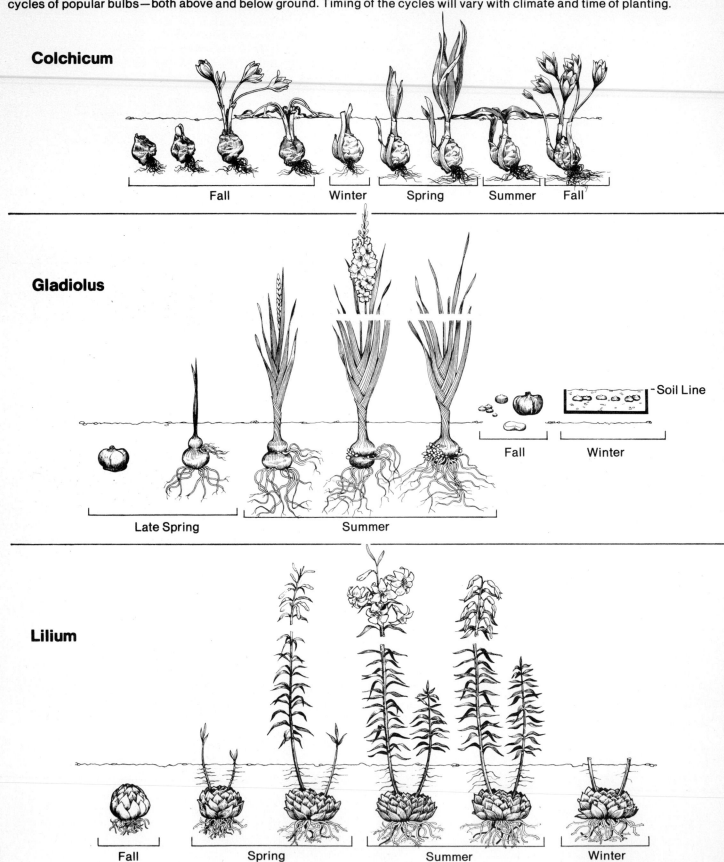

Colchicum

Fall   Winter   Spring   Summer   Fall

Gladiolus

Soil Line

Late Spring   Summer   Fall   Winter

Lilium

Fall   Spring   Summer   Winter

Dahlia

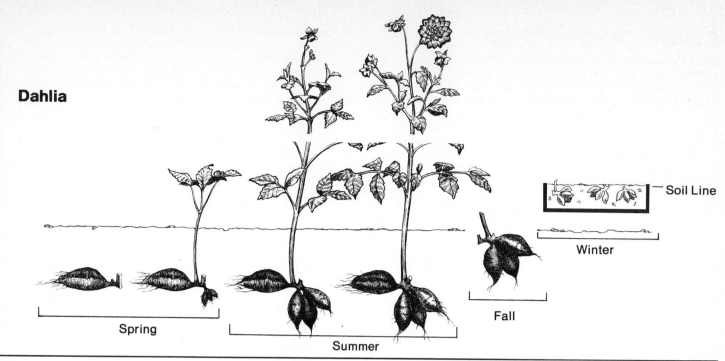

Soil Line

Spring

Summer

Fall

Winter

Crocus

Fall

Early Spring

Late Spring

Summer

Fall

Narcissus

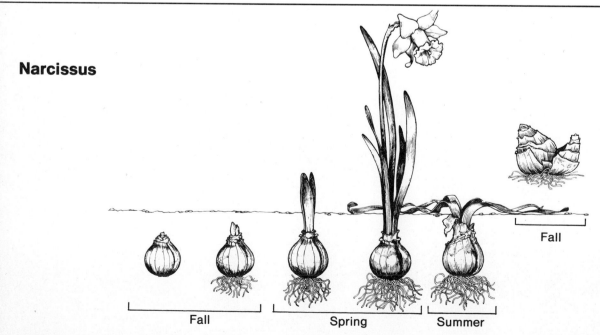

Fall

Spring

Summer

Fall

Bulbs by Mail

A wide selection of bulbs may be available from your local nursery, but sometimes you may not be able to find exactly what you need. Or, you may want to specialize in certain kinds of unusual bulbs. If this is the case, mail-order suppliers are dependable sources. Listed here are general and specialty suppliers of bulbs. Specialists are often the only source for rare bulbs.

General Suppliers

Breck's Dutch Bulbs
6523 N. Galena Road
Peoria, IL 61632
Catalog free.

Burpee Seed Co.
231 Burpee Building
Warminster, PA 18991
Catalog free.

DeJager Bulbs, Inc.
188 Asbury St. Dept. HPB
South Hamilton, MA 01982
Catalog free.

Dutch Gardens, Inc.
Box 400
Montvale, NJ 07645

International Growers Exchange
Box 397-P
East Farmington, MI 48024
Catalog $3.00.

John Scheepers
63 Wall St.
New York, NY 10005
Catalog free.

Mary Mattison Van Schaik
Cavendish, VT 05142
Catalog 50¢.

Messelaar Bulb Co.
Box 269
Ipswich, MA 01938
Catalog free.

Park Seed Co.
459 Cokesbury Road
Greenwood, SC 29647
Catalog free.

Quality Dutch Bulbs, Inc.
Dept. B
52 Lake Drive
Hillsdale, NJ 07642
Catalog free.

Wayside Gardens
503 Garden Lane
Hodges, SC 29695
Catalog $1.00.

White Flower Farm
Litchfield, CN 06759
Catalog $5.00.

Dahlia Specialists

Almand's Dahlia Gardens
2541 West Ave. 133
San Leandro, CA 94577

Blue Dahlia Gardens
G. Kenneth Furrer
San Jose, IL 62682

Forest View Gardens
Route 3, Box 136
Fairmont, WV 26554

Ruschmohr Dahlia Gardens,
H. Dewey Mohr, Prop.,
38 Vincent St. Box 884
Rockville Centre, NY 11571

White Dahlia Gardens
2480 S.E. Creighton Ave.
Milwaukie, OR 97222

Daylily Specialists

Cordon Bleu Farms
418 Buena Creek Road
San Marcus, CA 92069

Gilbert Wild & Son
1110 Joplin St.
Sarcoxie, MO 64862
Catalog $2.00.

Lee Bristol Nursery
Sherman, CN 06784
Send long, self-addressed, stamped envelope for catalog.

Louisiana Nursery
Route 7, Box 43
Opelousas, LA 70570

Seawright Gardens
134 Indian Hill
Carlisle, MA 01741
Catalog $1.00.

Tranquil Lake Nursery
45 River St.
Rehoboth, MA 02769
Catalog 25¢.

Gladiolus Specialists

Baldridge Glads
Sidney L. Baldridge
1729 19th Ave.
Greeley, CO 80631

Coastal Bulb Farm
John Ooosterwyk
Box 97
Hamstead, NC 28443

Flad's Glads
2109 Cliff Court
Madison, WI 53713

Gladside Gardens
Corys M. Heselton
61 Main St.
Northfield, MA 01360
Also carry *Dahlias* and tropical bulbs.

Kingfisher Glads
Sam N. Fisher
11345 Moreno Ave.
Lakeside, CA 92040

Noweta Gardens, Inc.
900 Whitewater Ave.
St. Charles, MN 55972

Pleasant Valley Glads
Gary Adams
163 Senator Ave.
Agawam, MA 01001

Valley Stream Farm
D.R. Woudstra
Orano, Ontario, Canada
L0B 1M0

Iris Specialists

Alpenflora Gardens
17985 40th Ave.
Surrey (Cloverdale) B.C.
Canada V3S 4N8
Good selection of Pacific Coast Natives.

Bay View Gardens
1201 Bay St.
Santa Cruz, CA 95060
Many species iris. Catalog $1.00.

Borbeleta Gardens
10078 154th Ave.
Elk River, MN 55330
Siberian iris only.

Cooley's Gardens
Box 126
301 S. James St.
Silverton, OR 97381
Tall bearded iris.
Catalog $2.00, deductible from first order.

Cordon Bleu Farms
418 Buena Creek Road
San Marcus, CA 92069

Louisiana Nursery
Route 7, Box 43
Opelousas, LA 70570
Louisiana iris.

Melrose Gardens
309 Best Road South
Stockton, CA. 95206
Catalog $1.00.

Schreiner's Gardens
3625 Quinby Road, NE
Salem, OR 97303
Many varieties. Color catalog $2.00.

David B. Sindt - Irises
1331 West Cornellia
Chicago, IL 60657
Pumilas and small-bearded iris.
Catalog on request.

Thompson and Morgan
Box 100
Farmingdale, NJ 07727
Iris seeds.

Tranquil Lake Nursery
45 River St.
Rehoboth, MA 02769
Catalog 25¢.

Vagabond Gardens
11115 Bodega Highway
Sebastopol, CA 95472
Bearded, Siberian, Louisiana and Pacific-Coast hybrids.
Reblooming irises. Catalog $1.00.

Gilbert Wild & Son
Box 338
Sarcoxie, MO 64882
Color catalog $2.00.

Lily Specialists

Rex Lilies
Box 774
Port Townsend, WA 98368

Strahm's Lilies
Box 2216
Harbor, OR 97415
Color catalog 50¢.

Narcissus Specialists

Blom's Daffodils
Leavesden, Watford
Hertfordshire, England
Color catalog.

Carncairn Daffodils
Carncairn Lodge, Broughshane
Ballymena BT43-7HF
County Antrim, Northern Ireland
Free catalog.

John Lea
Dunley Hall, Stourport on Severn
Worcestershire, England
Descriptive list available.

Grant E. Mitsch Novelty Daffodils
Box 218
Hubbard, OR 97032
Specialists in pinks and species hybrids.
Color catalog $2.50, deductible from first order.

P & G Phillips
P.O. Box 177
Otorohanga, New Zealand
Many Southern Hemisphere hybrids.

Rathowden
Knowehead, Dergmoney, Omagh
County Tyrone, Northern Ireland
Many show favorites. Color catalog available.

River's Edge Farm
Rt. 3, Box 228A
Gloucester, VA 23061

Mrs. J. Abel Smith
Orchard House, Letty Green
Near Hertford, England
Pinks specialist. Descriptive list available.

Nerine

Nerine Nurseries
Welland, Worcestershire
WR 13 6LN, England
Catalog $2.00.

Planting Bulbs

Too often, bulbs are thought to grow and bloom regardless of how they are planted. Although this is true to a certain extent, you can increase your success by supplying bulbs with good growing conditions.

EXAMINE BULBS

Before you plant, look bulbs over closely to determine their quality. Soft bulbs or those showing signs of rot should be discarded. If a particularly rare or valuable bulb shows damage, you might be able to save it by removing the bad spot with a sharp knife. Dust with sulfur or a fungicide to help prevent spread of disease. Bulbs that are lightweight are usually dehydrated or dead, and should be discarded. Lilies without protective covers often have dehydrated scales. You may be able to save them by placing them between wet towels or damp peat moss until the scales plump up again. *Anemones* that are overly dry may also benefit from this treatment. Refer to the chart on page 12 for additional information on how to buy bulbs.

PREPARE SOIL

Most bulbs prefer a soil that is not too acid. Any soil that has a pH 6.0 or below should be adjusted. It is a good idea to test the soil of a new planting area tested. Home test kits are available that will tell you the soil's pH. To be absolutely accurate, a laboratory soil test interpreted by an expert is best. State universities in all states except California and Illinois perform soil tests for a fee. Look in the white pages of your phone book under "county extension agent," "cooperative extension service," or contact your state university to determine the soil-testing laboratory nearest you. In California and Illinois, consult the Yellow Pages of your phone book for a listing of private soil-testing laboratories.

You can adjust the soil pH yourself by adding lime to the soil, but the trick is to know how much to add. You can add small amounts, testing soil after each application until the proper pH level was obtained.

In some areas, particularly in the Southwest, soil that is highly alkaline—having a pH of 9.0 and above—can be a problem. Alkaline soil can be adjusted by adding sulfur. Follow package directions closely.

Soak the soil two or three days before planting to make the soil easier to work. When the soil is moist but not muddy, turn it over and break up the clods. It is important that the soil drain well. Most bulbs rot if they sit in soggy soil too long. A heavy clay soil, which tends to drain slowly, can be improved by working in organic matter such as compost, peat moss or leaf mold. Organic materials added to sandy soil help retain moisture and nutrients in the root zone. Do not mix animal manures that are high in nitrogen into the soil. They may burn the bulbs.

Add superphosphate after organic matter has been mixed into the soil. Follow soil test recommendations or directions on package label. Work it into the future root zone of the bulbs. Unlike nitrogen, superphosphate takes a long time to move downward to the root zone, so do not apply it on the soil surface. After all materials have been added, rake the soil level. You are now ready to plant.

How Deep to Plant Bulbs?

As a general rule, plant bulbs at a depth equal to twice the height of the bulb. In heavy clay soil, plant slightly closer to the surface. Plant bulbs in containers as shallow as possible to allow maximum room for root growth. Bulbs that remain in the ground for more than a season will adjust, gradually moving to their preferred depth.

PLANTING

Before you plant bulbs, you should make some sort of plan. Use a stick or stakes and string to mark lines where each group of bulbs is to be located. For natural-looking plantings, you can toss the bulbs on the ground and plant them where they fall. This avoids even, unnatural spacing. The biggest concentration of bulbs should be at the center of a group. This mimics the appearance of bulbs that multiply naturally in the wild. For more on designing with bulbs, see pages 41 to 53.

Bulbs can be planted two different ways. One method is often used for large, formal beds. Remove the soil to an even depth. The bulbs can be placed an equal distance apart and covered with the proper amount of soil. This assures that bulbs of the same variety are planted at the same depth. They will bloom at the same time with stems of equal length.

A second method is to dig individual holes for each bulb with a trowel or other tool. If the ground is loose and well prepared, you can use a bulb planter. This is a conical-shaped device that looks like a tin can open at both ends, with a handle on the top. When pressed into the soil and pulled out, the bulb planter brings the soil with it, creating a hole. The bulb is placed in the hole and the soil is returned. Another device used in turf plantings is a short cylinder at the end of a pole. When pushed into the ground, it cuts out a circle of turf that can be replaced after the bulb is planted. See photo 1 below.

After planting bulbs, rake some fertilizer into the soil. Select a complete fertilizer low in nitrogen, such as a 5-5-5 or 5-10-10. *Complete* means that the major nutrients—nitrogen, phosphorus and potassium—are included.

1. Bulb planting tool makes individual planting holes. Markings are used as a depth gage. Recommended planting depth of bulb means to bottom of hole, not top of bulb. If planting depth for bulb is 6 inches, make hole 6 inches deep.

2. Place bulbs in individual holes. Growing tip should face up. If you can't identify the growing tip, place bulb on its side and it will adjust on its own. Check to be sure there are no air pockets beneath bulbs.

3. Water thoroughly and deeply to settle the soil after planting. Water requirements for newly planted bulbs vary considerably, depending on the bulb, the season planted and climate. Refer to the individual bulb descriptions on pages 58 to 157.

4. Add a layer of organic mulch to reduce evaporation of soil moisture, moderate temperatures and deter weeds. Many mulches are available. Or consider overplanting with a ground cover for a colorful, living mulch. See suitable list of ground covers on page 47.

Follow the instructions on the fertilizer label. See page 21.

Be sure to label the location and identity of your bulbs. If you don't, you may accidently injure them while digging in the bed at a later date, or plant over them. Plastic or metal labels last longer than wood. Mark with waterproof pens or pencils.

BULBS HAVE VARIED PLANTING DEPTHS

The fact that different bulbs are planted at various depths may seem odd when you consider that all bulbs originate from seeds dropped on the earth's surface. But over the years, bulb growers have found that tulips and daffodils planted near the surface break up into bunches of small bulbs. This is good for reproduction of the species, but not for the following year's bloom. Tall growers such as *Gladiolus* and lilies need the extra support of deep planting to hold them upright. Even then, they often require stakes for supports. *Lilium candidum* is one exception. It should be planted near the soil surface.

The general rule is to plant large bulbs at a depth equal to twice the depth of the bulb, and small bulbs slightly deeper than twice their depth. Bulbs in marginally cold areas benefit from slightly deeper planting to escape below-freezing temperatures. Bulbs in light, sandy soils should be planted a little deeper than normally recommended, and a little shallower in heavy clay soils.

Some bulbs have *contractile* roots that pull the bulb down to the natural desired depth. The beautiful *Leucocoryne,* glory-of-the-sun, has not learned when to cease its downward journey! A rock or piece of broken crockery can be placed under the bulb to halt its continuous descent.

The trench method of planting bulbs is often used for tulips and hyacinths. Remove soil to recommended depth. Level bottom of trench and place bulbs in trench. Bulbs planted at the same depth bloom at the same time and grow to the same maximum height.

Cover trench-planted bulbs with soil. Add soil carefully so that bulbs are not dislodged from their spots when first layer of soil is added.

If plants will need staking, drive stake into the ground at planting time. This is commonly recommended for *Dahlias.* The tuberous roots extend some distance to the sides and can be damaged if stakes are driven into ground after planting.

Gophers, mice, squirrels and chipmunks love tulips, *Crocus* and *Gladiolus* but ignore daffodils. Bulbs susceptible to rodent damage can be protected by encircling the bulbs in chicken wire.

Bulb Care

Ample water is the most important requirement for bulb growth. In nature, bulbs in cold-winter areas receive moisture from melting snow. In mild or warm regions, bulbs receive heavy seasonal rains. Good soil drainage is necessary when bulbs are subjected to large amounts of water. Without fast drainage, water stagnates in the root zone. This can suffocate and kill the bulbs.

When watering bulbs, water should go deep into the soil—one foot deep is not too much. This promotes deep rooting. Frequent, light sprinklings do not do the job properly. The soil surface remains moist, which encourages viruses, fungi, snails and slugs. Because the water penetrates into the top few inches of soil, the roots stay near the surface. This makes them susceptible to drying out in periods of warm and windy weather.

Give bulbs a long, slow soak when flower buds first appear. Watering at this time means less water is needed when the bulb is in bloom. This avoids problems caused when water accumulates on the flowers, which makes the stems sag and bend. In nature, *Crocus* and tulips eliminate this problem by closing their blooms tightly on cloudy, rainy days.

Sprinklers that spray or shoot water can be damaging to blooms. Soaker hoses or flood irrigation are probably the most effective ways to water and do not damage blooms.

Water bulbs regularly while they are blooming, and for a short time after bloom. Water is necessary because bulbs are building up food reserves for the next year. Generally, water bulbs until the leaves begin to turn brown. This stage signals that bulbs are beginning to rest and enter dormancy. After bloom, I often give my bulbs a diluted solution of liquid fish-based fertilizer.

WEED CONTROL

Weeds steal nutrients and moisture away from bulb plants. They are also unsightly. Some may be so vigorous that they actually cover the bulb foliage and reduce the amount of available sunlight. Weeds also harbor pests such as slugs, snails and cutworms. The best practice is to pull or hoe weeds when they are small, before they can reseed and return tenfold.

Tall-growing bulbs should be staked, especially if weather is likely to be windy or rainy. Tie plant to stakes in two locations so top will not snap off. A pencil-thick bamboo stake is plenty for *Gladiolus.* Use a heavy redwood stake for *Dahlia.*

Herbicides are tricky to use in a flower bed because of the diversity of plants. If weeds become a serious problem, weed seeds can be killed with *Vapam,* a soil fumigant, before preparing the bed for the following year.

GENERAL CARE

When cutting flowers for a bouquet or arrangement, leave as much of the foliage on the growing stem as possible. Leaves are important because they manufacture food that the bulb stores for future growth and flower production. If you remove too much foliage, the vigor of the bulb may be decreased the following year.

Snip off flowers as soon as they have passed their prime. Allowed to remain, the spent flowers form seeds, which takes a lot of the plant's energy. It is more important for the strength of the plant to go back to the bulb.

If flowering diminishes, it can be caused by overcrowding, or loss of sunlight due to the spreading branches of nearby shrubs and trees.

This often occurs with mature bulb plantings. To eliminate this problem, dig, separate and replant bulbs. See pages 24 and 25.

Some bulbs such as daffodils accept moderate watering throughout the year. Others, such as certain *Ranunculus, Anemone* and *Calochortus* species, rot during summer heat if the surrounding soil remains damp.

FERTILIZER

Supplementary feeding is valuable. For most bulbs, phosphorous and potash are more important than nitrogen. By reading the numbers on a fertilizer label, you can determine the amounts of these three primary nutrients in the package. They are always listed in the same order: *nitrogen, phosphorus* and *potassium.* A 2-10-10 or a 5-10-10 ratio, low in nitrogen, is better for bulbs than one high in nitrogen, such as 10-5-5. If minor nutrients such as iron are included in the formula, so much the better. If your soil is deficient in nitrogen, the foliage of the bulbs will take on a pale, yellowish cast. In this case, use a fertilizer that is slightly higher in nitrogen.

The best time to apply fertilizer is when the shoots first appear. Moisten soil and rake fertilizer into the top few inches. Avoid getting dry fertilizer on the foliage, or it will damage the plant. After the bulbs finish blooming and are storing energy before going dormant, apply fertilizer a second time.

MULCH

A mulch is a covering of material over the ground. In addition to making the garden look neater, a mulch helps reduce the weed population. A layer of organic mulch helps keep the soil cool, retains moisture and eventually breaks down to improve the soil composition. When adding a mulch, don't apply a thin covering. A layer 3 to 4 inches deep is best in most situations.

One of the best mulches is screened compost. Others include grass clippings, ground bark products and leaf mold. Some mulches are by-products of agriculture, and are available only in certain areas. These would include cottonseed hulls, peanut hulls and grape pomace. Check locally with your county extension agent or your nurseryman for recommendations and availability.

An organic mulch over the root area of bulbs is benefical. It looks attractive, reduces loss of soil moisture through evaporation and helps prevent weed growth.

As soon as flowers have passed their prime, snip them off. Flowers allowed to stay on the plant form seeds, which takes energy away from the bulb.

Pests and Diseases

Most bulbs, corms, tubers and rhizomes are relatively free of pests and diseases, but problems do occur. Many can be eliminated or controlled by planting bulbs at the correct depth and providing them with proper care.

One of the most important things you can do is watch for the first signs of a pest attack. By discovering and treating problems early, the damage to your bulbs will be minimized. Read and follow all label directions carefully when using insecticide and fungicide products.

Keep in mind that *you* can be your bulb's worst enemy. Learn their cultural requirements, so that you don't plant sun-loving bulbs in the shade or vice versa. You can mistakenly shorten the life span of bulbs by removing the foliage before the bulb is able to store up strength for the next year. Or, you may unknowingly place a trowel or shovel through a bulb hidden underground.

ANIMAL PESTS

Gophers and mice frequently attack bulbs, both in the ground and in storage. One exception is daffodils, which are normally left alone. Keep such pests away from bulbs in the ground by lining planting holes with chicken wire. Follow the same procedure when storing bulbs. Line the storage area with chicken wire to keep out animal pests.

Birds and rabbits love the tender, new buds of *Ranunculus* and lilies as the buds emerge from the ground. Until they toughen, cover buds with plastic bird netting or chicken wire.

INSECT PESTS

Aphids damage plants by sucking plant juices, weakening the plant and distorting growth. Some transmit plant diseases in the process. Aphids multiply fast, so take action as soon as you spot them. Spray infested plants with a soap and water solution consisting of 1 teaspoon of dish soap per gallon of water. Or, spray with the chemical malathion. *Systemic insecticides,* which are absorbed by the plant, are effective and last longer. Aphids that inhabit the soil attack roots. Eliminate them by drenching the soil around bulbs with malathion.

Mealybugs are wingless insects that cover themselves with a sticky, cottony substance. They usually hide at

Spray for gladiolus thrips at the first sign of discolored foliage. Use a *systemic* pesticide—one that is absorbed by the plant. Systemic granules worked into soil at the base of plant are slow acting but effective.

the base of bulbs that have strap-shaped leaves. You may not notice mealybugs until you see distorted leaves, caused by their constant sucking. Control with a systemic insecticide or oil spray.

Mites can enter a bulb that has been bruised or damaged during digging or handling. They begin to parasitize the bulb during storage. Cyclamen mites colonize on the undersides of leaves, stunting growth and causing leaves to curl. The surest way to control them is with a miticide such as dicofol, sold under the trade name Kelthane.

Narcissus flies prefer *Narcissus* species but damage other bulbs. They attack *Hymenocallis,* laying their eggs

on new foliage during late spring and early summer. There are two species of these flies. The larger lays one egg; the smaller lays several. You may notice them buzzing over dying bulb foliage. Both look like small bees but they have two wings instead of four. They lay eggs in the center of the foliage. Eggs mature into grublike pests that crawl down into the bulb and eat it. Grubs may also tunnel into the soil to the bulb's basal plate and eat into the bulb from there.

Infected bulbs are soft and spongy. The grubs can be found inside. Dust the foliage with diazinon early in the season before the flies have a chance to lay their eggs.

Normally, it is best to discard infected bulbs. But if a bulb is especially valuable, the grubs can be killed by soaking the bulb in hot water 110F (43C) for one hour. This might damage the bulb, but is the only way to save it. You can only plant the bulb and wait.

Nematodes damage bulbs by attacking bulb roots. A severe infestation is difficult to eliminate. They are most prevalent in the warm South, where the lack of cold temperatures allows them to proliferate. Susceptible bulbs should be grown in pots in a sterile potting soil.

Slugs and snails can be dispatched by hand picking, traps or poison bait. It helps to keep the garden area clean of trash and debris, which are their hiding places. Snails love to climb the stems and nibble the flowers of daffodils and other members of the *Amaryllis* family. Their presence is easily spotted in early morning by their slimy trails on paths and sidewalks. If they aren't too numerous, snails and slugs can be hand-picked and destroyed. Or, use snail bait containing metaldehyde or mesurol. Apply bait just after a rain or watering when snails and slugs are most active.

Thrips can be devastating to the usually tough *Gladiolus,* especially those planted late in the season. Thrips hide in the forming leaves and in the buds. When infestations are heavy, buds and leaves look distorted and often have silvery markings. Control by using a systemic insecticide such as Orthene. Thrips also hibernate on the corms through the winter. Scatter naphthalene flakes over them while in storage, or soak in water 110F (43C) for 20 to 30 minutes.

DISEASES

Mildew is a serious problem that plagues tuberous begonias, but it is one of the easiest diseases to prevent and control. Provide good air circulation and avoid watering plants at night so that foliage remains dry. Control mildew with a fungicide spray such as benlate as soon as you notice it.

Botrytis is a fungus disease identified by brown or gray spots that form on leaves. It can spread quickly. It kills bulbs gradually by sapping their strength. Lilies and tulips are especially susceptible to botrytis. It can spread to other bulbs of the same family, so remove and destroy diseased plants immediately.

It helps to check plants frequently for signs of pests and diseases. This gardener is using a magnifying glass to see if tiny thrips are damaging his *Gladiolus* blooms.

Basal rot is usually the result of poor drainage or high heat. Eventually, the *basal plate*—the area from which the roots grow—is destroyed and the bulb becomes soft. In warm climates, basal rot of trumpet daffodils is common. Control by planting the bulbs deep, to 8 inches, so soil temperature around the bulb does not exceed 75F (24C).

Viruses can be identified by streaked flowers and foliage. Occasionally, leaves and stems are twisted and distorted. Some virus-infected plants are not seriously damaged and actually produce unusual yet attractive colorations. For example, a virus was the cause of "broken tulips." Broken tulips were considered rare and unusual during Holland's period of "Tulipmania." You can grow broken tulips, but do not plant them with regular tulips or the virus may be transferred.

In most cases, a virus can cause a serious disease that may eventually kill the bulb. If you discover a lily infected with a virus, destroy it immediately before it spreads to other plants.

Viruses are often carried from one plant to another by aphids. Control these pests to reduce problems from virus diseases.

Mosaic virus damages lilies and bulbous irises. It causes spotting, streaking and stunting of the flower stem. No cure is known.

Propagating Bulbs

Bulbs are normally propagated in one of two ways: by seeds, or by dividing and planting some part of the plant—bulb offset, corm, bulbil—that is able to produce a new bulb.

SEPARATING BULBS

Many bulbs form new bulbs around the original. When they become so crowded that flowering starts to diminish, it is time to dig and separate them. For instance, daffodils form a large clump of bulbs after several years. When dug, the smaller bulbs normally fall away from the parent plant. If bulbs do not separate easily, use a sharp knife to separate them.

Treat cuts with a fungicide to reduce the potential for insect or disease damage. Each new bulb must have a section of basal plate or it will not be able to grow.

DIVIDING BULBS

Division is used to increase the stock of rhizomes, tubers and tuberous roots. A clean, sharp knife is usually required to divide them because they do not fall apart as easily as true bulbs.

Dig rhizomes such as *Iris* and *Cannas* when they become overly crowded. Use the knife to divide the rhizomes. Leave two new rhizomes with their fan of leaves connected with an old rhizome. This helps ensure the best bloom the following

year. Treat cuts with a fungicide. Allow them to dry and heal for one or two days before planting.

Daylilies can be dug and separated easily. Simply washing the soil away from the roots often separates the new plants. They should bloom with identical flowers the next year.

Tubers such as *Begonias* and *Cyclamen* can be divided as new growth begins. At that time, the location of buds on the tuber is most evident. This is important because each division requires a bud to grow. Dust cuts with a fungicide and replant after cuts have healed.

A tuberous root such as *Dahlia* must be connected to a living bud on the stem. The stem can be split with a

Daffodils, shown above, tulips, lilies, *Amaryllis* and bulbous iris are usually increased by separating offsets. When mature, offsets should pull apart easily. Be sure each offset has a section of basal plate—roots develop from it.

Rhizomatous iris are divided after four or five seasons of growth. After flowering—usually midsummer—dig, divide and replant. For fastest multiplication, divide into single fans, each with a section of rhizome.

Tuberous-rooted bulbs such as *Dahlias* are best divided in spring just before planting, and can also be divided in fall. Each divided section must have at least one bud. Buds are easiest to notice in spring, when they are beginning to grow.

Some lilies develop small bulbs, *bulbils,* in the leaf axils. Often, they develop into separate plants while still attached to the mother plant. Plant the small bulbs in flats of moistened potting soil before they fall to the ground.

knife. Often, buds are more apparent in the spring just prior to planting.

BULBILS, BULBLETS AND CORMLETS

Bulbils are miniature bulbs that form in the leaf axils on the stems of certain lilies such as *Lilium tigrinum* and *L. bulbiferum*. They sometimes form a rudimentary leaf and root. When mature, they disengage easily from the stem, and can be planted the same as a bulb.

Bulblets are similar but they form at the base of the stem, often underground. They can be removed when the stem dries. Plant bulbils and bulblets one inch deep. They generally bloom in one to three years.

Corms such as *Gladiolus*, *Freesia* and *Ixia* produce a new corm on top of the old, which withers away. However, small, numerous *cormlets*, or miniature corms, can be found around the base of the new corm. Plant the same as regular corms. They generally bloom after one year.

BULB SCALES

The fleshy scales of lilies can be removed to form a new bulb at their base. They should be inserted into a mixture of sand and leaf mold, or laid flat on damp peat moss. Keep humidity high by covering the flat with a clear plastic bag. For best results, maintain a temperature as close as possible to 70F (21C).

LEAF CUTTINGS

This method is confined almost entirely to the *Gesneriads*, which include the popular *Sinningia* and *Gloxinia*. Detach a leaf with a small section of stalk. Insert it upright to the base of the leaf in a mixture of peat moss and sand. *Begonias* and *Cyclamen* can also be propagated this way. It is possible to propagate a few bulbs such as *Muscari*, *Lachenalia* and *Haemanthus* by leaf cuttings, but this is not a common practice.

STEM CUTTINGS

Some bulbs can be propagated by *stem cuttings*. Stems cut from tuberous begonias and *Achimenes* bloom the same year they are planted.

Corms such as *Crocus* and *Gladiolus* are useless after they have flowered, but a new corm forms on top of the old one. Pull off and discard the old corm. *Cormels,* small corms that form around the base of the new corm, can be planted.

Many lilies are easy to propagate. Remove individual scales from bulb. Dip scales in hormone rooting powder and place in moistened perlite, shown above or sand, peat moss or vermiculite. A bubil will form at each scale base.

Tuberous begonias, *Dahlias* and *Achimenes* develop new bulbs from stem cuttings. A hormone powder aids root development and helps prevent decay.

Gloxinias are propagated by leaf cuttings. Well-developed green leaves are removed from the bulb top and placed in the rooting media. Bury stem several inches below the surface.

SCOOPING AND SCORING

The hyacinth is probably the most difficult of all bulbs to propagate. Although it reproduces itself each year, it multiplies slowly, and has to be coaxed into increasing its numbers. One common propagation method is called *scooping.* Using a knife with a curved blade, remove the entire basal plate from the bulb, including the main sprout. The bulb then forms bulblets at the base of each scale. These can be removed and planted.

Scoring is also used to propagate hyacinths. Using a straight knife, make three complete cuts across the base. Each cut should go through the center of the basal plate. In the fall, the mother bulb, along with the bulblets, can be planted about 4 inches deep. In the spring, the bulblets send up a lot of leaves as the mother bulb withers away.

Scooped bulbs produce up to 60 bulbs but take five years before they reach blooming size. Scored bulbs produce about half as many but require three to four years to mature.

SEEDS

Most bulbs can be grown from seeds. It is simple to do. Allow bulbs to flower and produce seeds. When seeds are completely dry, you can remove them for planting. Seeds started from bulb species usually produce a plant similar to the parent, but slight differences in height, size or shape of flower and color sometimes occur. This is called *natural variation.* When man creates new bulbs from seeds by *hybridizing,* changes are more drastic. Bulbs with good plant form are deliberately crossed with similar bulbs of particularly good color. The hope is that among the seedlings, one having the best attributes of both parents will appear.

When bulbs are hybridized, seedlings of mixed parentage are produced. Present-day tulips, *Gladiolus* and *Iris* look little like their ancestral parents. When naturally pollinated seeds of these hybrid plants are grown, variations usually result. Occasionally, a plant of considerable interest is produced. But because the mother plant was a *selected hybrid*—most often the best of a group of seedlings—her progeny are seldom as attractive.

Hybridizing between species can cause bulbs to produce sterile seeds. The same thing occurs in the animal kingdom. When a mare (horse) is bred with a donkey, the offspring, a mule, is sterile. Some of the beautiful show daffodils have reached the end of their evolution and are now producing sterile seeds.

To hybridize bulbs from seeds, you must do your own pollinating. To ensure production of many fertile seeds, select flowers of the same species. In general, the pollen from the male parent has more influence on the *color* of the flower. The female parent that produces the seeds has more influence on the *size* and *shape* of the flower. As an example, you may want to cross a pink daffodil with a white Triandrus daffodil, which has several flowers to a stem. The hope is that you will get a quality Triandrus with pink flowers.

After selecting flowers, it is necessary to protect them from outside pollination before you make your cross. Cover the immature blooms of the flowers you intend to cross with a paper bag and secure with a rubber band. This keeps insects from reaching them. Many bulbs are *self-fertile,* meaning they have the ability to polinate themselves. To prevent this, remove *anthers,* the male organ in the flower, as soon as they become evident.

To make the cross, remove the *anther* (male) of one flower and place its powdery pollen onto the *stigma* (female) of another flower. This is done by rubbing the anther onto the stigma. The best time to do this is when the stigma is sticky, which means it is receptive to the pollen. Look for glistening on the tip of the stigma.

After pollinating, cover flowers with paper bags to prevent insects from transferring any more pollen. Leave bags over flowers for several days. If your pollination is a success, seeds will form.

Harvest seeds after they are completely dry, then plant them in a soil mix in flats. Place the flats in a warm, sheltered location where they are protected from pests. Keep the soil mix moist until the seeds germinate. Water regularly until they can be transplanted to individual containers. When the seedlings reach sufficient size, they can be transplanted into the garden.

For the first three years, the immature bulb may produce only foliage. After this period, who knows what will happen?

A close-up look at a daffodil flower displays the *anthers,* the male organ of the flower, surrounding the *stigma,* the female organ.

Storing Bulbs

Many bulbs are dug and stored while they are dormant to protect them from cold, heat or moisture. Most commonly, they are stored to protect them from freezing in the ground during winter.

In cold areas, evergreen bulbs such as *Cliva*, *Agapanthus* and *Crinum* need light and water during winter. It is best to grow these bulbs in containers and bring them indoors during cold periods. Some, such as *Cannas*, continue to bloom indoors for several months if given sufficient light and warmth.

The majority of bulbs that require storage are deciduous kinds that would otherwise freeze in the ground. They are dug and stored in a loose material such as vermiculite, sand, perlite or peat moss. There should be enough material to keep the bulbs from touching. This helps protect them from bruising one another and reduces the spread of disease.

Bulbs and corms that have a protective coating or hard shells, such as *Gladiolus*, *Crocosmia*, *Tigridia*, *Freesia*, *Achimenes* and *Hymenocallis*, should be stored in a completely dry location. *Gladiolus* and other South-African corms can be tied up in loosely knit sacks or old nylon stockings and hung in an area sheltered from frost. Plastic bags are not recommended unless holes are punched in them to allow for air circulation.

Succulent, thin-skinned bulbs such as the tubers and rhizomes of *Dahlia*, *Calla*, *Canna*, *Ornithogalum* and *Gloriosa* lilies benefit from occasional drops of water added to the storage medium. This helps prevent the bulbs from drying out.

Bulbs in containers can be stored by stacking pots away from freezing temperatures. This works well with small bulbs such as *Freesia*.

Do not divide or separate bulbs before storing. It could encourage drying out where the cut is made. It also provides easy entry for diseases.

Some bulbs require protection from a combination of warmth and moisture. Otherwise, they rot. These include *Ranunculus* and *Calochortus*. If grown in a container, they can be stored easily in a dry location. Bulbs planted in the ground should be dug and put in an open box. Store them in a dry, shady spot.

1. After leaves have died back at least halfway, bulbs are ready to lift for storage. Daffodils, shown above, can be replanted immediately, or stored until fall planting time.

2. Remove bulbs by gently tapping them from container. If digging bulbs from the ground, use a spading fork to lessen the chance of injuring bulbs.

3. Remove bulbs from soil. This is easiest to do when the soil is dry. Keep bulbs separate and label them if you are sorting more than one kind of bulb.

4. Remove dried leaves from bulbs, and discard those that are soft. Don't separate individual bulbs at this time. Bulbs separate more easily after they are dried, just before planting.

5. Dusting bulbs with fungicide and insecticide is not necessary, but is recommended if you have had infestations of narcissus bulb flies or gladiolus thrips in the past.

6. Bulbs can be stored in a variety of ways. A selection of containers serve as holding bins during the dormant season. Here, they are kept in sand. Vermiculite or perlite can also be used.

3

Bulbs in Containers

For the most dramatic way to display a small number of bulbs, grow them in containers. On a grand scale, you might want to try three or four lilies in a large tub. Or perhaps an eye-catching display of miniature snowdrops in a bonsai pot is more your style. Both approaches are colorful and create their own special effect.

Bulbs in containers emphasize a focal point such as a doorway, or frame a scenic view. They can direct traffic along a path, or call attention to a pool or piece of garden sculpture. One of their best uses is indoors, brightening a room or a table setting. See page 33 for details on how to grow bulbs indoors.

Container bulbs have a great advantage over in-ground plants because they can be moved to a protected area in adverse weather or during heavy winds. If the pots are rotated regularly, the bulbs grow more evenly and with straight stems. When bulbs are grown in pots, they can be moved

out of view after bloom and replaced with other seasonal color.

It is generally more pleasing to use containers in groups rather than lining them up like soldiers. The bulbs do not have to be the same color, size or shape. Pots of tall, light-blue 'Wedgewood' Dutch iris are striking when combined with pots of golden trumpet daffodils. Low pots of purple or white *Crocus* work well in front of these.

Similarly, different colors of the same type of flower can also be used together. Pots of pink tulips combined with pots of lilac and white tulips of the same variety make an impressive display. A pot of lilies can steal the scene when placed at an entryway. A bonus is the lilies' nighttime fragrance. Potted bulbs also combine well with low pots of spring-blooming annuals such as pansies, violas or forget-me-nots.

Mixing different kinds of bulbs in a single container is not desirable.

Chances are that one bulb will bloom and decline before the others bloom. The spent flowers and fading foliage detract from the beauty of the planting. It is much better to plant a single variety in each pot so bulbs in each pot bloom simultaneously.

There is no better way of displaying a small bulb than in a bonsai pot. Small species of *Narcissus* and *Crocus* are particular favorites in these containers. Placing a piece of lava rock or driftwood in the background of the container adds a natural touch.

When grouping bulbs in containers, it is not necessary to have pots that are the same size, height or shape. It helps to have them of the same material and color. If simplicity is your style, one beautiful pot of daffodils by a front door gives a feeling of warmth and welcome to arriving guests.

A fun way to grow small bulbs is to use them as a colorful ground cover in large containers. Try them beneath plants such as dwarf citrus, dwarf fruit

Left: Dutch hyacinths in simple, redwood boxes are unusual and attractive. Bulbs are planted, then boxes are covered with sphagnum moss and chicken wire. Allow normal growth until stalks emerge, then hang at nose level. Above: Wine carafes are perfectly suited to house Dutch hyacinth bulbs, grown in water indoors.

Bulbs in Containers **29**

Pots of tulips, hyacinths, daffodils and *Ipheion* make a striking springtime display.

Flowers of paper-white *Narcissus* enhance outdoor living areas with their beauty and their fragrance.

'February Gold' daffodils in foreground are spaced as closely as possible to produce this compact planting. In the background are gold *Freesias* and white *Azaleas.*

A container grouping on the author's terrace: Counterclockwise from front is *Ipheion, Anemone coronaria,* two-toned Picotee hybrid *Ranunculus, Tritonia crocata* with lime tree in clay container, 'Jewel of Spring' tulips, 'Mt. Hood' large cup *Narcissus,* 'Thalia' *Triandrus Narcissus,* 'Lady Derby' pink hyacinth and a red Darwin tulip.

Tight, "shoehorn" planting of 'Pink Pearl' hyacinths in a terra-cotta pot makes a striking display.

Haemanthus katharinae makes an outstanding display at a terrace door. This rare and exotic South-African native is attractive in any setting.

trees, tree roses and tree wisteria. In mild climates, *Freesia,* 'Grand Duchess' *Oxalis, Ipheon, Lapeirousia* and *Tritonia* accept the restricted root space. In colder climates, try dwarf varieties of *Anemone,* species *Cyclamen, Eranthis, Ipheion, Muscari* or *Oxalis adenophylla.*

CHOOSING CONTAINERS

Containers for bulbs are available in many sizes, shapes and kinds. You can choose from brightly glazed clay pots, plastic pots, wooden boxes and tubs, Japanese bonsai pots, metal pots and glass jars.

Each type of container has advantages and disadvantages.

Glazed and plastic pots do not allow water to evaporate through the sides. This means that less moisture is lost, and watering is less frequent than with unglazed containers. But because evaporation is reduced, the pots tend to heat up with warm weather. Too much heat can damage or kill the roots of plants.

Glazed and plastic pots are often available only in bright colors. You notice the pot and not the plant. However, a plastic pot with an attached saucer, no matter what the color, works well placed inside a basket, metal pot or urn.

Clay pots "breathe," which allows air circulation. This also allows water to evaporate from the sides, providing good drainage. But this means that watering has to be more frequent. In warm-summer areas, watering may be necessary every day. In addition, when the water evaporates, soil salts are left behind on the pot, which can be detrimental to the plant. This does not occur with plastic pots.

Wooden tubs and boxes have a natural look that lends itself well to informal settings. Wood is a good insulator that helps keep the soil cool in warm weather. Redwood and cedar are best because of their natural resistance to moisture and decay. To prevent rot and to increase the longevity of wooden containers, raise them off the ground with small blocks.

No matter what kind of container you choose for your bulbs, be sure that it allows for good drainage. All containers should have one or more holes in the bottom to allow excess water to drain away after each watering. Many pots are manufactured with a removable plug.

SOIL FOR CONTAINERS

Drainage is the most important consideration when choosing soil for containers. Most garden soils are too heavy, especially clay soils, and do not allow for fast drainage. Therefore, it is best to plant bulbs in a prepared soil mix. Ingredients such as sand, *perlite,* a porous volcanic rock, and *vermiculite,* expanded mica, are excellent for providing drainage. Perlite and vermiculite are lightweight so pots are easy to move. The standard mix of one-third leaf mold, one-third peat moss and one-third sand is one of the best combinations for potting.

Several brand names of soil mixes are available at retail outlets. Many are based on mixes developed by the University of California and Cornell University. These mixes are free of soil-borne diseases.

Before filling the containers with soil, moisten the mix slightly before putting it into the pots. Bone-dry soil often resists water penetration. Also mix in some superphosphate, which supplies phosphorus. Follow directions on the package label as to amount. Bulbs use more phosphorus than other nutrients, so it is a good idea to have sufficient amounts in the mix for use when the bulb needs it.

Most bulbs are satisfied with a standard soil mix, as described previously.

A few tropical bulbs prefer a more water-retentive mix, so add in some sphagnum peat moss. Among these are tuberous begonia, *Gloxinia, Eucharis* and *Achimenes.* Others, such as the many South-African bulbs that grow in sand or gravel in the wild, prefer faster drainage. With these bulbs, it is helpful to add a little sand to the soil mix.

POTTING BULBS

Before putting soil into containers, place a piece of broken clay pot, screening or other material over the drainage hole in the bottom. This allows the water to drain freely yet prevents the soil from washing out. A handful or two of sand over the broken piece ensures even drainage.

Fill the pot with soil to the desired depth. In containers, bulbs are planted closer to the surface than in the ground so roots will have the most room. They are also planted closer together than in the ground to make a full, attractive display, but not so close that they touch sides. When planting tulips, face the flat side of the bulb toward the outside of the pot. The leaves will then grow in a way that makes a prettier display.

After the first shoots appear, keep the soil damp. Watering every day will do no harm if soil drainage is ade-

quate. Apply water at low pressure so it trickles onto the soil. High-pressure watering washes out the soil and pushes over the foliage when it appears.

HANGING-BASKET BULBS

Certain bulbs have a trailing growth habit and pendulous flowers, such as the hanging varieties of tuberous begonias and *Achimines.* Bulbs of this type look best displayed in a hanging basket. These are wire baskets lined with sphagnum moss. The moss remains moist after watering and increases the humidity around the plant. The wire forms and moss are available at nurseries.

When you make hanging baskets, don't skimp on the moss. Moisten the moss before placing it in between the spaces of the wire basket. Fill it in until the moss is about 1 inch thick. It helps to add extra moss in the bottom of the basket to prevent the soil from washing out. Fill the basket with a house-plant soil mix, and you are ready to plant the bulbs.

Because they are highly exposed to wind and sunlight, hanging baskets dry out rapidly. They require water on a regular basis. If you plan to display several containers, consider installing a drip-irrigation system to water the baskets.

Bulbs in a fanciful container make a unique gift. Ingredients are few: bulbs, planter mix, milled sphagnum peat moss, planter, wrapping paper and ribbon.

You have an option as to when to give your gift of bulbs. You can present the preplanted container . . .

. . . or time your planting so that bulbs will be in full bloom for that special occasion.

Bulbs Indoors

Bulbs are easy to grow indoors if you provide the proper light, humidity and temperature. Flowering bulbs need more light than most indoor foliage plants. This does not mean that all bulbs need the same amount of light. However, for most bulbs, the more light you can provide the better. Bulbs preferring shade outdoors naturally prefer similar light conditions indoors. Indoor "shade" means an exposure to an eastern window, or indirect light from a south or west window.

The humidity of most homes is lower than that preferred by the majority of bulbs. But it is not hard to increase humidity. A saucer or tray filled with gravel placed under the pot collects drainage water. As the water evaporates, it raises humidity around the plant. Grouping plants also helps increase humidity. Keep in mind that bulbs native to humid areas, such as *Gloxinia* and *Eucharis,* need additional humidity. Daily misting of the potted bulbs helps somewhat, but the increased humidity lasts for a short time.

Temperature is one of the main environmental factors that controls bulb growth and development. Heat is actually more intense inside near a sunny window than outside, because of the heat absorption and reduced air circulation. Modify excessive heat with shades, screens or blinds.

If you are curious about the temperatures of various indoor locations, place a thermometer in the area where you are considering locating plants. It might be warmer or colder than you imagine. As a guide, spring bulbs bloom before the weather warms. They like it cooler than the indoor temperatures of most houses. It is best to keep all bulbs away from drafts from doors or windows, furnaces, heaters and air conditioners.

Indoor foliage plants combine beautifully with pots of colorful bulbs. It is interesting to stage combinations of bulbs and house plants in locations where they will be noticed. Some bulbs also serve as evergreen plants indoors. Most need a sunny window to bloom well. *Clivia, Eucharis* and *Zantedeschia* sometimes flower in the low light of a north window. The chart at right lists the best bulbs for growing indoors. These also serve as evergreen foliage plants.

Tulips induced into early flowering bring spring indoors while snow covers the outside garden.

Daffodils add grace to office desk. These are large-cup, bicolored types, but almost every type of daffodil adapts well to container culture.

Bulbs Indoors

Bulb	Comments
Agapanthus	Beautiful, blue or white flowers in summer. Handsome, dark-green, strap-shaped foliage. Dwarf varieties are most adaptable indoors.
Canna	Select from dwarf forms, available in many colors. Long-blooming tropical flowers. Foliage may be green or bronze. Remove shoots after bloom has finished to make room for new ones.
Clivia	Handsome, dark-green, strap-shaped foliage. Large yellow and orange flowers appear in early spring.
Crinum	Pink or white, trumpet-shaped flowers are fragrant, held above foliage. Relatively large plant. Blooms in summer.
Dietes	Stiff, gray-green, strap-shaped leaves with white, irislike flowers. Intermittent bloom.
Eucharis	Handsome, shiny, dark-green leaves, fragrant, pure-white flowers. Prefers warmth, humidity and light, but not direct sunlight.
Sprekelia	Narrow, strap-shaped leaves and large, orchidlike scarlet flower. Blooms in spring.
Tulbaghia	Small clusters of lavender flowers are held above foliage. Leaves resemble chives and can be used for culinary flavoring in place of chives. Blooms over half the year after established.
Zantedschia	Dwarf forms are more adaptable to indoor conditions. Spade-shaped leaves are large and handsome. Yellow and pink callas are deciduous.

4

Forcing Flowers

Spring bulbs that are *forced* to flower in midwinter are special attractions. A pot of flowering bulbs for a birthday or other special occasion is a wonderful gift to give or receive.

Forcing is not the best term to describe the process. *Manipulating, influencing* and *cajoling* are probably more descriptive. Actually, flowers *cannot* be forced. What you are doing is simulating the natural conditions that cause bulbs to bloom. The end results are flowers that bloom months before the usual cycle.

Perhaps you have tried to force spring bulbs in the past, only to watch weak stems flop over, or have the flowers drop just before opening. This is common, and is most often caused by lack of an adequate cool period. The majority of spring-blooming bulbs need 12 to 16 weeks of 45F (7C) temperatures after they are potted to develop roots strong enough to support plants and flowers. Home gardeners lacking special facilities may have a tough time supplying this cool period. A closet or cupboard,

often recommended, is rarely cold enough. Even outdoors, sufficient cold does not occur until mid-October or November in many areas.

The secret of forcing is to plant early enough to allow plenty of time for strong root systems to develop, with cool temperatures during that period. See page 39 for sample schedules for forcing bulbs.

FOUR STAGES OF GROWTH

Growth of spring bulbs, and corresponding temperatures, can be divided into four stages. Duplicate conditions natural for the bulbs and they will flower earlier than normal.

Stage one is dormancy, or near dormancy. This is when bulbs are planted. Stage two is root growth. Light is not necessary for this stage, and temperatures should be in the 45F (7C) range. If temperatures approach freezing, roots cease to grow. When temperatures go above 55F (13C), top growth may begin prematurely. Stage three is when top growth begins. Light should be

strong, but temperatures should be cool, in the 55F to 65F (13C to 19C) range. After two or three weeks at stage three, move into warmer 75F (24C) temperatures, about 75F (24C) and watch the sight of healthy flowers unfolding, which is stage four.

One of the best ways to maintain a temperature near 45F (7C) during the rooting stage is to bury potted bulbs in a trench. Dig the trench below the freezing level if you live in a cold-winter area. Be sure water drains away from the trench. Cover pots with a soft, non-compacting material such as vermiculite, hay, fir bark or peat moss. In most parts of the United States and Canada, this trenching keeps the bulbs at the proper temperature.

A simpler method is shown on page 36. Build a raised bed in the coolest part of the yard, ideally out of direct sunlight. Set pots of bulbs inside and cover with a coarse material such as fir bark. If the covering material is kept moist, evaporation reduces temperatures around bulbs by 10F to 15F.

Left: Daffodils forced into bloom bring spring early to this patio setting. Above: New shoots of forced bulbs emerge from container, ready to begin growth.

When the time arrives that you think the roots are mature enough to support top growth, lift a couple of pots and examine the roots. If roots are emerging from the bottom of the pot, the bulb is ready to bring out to warmer temperatures. If you can't see the roots, turn the pot upside down and tap it gently until the bulb and soil slip out. If the roots are not developed, place the bulb and soil back in the pot and return to the rooting area.

The many kinds of bulbs prefer slightly varying treatments. Different varieties of the same kind of bulb respond to different treatments. The Dutch have mastered the science of forcing bulbs. If you are serious about producing out-of-season flowers from bulbs, write to the Netherlands Flower Bulb Institute: 5 World Trade Center, Suite 6217, New York, NY 10048. Ask for information about their *Holland Bulb Forcer's Guide*.

SCHEDULING BLOOMS

Many bulbs are available in bloom in florist shops throughout the year. This is because commercial growers of these flowers are able to supply carefully controlled temperatures at the proper time. If you have the facilities to manipulate temperatures within a few degrees, you can have flowers of most bulbs any day of the year. Most home gardeners do not have this luxury, and must work within their own situation.

Precooling is an integral part of forcing flowers to bloom out of season. Bulbs are exposed to enough warmth to initiate internal growth, then chilled to simulate winter cold. Precooling is done by the supplier, usually in Holland. Precooled bulbs must be specially ordered, and are used to produce extra-early blooms. Availability of precooled bulbs varies, so contact suppliers early. Store precooled bulbs until the planting date in a cool, above-freezing location.

Dark root growth is the stage when root systems develop. Bulbs are stored in containers in a dark location such as a trench in the ground or a raised bed. Cool temperatures are usually necessary for this step. Ideal temperatures for this period of root growth are 50F to 55F (10C to 13C), gradually decreasing over a month to between 35F and 41F (2C to 5C).

After growth of an extensive root system, most bulbs need light and warmer temperatures. This encourages top growth and eventually produces flower buds. Ideal temperatures for this period vary according to the bulb. Try to keep tulips between 55F and 65F (13C to 18C); hyacinths between 55F and 73F (13C to 23C); daffodils between 55F and 63F (13C to 17C); and *Crocus* between 55F and 60F (13C to 16C).

1. To force flowers, plant bulbs in containers. Place bulbs close to surface to allow for maximum root growth. With large-flowered bulbs, leave space between bulbs.

2. Store bulbs in a cool, constantly shaded spot to provide the low temperatures necessary in the beginning stages of forcing. Water bulbs thoroughly.

3. Cover containers with an insulating material such as fir bark, perlite, polystyrene beads or sand. If containers will be exposed to winter rains, place a layer of bark, sand or gravel underneath pots to supply the necessary drainage.

4. After 16 weeks shoots are about 2 inches high, and an extensive root system is visible. Bulbs are ready to force. Place pots in bright shade, away from direct sun. After shoots are green, begin *gradual* exposure to sun.

Bulbs That Force Easily

The following bulbs were tested at Michigan State University for the Netherlands Flower Bulb Institute.
All are generally available in garden centers, nurseries or by mail order.

Bulb	Color	*Flowering Time
Crocus		
'Flower Record'	Purple	Mid to late
C. purpureus grandiflorus	Purple	Early to late
'Remembrance'	Purple	Early to late
'Victor Hugo'	Purple	Early to late
'Joan of Arc'	White	Early to late
'King of the Striped'	Striped	Early to late
'Pickwick'	Striped	Early to late
'Yellow'	Yellow	Late
Daffodils		
Trumpet		
'Dutch Master'	Yellow	Early and late
'Explorer'	Yellow	Early and late
'Gold Medal'	Yellow	Early and late
'Joseph MacLeod'	Yellow	Early
'Magnet'	Yellow trumpet, white perianth	Early and late
'Mount Hood'	White	Early and late
'Unsurpassable'	Yellow	Early and late
Large cup		
'Carlton'	Yellow	Early
'Flower Record'	Yellow and orange white perianth	Late
'Ice Follies'	Cream cup with white perianth	Early and late
'Yellow Sun'	Yellow	Early and late
Small cup		
'Barrett Browning'	Orange cup with white perianth	Early and late
Double		
'Van Sion'	Yellow	Late
Cyclamineus		
'February Gold'	Yellow	Early and late
Hyacinths		
'Jan Bos'	Red	Early
'Amsterdam'	Pink	Early and late
'Anna Marie'	Pink	Early
'Delight'	Pink	Early
'Lady Derby'	Pink	Early
'Marconi'	Pink	Late
'Pink Pearl'	Pink	Early and late
'Bismark'	Blue	Early
'Blue Giant'	Blue	Late
'Blue Jacket	Blue	Late
'Delft Blue'	Blue	Early to mid
'Marie'	Blue	Late
'Ostara'	Blue	Early to late
'Perle Brillante'	Blue	Mid
'Carnegie'	White	Mid
'Colosseum'	White	Early
'L'Innocence'	White	Mid to late
'Madame Kruger'	White	Early to late
'Amethyst'	Violet	Late

Bulb	Color	*Flowering Time
Muscari		
'Early Giant'	Blue	Early to late
M. armeniacum	Blue	Early to late
Iris reticulata		
'Harmony'	Blue	Early to late
'Hercules'	Purple	Early to late
Iris danfordiae		
'Yellow'	Yellow	Early
Tulips		
'Bing Crosby'	Red	Early and late
'Paul Richter'	Red	Early
'Olaf'	Red	Early and late
'Cassini'	Red	Early
'Charles'	Red	Early
'Coleur Cardinal'	Red	Late
'Danton'	Red	Early and late
'Diplomat'	Red	Mid
'La Suisse'	Red	Late
'Prominence'	Red	Early to mid
'Robinea'	Red	Early
'Ruby Red'	Red	Early to mid
'Stockholm'	Red	Early
'Topscore'	Red	Early
'Trance'	Red	Early
'Bellona'	Yellow	Early and late
'Kareol'	Yellow	Early
'Makassar'	Yellow	Late
'Monte Carlo'	Yellow	Early
'Yellow Present'	Yellow	Late
'Yokohoma'	Yellow	Early to mid
'Hibernia'	White	Early to late
'Pax'	White	Early
'Snowstar'	White	Early
'Angelique'	Double pink	Late
'Blenda'	Pink	Early
'Christmas Marvel'	Pink	Early
'Peerless Pink'	Pink	Late
'Preludium'	Pink	Early
'Edith Eddy'	Red, edged white	Late
'Invasion'	Red, edged white	Early
'Mirjoran	Red, edged white	Early
'Golden Eddy'	Red, edged yellow	Late
'Karel Doorman'	Red, edged yellow	Early
'Kees Nelis'	Red, edged yellow	Early
'Madame Spoor'	Red, edged yellow	Early
'Paris'	Red, edged yellow	Mid to late
'Thule'	Yellow with red	Early
'Apricot Beauty'	Apricot	Early

*All the bulbs listed above naturally bloom during the spring months, but do not bloom at the same time. Use the Flowering Times listed—early, midseason and late—as a guide to acceptable periods of forcing these bulbs into bloom. If you force flowers with varied bloom times, blooms appear throughout the season instead of all at one time. Some bulbs, such as Crocus, can be forced over a period of time.

WATER CULTURE

Some bulbs store so much food for the following year that all they need is water to bloom. Hyacinths, *Crocus* and *Narcissus* are well adapted for water culture. Tulips are not, because they need the additional nutrients available in the soil.

Autumn crocus, *Colchicum* species, does not even require water to bloom. When brought into normal room temperature, the bloom can't be stopped. Because it requires no care or effort from the gardener, it makes a great gift. Everyone seems to enjoy watching its daily growth, ending with a cluster of beautiful flowers.

Hyacinths and *Crocus* are commonly grown in jars made especially for water culture. Clear glass jars are commonly used so you can watch the roots develop. It helps to add some activated charcoal to prevent algae growth.

Paper-whites, Chinese sacred lilies and 'Soleil D'Or', varieties of *Narcissus tazetta,* grow well in low bowls filled with gravel. Use plenty of gravel so roots have something to hold onto because plants become top-heavy. Placing gravel around the sides of the bulbs helps, but keep the water level below the bulb base once roots start to grow. Add a small amount of activated charcoal to help keep water fresh.

Paper-whites for Christmas are normally started about the middle of November. By starting at the end of October and planting at 2- to 3-week intervals, you can have a succession of blooms. Chinese sacred lilies naturally bloom later, and 'Soleil D'Or' later still. After growth of these *Narcissus* begins, do not leave them in the dark. They will stretch for light until they topple over.

Keep hyacinths, *Crocus* and *Muscari* in a cool, dark place until roots are well developed and top growth is under way. Bring them into light when the buds on *Crocus* are a couple of inches tall. Hyacinth buds should be about 4 inches tall with flower buds showing through leaf sheaths.

Most bulbs grown in water become weak. They are generally discarded after flowering.

Forcing Dutch Amaryllis for Christmas Bloom

Bulbs can be purchased in nurseries or by mail order, prepotted and ready to grow. Increase amount of water as the bulbs grow. Rotate pots to prevent bending of stem toward light. If you live in a mild-climate area, bulbs can be planted in the garden after bloom has passed. If you live in a cold-climate area, water and fertilize lightly to maintain growth until bulb goes dormant in summer. Maintain summer dormancy until Thanksgiving. At this time, increase watering for a repeat bloom at Christmas.

November 28

December 7

December 14

December 19

December 23

Christmas Day

Forcing Bulbs for Seasonal Blooms

Paper-White Daffodil for Christmas Bloom
Chinese Sacred Lily Daffodil for Chinese New Year
Precooling: Not necessary.
Planting time: Third week of November for paper-white. Six weeks before Chinese New Year for Chinese sacred lily.
Dark root growth period: Not necessary.
Light top growth period: Not necessary.
With both bulbs, bring indoors right after potting, ideally to a cool location. Low light promotes weak top growth that may topple. High heat forces top growth at expense of roots. If grown in water and gravel, use enough gravel to support roots and some activated charcoal to keep water clear and algae-free.

'February Gold' Daffodil for Christmas
Precooling: Order precooled bulbs from a dependable supplier in early summer. Keep bulbs in the vegetable compartment of the refrigerator at above-freezing temperatures until planting date.
Planting time: Last week of August.
Dark root growth period: 15 weeks.
Cool light growth period: 3 weeks.
Bring indoors when buds are well formed, just before they open.

'February Gold' Daffodil for January
Precooling: Not necessary.
Planting time: Last week of September.
Dark root growth period: 15 weeks.
Light top growth period: 2 weeks.
Bring indoors when buds are well formed, just before they open.

'Olaf' Tulip for Valentine's Day
Precooling: Not necessary.
Planting time: First week of October.
Dark root growth period: 16 weeks.
Light top growth period: 3 to 4 weeks.
Bring indoors when buds are well formed, just before they open.

'Peerless Pink' Tulip for Mother's Day
Precooling: Not necessary.
Planting time: Second week of December.
Dark root growth period: 16 weeks.
Light top growth period: 3 weeks.
Bring indoors when buds are well formed, just before they open.

'Anna Marie' Hyacinth for Valentine's Day
Precooling: Not necessary.
Planting time: First week of October.
Dark root growth period: 13 weeks.
Light top growth period: 2 weeks.
Bring indoors when buds are well formed, just before they open.

'Grote Gele' Dutch Crocus for January
Precooling: Order precooled bulbs from dependable supplier in midsummer. Keep in refrigerator, above freezing, until planting date.
Planting time: Second week of September.
Dark root growth period: 16 to 17 weeks.
Light top growth period: 3 weeks.
Bring indoors when buds are well formed, just before they open.

Lily-of-the-Valley for June 15 Wedding
Precooling: Not necessary. Keep roots chilled and above freezing until planting date to prevent growth.
Planting time: Third week of May.
Dark root growth period: Not necessary.
Light top growth period: Not necessary.
Bring indoors immediately after planting to begin growth and flowering.

Paper-white *Narcissus* are among the most reliable and fragrant bulbs for forcing indoors.

Tulips need a long, cool period to develop a strong root system. Start with precooled bulbs, grow in pots and bulbs will flower months before spring.

Bulbs in the Landscape

Many of the basics of landscape design apply to the bulb garden. The primary purpose is to bring all garden elements together in a way that is pleasing to the eye. The garden should include interesting accents, with a common element or unifying theme.

Depending on how bulbs are grouped and the supporting landscape materials and architecture, a garden can project many moods. For example, one daffodil enthusiast may want a formal garden. He could divide an area into equal squares and edge them with a finely trimmed hedge. A piece of sculpture would provide a focal point at the center of the garden where the squares converge. The daffodils, many of them rare, could be planted and labeled in groups within the squares.

Using the same daffodil varieties, another bulb enthusiast may wish to take an informal approach. The daffodils could be planted in labeled drifts in a small, natural meadow, using

stones and weathered logs to complement the natural theme. What a difference from the formal garden!

THE IMPORTANCE OF PLANNING

Whether you want to design a formal or informal garden, or add some simple bulb plantings to your existing garden, it is important to begin with a plan. A plan can be as simple as a rough sketch on the back of an envelope, or measured to exact specifications on graph paper.

Certain obvious factors limit what you can do. The most important include garden space, and available time and money. In addition to these major factors, you need to consider the following:

Climate—Narrow your selection of bulbs to those that will do well in your particular climate. Although many bulbs are adaptable, certain bulbs naturally grow better in certain types of climates. Bulb growers in cold-winter areas have a different group of

bulbs to select from than those in mild-winter areas. See the section on climate, page 56, and the lists of bulbs on pages 46 and 47.

Garden Location—Observe the nature of the proposed garden site. Does the location receive full sun, light shade or full shade? Are there trees nearby that will compete for light? *Endymion, Clivia,* lily-of-the-valley, *Fritillaria* and *Cyclamen* are well adapted to light shade. *Crocus* and *Ixia* need the warmth of full sun to bloom. Does the soil drain well, and is it of sufficient quality? If not, soil amendments may have to be added.

Color—Selecting bulb color is a personal choice, depending on the effect you want to create. Consider how various colors combine. White or blue goes with anything, and pastels are forgiving colors. But you might find a brilliant orange next to a strong magenta a bit overwhelming. It doesn't hurt to experiment. Grouping color opposites, such as blues with oranges and purples with yellows, in-

Left: Red and white flowers of *Hippeastrum* are perfect complement to brick walk.
Above: 'Gudoshnik' tulip typically has great color variation from flower to flower.
Plant them in groups to accent their subtle variations.

tensifies the colors in your garden. If you are planning certain color combinations, keep in mind that there are early, midseason and late varieties of tulips, daffodils, hyacinths, *Irises* and *Crocus.* You must match up the seasons to successfully coordinate your color scheme.

Groups of the same color are most often more effective than mixing several colors. This is especially true when plantings are viewed from a distance. For example, grouping yellow daffodils of the same variety is more natural and pleasing than different colors and sizes. Likewise, *Ranunculus* provides a more effective show of color if the colors are separated into groups.

Timing—Generally, a garden can be planned to bloom in one of two ways: It can produce an outstanding show of color for a short period, with bulbs scheduled to bloom all at one time. Or, by planting a selection of bulbs with early, midseason and late bloom times, you can have color throughout the year. Either schedule requires careful planning. It is extremely helpful to keep records of the bloom dates of your bulbs. The weather may change the actual date of blooms from year to year, but the time relationship between different bulb types remains the same.

Height—Learn the mature height of bulbs before you plant. A tall-growing bulb can be planted in the foreground for variety, but low-growing bulbs planted behind them will be hidden from view. Don't assume that all bulbs of one species are the same general height—most range from high to low. For example, *Agapanthus* grows from 1-1/2 feet to 5 feet high, depending on the named variety. Kaufmanniana tulips grow to 5 inches high, but cottage tulips reach 30 inches high. The mature height of bulbs is usually given in mail-order catalogs, or at retail outlets where bulbs are sold.

It is best to plant early blooming bulbs toward the rear of a flower bed or border. Daffodils invariably bloom before tulips. If daffodils are planted in the foreground, you will have to look past their spent flowers when tulips begin to bloom.

Relationships—This is a difficult concept to explain, but certain plants and landscape materials look "right" when planted together. Generally, it

Landscape planting features rich color combinations, including violet-colored fairy primrose, *Primula malacoides,* against earth-toned wall. Bright-purple pansies in front contrast nicely with white tulips, their white repeated by candytuft ground cover in center.

Author's garden combines many kinds of bulbs for an attractive, casual effect. White border is candytuft, *Iberis sempervirens.* Yellow flowers in foreground are *Freesia.* Golden flowers at left front are *Narcissus bulbocodium.* Blue anemone link clumps of daffodils at left rear, and Dutch hyacinths, right center.

is a matter of blending texture, form and color into a pleasing combination. For example, formal, precise plant forms do not look at home in a woodland situation. Likewise, a formal, contained garden will not welcome a bulb that spreads and naturalizes rapidly. Study gardens that appeal to you. If you look closely enough, you will see factors that unify the different bulbs, plants and materials.

KEEPING RECORDS
Keeping accurate records of planting and bloom dates is necessary to repeat a star performance, or adjust a planting so it will be more attractive the following year. As mentioned, the actual bloom dates may not fall on the same calendar day each year, but the timetable between the different bulb types remains constant. Also keep notes of the bulbs that bloom at the same time in your neighborhood.

SAMPLE PLANS
Sample plans for bulb borders are shown on pages 44 and 45. Two plans are supplied: one for mild climates and one for cold climates. If planted as shown, these gardens require little maintenance and are long-lived. If you happen to have the area to accommodate dimensions of the sample plan—perfect! If not, it is simple to adjust the size, and adapt the plan and plants.

BULBS WITH BEDDING PLANTS AND GROUND COVERS
Many bulb growers plant compatible bedding plants or ground covers over a bulb planting. *Overplanting* bulbs is simple to do. First, plant the bulbs. Then rake the area smooth and plant seeds or bedding plants of ground covers over the same area.

Bedding plants are often placed over bulbs for additional color and contrast. Imagine pink tulips with blue forget-me-nots, or white Dutch iris with yellow violias.

Planting over bulbs also prolongs color. After the bulbs finish, summer annuals such as petunias begin to bloom, blending one season of color into the next. As soon as summer annuals become available, plant them between bulbs to prolong the life of a colorful border. Star performers include ageratum, marigolds and asters. They hide the dying leaves of the bulbs as they grow.

Bedding plants and ground covers having neutral-colored flowers are usually best combined with brightly colored bulbs. However, don't be afraid to try pink tulips with purple pansies. But, avoid a white-flowered ground cover if your bulbs have white flowers. White daffodils with white alyssum do neither any service. The same is true of planting yellow daffodils with yellow English primroses.

White and yellow daffodils are much more effective with contrasting blue violas or pansies.

Bedding plants or ground covers should be a single color, not a mix. Various colors of violas or pansies call more attention to themselves than to the flowering bulbs.

Ground Covers—Many bulbs are happy to rise through an established ground cover of violets, *Ajuga, Vinca minor* or English ivy. The height relationship between the ground cover and bulb flower is important. As a rule, the ground cover should be no more than half the height of the bulb flower. *Freesias, Sparaxis* and *Tritonia* thrive under a border of candytuft. *Crocus,* on the other hand, suffocates under any but the lowest ground covers. It does well in lawns as long as the first mowing is made after foliage has matured.

A ground cover supports bulb stems and protects flowers from mud splashed by rain or sprinklers. An overplanting of ground cover also acts as a mulch to cool soil temperatures. For example, lilies thrive with shallow-rooted ferns at their base, shading the soil.

On page 47 is a list of ground-cover plants that serve well as bulb covers. For more information see *Lawns and Ground Covers: How to Select, Grow and Enjoy,* by Michael MacCaskey, published by HPBooks.

Babiana stricta is delicate and low growing—perfect for viewing close up, such as between steppingstones.

An expanse of color can be created with large beds, such as these 'Renown' tulips.

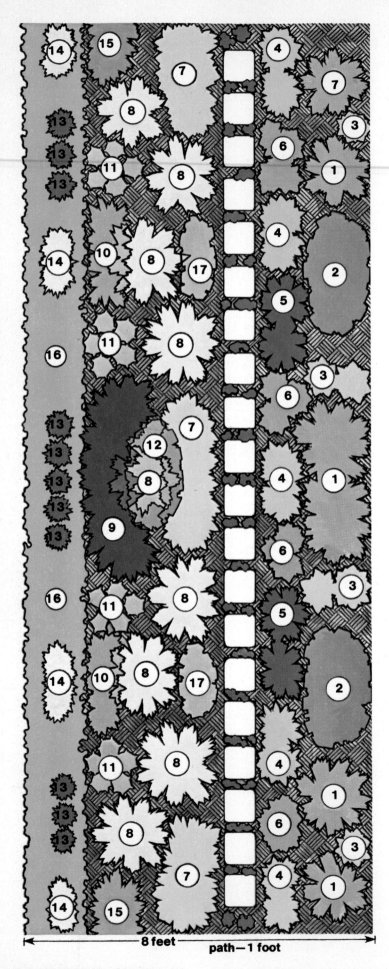

Plan for Mild-Climate Bulb Garden

If you live in a mild-climate region, you have the opportunity to grow color plants the year round. Annuals make an attractive, colorful display, but take a lot of time. Bulbs are excellent for easy-care color. After they are planted, they return year after year. Many have evergreen foliage, adding to their landscape value. These include *Agapanthus*, *Hemerocallis*, *Canna* and *Cliva*.

The plan at left includes many plants with varied bloom periods to provide color through the whole year. The numerals following the plant names are recommended numbers of plants for the best effect. Adjust the number of plants to fit your own situation.

1. Tall, dark *Agapanthus:* 2
2. Pink or white *Crinum:* 2
3. White or dark-pink *Amaryllis belladonna:* 2
4. Tall, yellow, bearded iris: 1 or 2
5. Dwarf blue *Agapanthus:* 2
6. *Lycoris africana:* 4 or 5
7. Dutch iris 'Wedgewood': 1 dozen
8. Deciduous *Hemerocallis:* 1
9. Daffodil 'February Gold': 2 dozen
10. Daffodil paper-white: 1 dozen
11. *Nerine bowdenii:* 5
12. Daffodil 'Professor Einstein': 1 dozen
13. *Lycoris radiata:* 3 to 5
14. Yellow *Freesias:* 1 dozen
15. Daffodil 'Soleil d'Or': 1 dozen
16. Ground cover: *Iberis sempervirens*
17. Dutch iris 'Blue Ribbon': 1 dozen

Plant *Oxalis* 'Grand Duchess' between pathway steppingstones.

Bloom Sequence

Spring
Daffodils
Dutch iris
Freesias
Oxalis 'Grand Duchess'

Early Summer
Hemerocallis
Agapanthus
Bearded iris

Summer
Hemerocallis

Late Summer and Fall
Crinum
Amaryllis belladonna
Lycoris

Christmas
Paper-white daffodil
Nerine
Oxalis 'Grand Duchess'

8 feet
path—1 foot

Plan for Cold-Climate Bulb Garden

After a winter of gray and white, gardeners in cold-climate regions have the chance to enjoy a tremendous display of spring-blooming bulbs. Many bulbs have waited for the cold weather to pass before bursting into bloom, creating a riot of color. Blooms of daffodils, tulips, *Crocus* and others are a firm affirmation that winter has ended.

Many mild-climate bulbs can be planted after danger of frost has passed. They must be dug and stored after bloom and before fall frost.

The plan at right features bulbs with varied bloom periods for color through most of the year. The numerals following the plant names are recommended numbers of plants for the best effect. Adjust the number of plants to fit your own situation.

1. *Eremurus robustus:* 1
2. *Lilium auratum:* 3
3. Tall bearded *Iris,* your favorite color: 3
4. *Galtonia candicans:* 1
5. *Lilium speciosum:* 5
6. *Lilium,* Bellingham Hybrid: 3
7. Deciduous *Hemerocallis:* 2
8. Tall perennial tulips: 1 dozen
9. *Fritillaria imperialis:* 2
10. *Chionodoxa luciliae:* 4 dozen
11. *Eranthis hyemalis:* 4 dozen
12. Low botanical tulips, *Tulipa kaufmanniana* or *T. fosterana:* 1 dozen
13. Daffodils planted around *Hemerocallis:* 1 or 2 dozen
14. *Crocus speciosus:* 1 dozen
15. Ground cover: *Vinca minor* or *Iberis sempervirens*

Plant *Muscari, Eranthis* and *Crocus* species between pathway steppingstones.

Bloom Sequence

Early Spring
Eranthis
Chionodoxa
Botanical tulips

Spring
Daffodils
Tulips
Fritillaria
Muscari
Crocus
Eremurus

Early Summer
Hemerocallis
Lilium Bellingham Hybrid
Bearded iris

Late Summer and Fall
Galtonia
Lilium speciosum
Lilium auratum

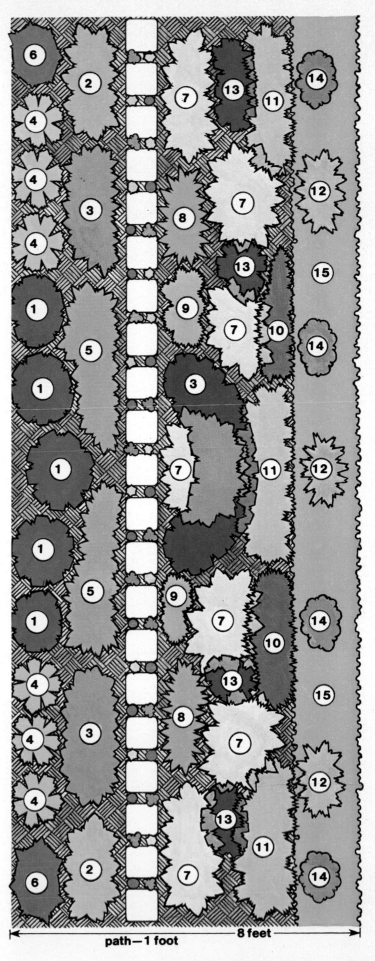

path—1 foot   8 feet

Bulb Selection Guide

Bulbs for Containers

Any bulb can be grown in a container for at least one season. Tulips, hyacinths, *Narcissus, Crocus* and Easter lilies are favorites. Because of their naturally extensive root systems, they seldom flower well year after year. Rhizomatous bulbs such as bearded iris and *Canna* grow horizontally and quickly push to the side of the container.

Some bulbs thrive under crowded conditions. They can remain in the same pot for years. Eventually, they have to be separated and repotted. The best include:

Agapanthus
Clivia
Eucharis
Eucomis
Freesia
Haemanthus
Hippeastrum
Hymenocallis
Ipheion
Ixia maculata
Lapeirousia
Muscari
Nerine
Oxalis
Pancratium
Sparaxis
Tritonia
Urginea
Velthemia

Muscari armeniacum

Bulbs for Fragrance

Many bulbs produce some fragrance. The following have a strong and pleasant scent.

Acidanthera bicolor
Amaryllis belladonna
Chlidanthus fragrans
Convallaria majalis
Crinum americanum
Crinum moorei
Eucharis amazonica
Freesia refracta
Gladiolus tristis
Hyacinthus orientalis
Hymenocallis species
Iris x germanica var. florentina
Leucocoryne ixioides
Lilium species, especially trumpets
  and bowl shaped
Lycoris squamigera
Narcissus jonquilla
Narcissus tazetta
Pancratium
Polianthes tuberosa

Bulbs that Naturalize

If conditions are ideal for growth most bulbs *naturalize*—grow and multiply on their own. Some are especially suited to naturalizing because they are long-lived, or because they multiply rapidly. Naturalized bulbs require little care after they are established.

*Agapanthus
Allium
*Amaryllis
Anemone
Belamcanda
Brodiaea
*Chasmanthe
Chionodoxa
Crocus
Cyclamen
Endymion
Eranthis
*Freesia
Fritillaria
Galanthus
Gladiolus tristis
Hemerocallis
Hippeastrum
Ipheion
Iris
*Ixia
Leucojum
Lilium
Muscari
Narcissus
*Narcissus tazetta
*Oxalis
Scilla
*Sparaxis
*Tritonia
Tulipa clusiana
*Zantedeschia

*mild climates only

Bulbs for a Rock Garden

Vigorous-growing bulbs such as *Muscari* are not used in rock gardens because they eventually crowd out other bulbs.

Anemone
Babiana
Calochortus
Chionodoxa
Crocus
Cyclamen
Eranthus
Habranthus
Iris, small kinds
Lapeirousia
Narcissus
Oxalis
Rhodohypoxis
Sternbergia
Tritonia
Tulipa
Zephyranthes

Narcissus bulbocodium obesus

Bulbs for Hanging Baskets

Only a few bulbs have the trailing growth habit and long bloom period particularly adapted to hanging baskets. These include:

Achimenes
Begonia
Oxalis

Convallaria and *Freesias* can be planted in a hanging basket. A bonus is their delightful fragrance. However, their bloom period is relatively short.

Regional Favorites

Many bulbs are widely adapted. Others are best suited to certain climates. Here are some listings to guide your selections.

Cold Climates

Allium
Anthericum
Belamcanda
Bulbocodium
Chionodoxa
Convallaria
Crocus
Eranthis
Galanthus
Hemerocallis
Iris reticulata
Leucojum
Lilium Bellingham
  hybrids
Muscari
Puschkinia
Scilla
Tulipa

Warm and Humid Climates

Achimenes
Agapanthus
Amaryllis
Caladium
Canna
Clivia
Colocasia
Crinum
Dietes
Eucharis
Gloriosa
Habranthus
Hemerocallis
Hippeastrum
Hymenocallis
Pancratium
Polianthes
Sauromatum
Zantedeschia
Zephyranthes

Mild Climates

Agapanthus
Allium
Amaryllis
Anemone
Babiana
Brunsvigia
Bulbinella
Canna
Chasmanthe
Clivia
Crinum
Crocosmia
Crocus—selected
  species
Dietes
Endymion
Freesia
Gladiolus
Gloriosa
Habranthus
Haemanthus
Hemerocallis
Hippeastrum
Hymenocallis

Ipheion
Iris
Ixia
Lachenalea
Lapeirousia
Leucojum
Lycoris
Muscari
Narcissus
Nerine
Ornithogalum
Oxalis
Ranunculus
Scilla
Sparaxis
Sprekelia
Tritonia
Tulbaghia
Tulipa—selected
  species
Watsonia
Zantedeshia
Zephyranthes

Desert Climates

Amaryllis
Brodiaea
Calochortus
Canna
Habranthus
Hemerocallis
Ipheion
Iris
Milla
Oxalis
Ranunculus
Sparaxis
Tulbaghia
Tulipa species
Zephyranthes

Bulbinella species

Ground Covers for Overplanting

Many ground covers complement bulbs. They act as a living mulch, moderating temperatures and conserving moisture. They help keep down mud splashes from rain and irrigation. Choose a ground cover that will be no more than half the height of the bulb flower. Examples are:

Arabis
Arenaria
Aubrieta
Aurinia
Campanula
Cerastium
Chamaemelum
Cotula
Cymbalaria
Erodium
Ferns, low kinds
Galium
Geranium
Hedera helix
Herniaria
Iberis
Lamiastrum

Lamium
Laurentia
Lobelia
Lobularia
Lysimachia
Mazus
Mentha
Myosotis
Omphalodes
Phyla
Potentilla
Sedum
Soleirolia
Thymus
Vancouveria
Veronica
Vinca minor

Bulbs for Special Cultural Conditions

These bulbs are adapted to some of the more common problems of shade, moist soil, and acid or alkaline soil.

Shade

Achimenes
Anemone
Anthericum
Begonia
Clivia
Convallaria
Cyclamen
Endymion
Erythronium
Eucharis
Fritillaria
Galanthus
Muscari
Scilla
Trillium
Zantedeschia

Acid Soil

Allium moly
Convallaria
Endymion
Eranthis
Erythronium
Galanthus
Leucojum
Lilium auratum
Lilium canadense
Lilium superbum
Narcissus cyclamineus
Oxalis
Puschkinia
Scilla
Trillium
Tulipa
Zephyranthes

Moist Soil

Caladium
Camassia
Canna
Colocasia
Convallaria
Eranthis
Hemerocallis
Iris, some species
Zantedeschia

Alkaline Soil

Allium
Amaryllis
Anemone
Brodiaea
Cyclamen
Iris
Narcissus
Nerine
Ornithogalum

Canna species

Bulbs for California

California has a unique climate. Many bulbs will thrive there that are normally short-lived in other areas. The climate is perfect for bulbs adapted to dormant, semidry conditions generally free of freezing temperatures. Many bulbs from the Mediterranean, South Africa and Mexico are adapted to this type of climate.

Bulbs that do better with cold-dormant periods are more difficult to grow here. Those that like humidity must be coddled. Many of the bulbs that grow in southern California are not well known in other areas.

In choosing bulbs for a permanent spot in a California garden, it helps to select those originating from the similar climates mentioned. This is true up to a point. You would naturally consider native California bulbs the best for the California garden, but this isn't always the case. Most California natives are too well adapted to the hot, dry summers. Regular moisture from landscape irrigation around the home causes them to rot when the soil is warm.

In choosing long-lasting bulbs, some of the best are native to the southern tip of Africa. From this region comes a wide variety of bulbs and corms.

Perhaps the best known South-African bulb is the delightfully fragrant *Freesia.* The original variety may be found in many old, established gardens. It is not generally available from conventional sources, and must be acquired from an existing planting. The white, tubular flowers have slight, purple veins.

Because of its fragrance and keeping quality as a cut flower, hybridizers have done a great deal of work with *Freesia.* It is available with larger flowers and longer stems, in pure white, white with yellow throats, yellow, golden orange, pink, red and lavender-blue. Hybridizers in Holland have developed double-flowered varieties.

Tritonias are similar to *Freesias,* but lack fragrance and have more open flowers. They bloom later than *Freesias,* in shades of salmon, coral, peach, orange and cream.

Ixias have clusters of smaller flowers on long, extremely thin stems. They are a favorite of European florists, who add them to mixed

Like a successful work of nature, colorful, fragrant *Freesias* grace poolside with ornamental grasses, herbs and daffodils.

bouquets. The colors are white, buff, orange, carmine or blue. The beautiful, peacock blue-green variety, *Ixia viridiflora,* is difficult to grow. It must be ordered from specialists.

Sparaxis usually comes in bright orange and black or yellow and black. Where well adapted, seedlings come up around the original plants.

Babiana has pleated leaves and flowers in shades of blue, lavender or white, on 10- to 12-inch stems.

Watsonia closely resembles *Gladiolus.* It has similar, straight stems that grow to 3 feet high. It is a good cut flower for the home gardener and is reliable.

Oxalis 'Grand Duchess' does not resemble any of the previously mentioned bulbs. It is low and spreading, with fresh, green, shamrocklike leaves. Flowers are showy and come in bright pink, white, or lavender with yellow throats. Plants do not mind

crowded conditions and grow well among tree roots if they receive some sunlight. They are decorative around the base of tree roses or shrubs grown in containers.

Dutch iris, which originates in Spain, also does well. Varieties colored clear, light blue and dark blue are especially attractive. Others are available in white, yellow, purple, mauve and brown.

Blue *Scilla campanulata* from Spain does well in California. It grows best with partial shade. In some established gardens, plantings have become large masses. It resembles its relative, the English blue bell. You may find it listed under the new name botanists have given it: *Endymion hispanicus.*

The popular *Ranunculus,* originally from the Near East, is well adapted to California's long, cool, winter season. If you want to use them year after year, dig and store after the foliage turns brown. If the area is kept absolutely dry until fall, *Ranunculus* can remain in the ground. Florist-type *Anemone* also prefers dry conditions during the summer.

Leucojum vernum, spring snowflake, comes from France. It resembles a large lily-of-the-valley, and does well in sun or shade.

From Argentina and Uruguay comes *Ipheion uniflorum,* a low-growing bulb that multiplies rapidly. White-centered, starlike flowers can be light blue or dark blue.

Also from South America comes the large-flowered *Hippeastrum,* whose hybrids are known as *Dutch amaryllis.* It is often grown as a Christmas plant. Dutch amaryllis adapts beautifully to a California setting, as long as plants are protected from snails. In the Southern Hemisphere, it blooms in November—the beginning of summer. When brought to the Northern Hemisphere, it blooms in November the first year. After it becomes acclimated, it blooms in May.

Other South-African bulbs adapted to California gardens include different varieties of *Lachenalia* in red, yellow, blue or silver-white. *Ornithogalum thyrsoides,* an excellent white cutting flower, and *Nerine* species, with delicate clusters of flowers in coral, pink, orange or white, also do well. Plant all of the preceding in the fall.

The Mediterranean region is home to other groups of bulbs for warm, California gardens. Some members of trumpet *Narcissus* do well in southern California, as long as the soil is kept cool during summer. The small, early blooming 'February Gold' often forms large clumps. Paper-whites, Chinese sacred lily and 'Soleil D'Or', all varieties of *N. tazetta,* thrive in southern California.

The wild *Crocus* from southern Italy and Greece does well as a permanent planting. Among the best are *C. imperati* from Naples and *C. goulimyi* from Sparta. The large *Crocus* that come from the Alps grow and bloom for one year only.

Some of the blue grape hyacinths, especially *Muscari armeniacum,* cover large areas.

From the Mediterranean, *Ornithogalum arabicum* does well in irrigated summer gardens. It grows 2 feet tall with white, star-shaped flowers that have a shiny, black, beadlike ovary in the center.

Ranunculus is a popular California bulb. Here it makes an unusual container planting.

Crocus species are well adapted to California climates.

Ixia hybrid is striking in a container.

Early Spring Blooming

Anemone x fulgens
Bulbinella floribunda
Chionodoxa, all species
Crocus biflorus
Crocus chrysanthus
Crocus flavus
Crocus sieberi
Crocus angustifolius
Crocus tomasinianus
Cyclamen coum coum
Eranthis hyemalis
Galanthus nivalis
Iris danfordiae
Iris reticulata
Lachenalia pendula
Narcissus, some species
Tulipa, some species

Spring Blooming

Allium aflatunense
Allium karataviense
Allium neapolitanum
Allium triquetrum
Anemone appenina
Anemone coronaria
Anthericum liliago
Babiana, all species
Calochortus albus
Chasmanthe aethiopica
Clivia, all species
Convallaria majalis
Crocus aureus
Crocus kotschyanus
Crocus oliveieri
Crocus vernus
Crocus, Dutch hybrids
Cyclamen coum
Cyclamen hybrids
Cyclamen repandum
Dietes bicolor
Dietes vegeta
Eremurus, all species
Erythronium species
Eucharis grandiflora
Eucomis bicolor
Freesia, all species
Fritillaria meleagris
Galanthus elwesii
Gladiolus x colvillei
Gladiolus tristis
Hippeastrum
Hyacinthus
Hymenocallis caroliniana
Ipheion uniflorum
Iris cristata
Iris douglasiana
Iris, Dutch hybrids
Iris foetidissima
Iris innominata
Iris orientalis, Spurias
Iris, Regeliocyclus hybrids
Iris sibirica
Iris tectorum

Iris unguicularis
Ixiolirion tataricum
Lachenalia pearsonii
Lachenalia tricolor
Lapeirousia laxa
Leucocoryne ixiodes
Leucojum aestivum
Leucojum vernum
Lilium pumilum
Moraea pavonia
Muscari, all species
Narcissus asturiensis
Narcissus bulbocodium
Narcissus cyclamineus
Narcissus hybrids
Narcissus jonquilla
Narcissus poeticus
Narcissus pseudonarcissus
Narcissus tazetta
Narcissus triandrus
Ornithogalum arabicum
Ornithogalum thyrsoides
Oxalis adenophylla
Oxalis bowiei
Oxalis pes-caprae
Oxalis purpurea 'Grand Duchess'
Puschkinia scilloides
Ranunculus asiaticus
Rhodohypoxis baurii
Scilla peruviana
Scilla siberica
Sparaxis tricolor
Sternbergia fischerana
Streptanthera cuprea
Trillium, all species
Triteleia—see *Brodiaea*
Tritonia crocata
Tulipa garden hybrids
Veltheimia capensis
Watsonia garden hybrids
Zantedeschia aethiopica

Late Spring Blooming

Allium aflatunense
Allium karataviense
Allium moly
Allium neapolitanum
Allium triquetrum
Alophia pulchella
Anthericum liliago
Calochortus albus
Clivia nobilis
Dietes bicolor
Dietes iridiodes
Eucharis grandiflora
Fritillaria imperalis
Gladiolus recurvus
Hemerocallis garden hybrids
Hyacinthus orientalis
Iris douglasiana
Iris foetidissima
Iris innominata
Iris x germanica, bearded
Iris, Louisiana group
Leucojum aestivum
Lilium pumilum
Moraea villosa
Muscari comosa
Narcissus poeticus
Oxalis adenophylla
Oxalis bowiei

Plant in Early Spring

Achimenes
Agapanthus
x *Amarcrinum*
Begonia
Bletilla striata
Chasmanthe aethiopica
Chlidanthus fragrans
Clivia
x *Crinodonna*
Dietes

Eucharis grandiflora
Sinningia
Sprekelia formosissima
Tulbaghia

Plant in Spring

Achimenes
Acidanthera bicolor
Agapanthus, all species
Alstroemeria, all species
x Amarcrinum
Begonia tuberous kinds
Belamcanda chinensis
Bessera elegans
Bletilla striata
Bulbinella floribunda
Caladium x hortulanum
Canna, all species
Chlidanthus fragrans
Clivia
Colocasia esculenta
x Crinodonna
Crinum, all species
Cyclamen hederifolium
Dahlia garden hybrids
Dietes bicolor
Dietes iridoides
Eucharis grandiflora
Galtonia candicans
Gladiolus alatus
Gladiolus byzantinus
Gladiolus carinatus
Gladiolus caryophyllaceus
Gladiolus hybrids
Gladiolus natalensis
Gloriosa rothschildiana
Habranthus, all species
Haemanthus, all species
Hemerocallis, all species and hybrids
Homeria breyniana
Hyacinthus orientalis
Hymenocallis amancaes
Hymenocallis x festalis
Hymenocallis narcissiflora
Iris x germanica, bearded
Leucojum autumnale
Lilium auratum
Lilium davidii
Lilium henryi
Lilium lancifolium
Lilium longiflorum
Lilium pardalinum
Lilium regale
Lilium speciosum
Lilium superbum
Milla biflora
Polianthes tuberosa
Sauromatum guttatum
Sinningia
Smithiantha
Tigridia pavonia
Tulbaghia fragrans
Tulbaghia violacea
Vallota speciosa
Zantedeshia, all species
Zephyranthes, all species

SUMMER

Early Summer Blooming

Allium aflatunense
Allium karataviense
Allium moly
Allium neapolitanum
Allium triquetrum
Alophia pulchella
Alstroemeria, all species
Anthericum liliago
Calochortus, all species
Camassia, all species
Dietes iridiodes
Dietes tricolor
Eucharis grandiflora
Hemerocallis species and hybrids
Iris douglasiana
Iris foetidissima
Iris innominata
Ixia maculata
Ixia viridiflora
Leucojum aestivum
Lilium pumilum
Moraea villosa
Muscari comosa
Narcissus poeticus
Oxalis adenophylla
Oxalis bowiei
Sauromatum guttatum
Zantedeschia, all species
Zephyranthes atamasco

Summer Blooming

Achimenes
Acidanthera bicolor
Agapanthus
Allium caeruleum
Allium christophii
Allium giganteum
x Amarcrinum
Begonia, tuberous kinds
Belamcanda chinensis
Bessera elegans
Brodiaea, all species
Caladium x hortulanum
Canna garden hybrids

Chlidanthus fragrans
Colocasia esculenta
x Crinodonna
Crinum, all species
Crocosmia, all species
Dahlia garden hybrids
Dietes bicolor
Dietes iridiodes
Eucomis bicolor
Galtonia candicans
Gladiolus alatus
Gladiolus byzantinus
Gladiolus carinatus
Gladiolus caryophyllaceus
Gladiolus hybrids
Gladiolus liliaceus
Gladiolus natalensis
Gloriosa rothschildiana
Habranthus, all species
Haemanthus coccineus
Haemanthus katharinae
Homeria breyniana
Hymenocallis amancaes
Hymenocallis x festalis
Hymenocallis narcissiflora
Iris kaempferi
Iris xiphioides
Lilium, many species
Lycoris radiata
Milla biflora
Sinningia hybrids
Smithiantha hybrids
Sprekelia formosissima
Tigridia pavonia
Tulbaghia violacea
Zephyranthes grandiflora

Late Summer Blooming

Achimenes
Acidanthera bicolor
Amaryllis belladonna
Begonia, tuberous kinds
Brunsvigia josephinae
Canna hybrids
Crinum species
Crocosmia, all species

Dahlia garden hybrids
Dietes bicolor
Dietes iridiodes
Galtonia candicans
Gladiolus alatus
Gladiolus natalensis
Haemanthus albiflos
Lilium auratum
Lilium lancifolium
Lilium speciosum
Lycoris radiata
Polianthes tuberosa
Urginea maritima
Vallota speciosa
Watsonia beatricus
Zephyranthes candida
Zephyranthes tubiflora

Plant in Early Summer

Agapanthus
x Amarcrinum
Clivia
x Crinodonna
Cyclamen hederifolium
Dietes bicolor
Dietes iridiodes
Eucharis grandiflora
Tulbaghia violacea

Plant In Summer

Agapanthus africanus
x Amarcrinum
Brunsvigia josephinae
Clivia
Colchicum, all species
Crocus goulimyi
Crocus longiflorus
Crocus nievus
Crocus sativus
Crocus speciosus
Cyclamen coum coum
Dietes bicolor
Dietes iridiodes
Eucharis grandiflora
Iris cristata
Iris douglasiana
Iris foetidissima
Iris innominata
Iris sibirica
Iris tectorum
Lycoris africana
Lycoris radiata
Moraea polystachya
Nerine species
Tulbaghia fragrans
Tulbaghia violacea
Urginea maritima

Plant In Late Summer

Agapanthus africanus
Amaryllis belladonna
Clivia
x Crinodonna
Dietes bicolor
Dietes iridoides
Eucharis grandiflora
Tulbaghia fragrans

FALL

Early Fall Blooming

Achimenes
Acidanthera bicolor
Amaryllis belladonna
Begonia x tuberhybrida
Brunsvigia josephinae
Canna hybrids
Crinum, all species
Crocosmia, all species
Dahlia hybrids
Dietes bicolor
Galtonia candicans
Gladiolus alatus
Gladiolus natalensis
Haemanthus albiflos
Lilium auratum
Lilium lancifolium
Lilium speciosum
Lycoris africanus
Polianthes tuberosa
Urginea maritima
Vallota speciosa
Zephyranthes candida
Zephyranthes tubiflora

Fall Blooming

Achimenes
Acidanthera bicolor
Amaryllis belladonna
Begonia x tuberhybrida
Canna hybrids
Colchicum, all species
Crocosmia, all species
Crocus goulimyi
Crocus longiflorus
Crocus niveus
Crocus sativus
Crocus speciosus
Cyclamen hederifolium
Cyclamen neapolitanum
Dahlia hybrids
Dietes bicolor
Dietes iridoides
Galtonia candicans
Gladiolus alatus
Gladiolus natalensis

Leucojum autumnale
Lilium auratum
Lilium lancifolium
Lilium speciosum
Lycoris africanus
Moraea polystachya
Narcissus viridiflorus
Nerine bowdenii
Nerine sardensis
Sternbergia lutea
Urginea maritima

Late Fall Blooming

Colchicum, all species
Crocus goulimyi
Crocus niveus
Dietes bicolor
Dietes iridiodes
Narcissus tazetta paper-white
Nerine bowdenii

Plant in Early Fall

Agapanthus, all species
Allium, all species
Alophia pulchella
x Amarcrinum
Amaryllis belladonna
Anemone, all species
Anthericum liliago
Babiana stricta
Brodiaea, all species
Calochortus, all species
Camassia, all species
Chionodoxa, all species
Clivia, all species
Convallaria majalis
x Crinodonna
Crocus angustifolius
Crocus aureus
Crocus biflorus
Crocus chrysanthus
Crocus flavus
Crocus imperati
Crocus kotschyanus
Crocus olivieri
Crocus sieberi
Crocus tomasinianus
Crocus vernus

Cyclamen coum coum
Cyclamen persicum
Cyclamen repandum
Dietes iridiodes
Endymion hispanica
Endymion hispanica
Eranthis, all species
Eremurus, all species
Erythronium, all species
Eucharis grandiflora
Freesia refracta
Fritillaria, all species
Galanthus, all species
Gladiolus x colvillei
Gladiolus liliaceus
Gladiolus recurvus
Gladiolus tristis
Hippeastrum species and hybrids
Homeria breyniana
Hyacinthus orientalis
Hymenocallis caroliniana
Ipheion uniflorum
Iris danfordiae
Iris, Dutch hybrids
Iris kaempferi
Iris, Louisiana group
Iris orientalis, Spurias
Iris, Regeliocyclus hybrids
Iris reticulata
Iris unguicularis
Iris xiphioides
Ixia, all species
Ixiolirion tataricum
Lachenalia, all species
Lapeirousia, all species
Leucocoryne ixiodes
Leucojum aestivum
Leucojum vernum
Lilium, most kinds
Lycoris africana
Milla biflora
Moraea villosa
Muscari, all species
Narcissus asturiensis
Narcissus hybrids
Narcissus poeticus
Narcissus tazetta
Ornithogalum arabicum
Ornithogalum thyrsoides
Oxalis, all species
Puschkinia scilloides
Ranunculus asiaticus
Rhodohypoxis baurii
Scilla peruviana
Scilla sibirica
Sparaxis
Sternbergia, all species
Streptanthera cuprea
Trillium, all species
Tritonia crocata
Tulbaghia fragrans
Tulbaghia violacea
Tulipa, all kinds
Veltheimia capensis
Watsonia, all species and hybrids
Zantedeschia aethiopica

Winter Blooming

Anemone blanda
Crocus angustifolius
Crocus biflorus
Crocus chrysanthus
Crocus flavus
Crocus imperati
Crocus niveus
Crocus sieberi
Crocus tomasinianus
Cyclamen coum coum
Cyclamen persicum
Eranthis hyemalis
Galanthus nivalis
Iris danfordiae
Iris reticulata
Narcissus minor
Narcissus tazetta

Narcissus tazetta paper-white
Oxalis hirta
Oxalis purpurea
Tulbaghia fragrans

Winter Blooming As House Plants

Convallaria majalis
Crocus species
Eucharis amazonica
Freesia refracta
Hippeastrum hybrids
Hyacinthus orientalis
Muscari armeniacum
Narcissus tazetta
Oxalis purpurea
Sinningia hybrids
Tulipa species and hybrids
Zantedeschia aethiopica

Encyclopedia of Bulbs

This encyclopedia describes more than 250 of the diverse plants known as *bulbs*. Even though they are a varied group, bulbs have much in common. By definition, all are adapted to endure unfavorable weather by storing food underground. This may be accomplished by the formation of bulbs, corms, rhizomes, tubers or tuberous roots.

In the following descriptions, the ''vital statistics'' that follow each bulb name provide much valuable information. Details are noted on bloom season and length, available colors, height, planting time and depth, and specific cultural requirements. Helpful information such as climate adaptation, design use and superior species for garden use are provided in the descriptive copy.

The vast majority of bulbs belong to one of three plant families: *Iridaceae, Iris; Amaryllidaceae, Amaryllis;* and *Liliaceae, Lily.* The lily family include *Allium, Lilium, Tulipa, Muscari* and *Trillium. Amaryllis, Narcissus* and *Nerine* belong to the *Amaryllis* family. *Crocus, Freesia, Gladiolus* and *Iris* are part of the *Iris* family.

Only three bulbs—*Dahlia imperialis, Eremurus robustus* and *Urginea maritima*—grow taller than 7 feet. No bulbs develop woody stems. Only one, *Gloriosa rothschildiana,* can be considered vinelike in its growth habit.

Bulb Names

Compared to most plant groups, bulbs comprise a wide array of botanical and common names. In this book, bulbs are listed alphabetically by their botanical name according to the standard horticultural reference, *Hortus Third.* Exceptions are *Dichelostemma* and *Triteleia,* which are found under *Brodiaea.* In the text, botanical names are shown in italics. In some cases the botanical name and common name are the same, such as *Iris, Dahlia* and *Gladiolus.* Note the sample below for a further explanation of botanical nomenclature.

Genus: Plants consisting of one or more species sharing many characteristics, usually flowers and fruit. Plural is *genera.*

Species: Plants with certain differences compared to other plants of the same genus. Characteristics normally continue from generation to generation. Variations in species that occur in nature are *varieties,* designated in this book as var.

Bessera elegans
Coral-drops

Family: Amaryllidaceae.

Family: Plants within a family share some general characteristics, but differ enough to be further categorized into genera.

Common Name

Hybrid crosses are sometimes made between different species or genera. It is designated by an ''x.'' Example: *Begonia x tuberhybrida.*

Bulb flowers come in many forms, both common and unusual. Left: *Nerine* species. Above: *Lachenalia aloides.*

Bulbs and Climate

If you are looking for bulbs that are easy to grow, choose those that originate in climates similar to your own. For example, bulbs from England thrive in the Pacific Northwest and British Columbia. Bulbs native to the humid tropics thrive in Florida. Those from South Africa flourish in southern California. See Bulbs and Their Origins, pages 8 and 9.

Many bulbs can be grown successfully in climates differing from their native homes. This often requires special care, but some gardeners love to try something different and challenging. This ambition and curiosity is what makes gardeners grow tulips in southern California and *Gladiolus* in Nebraska. To be successful, tulips in California require preplanting chilling. They should be planted after the soil cools—normally after Thanksgiving. *Gladiolus* grown in Nebraska must be dug in the fall and stored away from freezing temperatures during the winter months.

Climate and latitude have a great effect on the bloom period of bulbs. It's possible for a person in San Diego to see his pampered tulips bloom and fade, then fly to Washington D.C. and see tulips at their prime. He could then fly to Holland and see the tulip season again. If he were a true tulip fanatic, he could then dash to Scotland for another show. The farther north, the later spring arrives, and with it, a corresponding period of bloom.

Year-to-year weather patterns also cause change. In a warm year, spring bulbs bloom earlier. When winter cold lingers on, they bloom later in the season.

MICROCLIMATES

Microclimates are small climates that exist within a larger climate. They can have a great influence on how well bulbs adapt to a certain area. Daffodils will bloom a week or two later on a cool, north slope than they will on a warm, south-facing slope.

You can increase your success by recognizing these climates, and using them to your advantage. Before you plant your bulbs, take a walk around your home. You will notice subtle differences in temperature and accumulation of moisture. The northern exposure of your home does not receive afternoon sunshine, so temperatures are cooler, and the ground is often more moist. Conversely, the south and west exposures are warmer and drier due to the additional sunshine they receive. Bulbs that thrive in full sun or those that require heat to bloom should be planted here. If you live in a cold-climate area, or in a coastal region where cloudy conditions reduce sunshine, it would be helpful to plant heat-loving bulbs against a south wall. Extra heat is released onto the bulb plant. Heat absorbed by the wall during the day is released at night to increase the temperature around plants.

In some areas, placement in the garden can make a great difference in how the bulb grows. Because cold air sinks and warm air rises, a garden on a hillside is warmer than one in the valley below. A few degrees can make a difference to plants. Similarly, large bodies of water such as oceans or lakes *increase* temperatures of the surrounding area in the winter, and *decrease* temperatures in the summer.

CLIMATE ZONES

Pacific Northwest—The climate of much of this region is ideal for commercial bulb culture. Many daffodil, *Iris* and lily growers are located here. *Dahlias* are grown, but roots must be dug and stored during winter. Even though *Gladiolus* and tuberous begonias do well, they also must be protected from cold weather.

For some bulbs, there is not enough summer heat in the Pacific Northwest. Without sufficient heat, tulips left in the ground in summer are unable to produce buds for the next year. It is necessary to utilize microclimates to the fullest to grow bulbs such as *Eucharis, Gloriosa* and *Polianthes,* which need heat while actively growing.

Southern California—Winter rains and arid summers makes this area perfect for most bulbs from South Africa. Problems arise with bulbs such as tulips that require a period of cold temperatures. Tuberous begonias are at their best close to the coast, but farther inland they become temperamental. Lily-of-the-valley is difficult to establish because it requires cold. Winter aconite, dwarf species of *Iris,* snowdrops and many *Crocus* also require cold. Trumpet daffodils, a joy in other areas, are subject to basal rot, which destroys the bulb when the soil temperature goes over 70F (21C). But the early blooming Tazetta daffodils thrive here.

Desert Areas—Bulbs that bloom in early spring, before high heat arrives, are best for hot-summer regions. *Ranunculus* thrives in desert regions but must be kept dry during the summer. Some of the unusual, South-African bulbs that are native to regions with dry summers do well here. Species tulips, which come from areas in Turkey with cold winters and long, hot, dry summers, may do well in some of the high-elevation deserts. Desert summers are usually too hot and arid for lilies, tuberous begonias and *Caladiums.* Conditions can be modified by planting under lath and by increasing humidity around plants.

The South—The Gulf Coast, from Texas to Florida, has the heat and humidity ideal for *Caladium, Crinum* and *Achimenes.* Louisiana iris thrives here, but bearded iris is subject to rot and fungus. Tropical *Cannas* are superb. The standard spring bulbs—tulips, daffodils, hyacinths and *Crocus*—thrive throughout much of the upper South.

Midwest and North—Farther north, the standard spring bulbs are easier to grow. Bulbs that bloom in the winter and early spring but cannot tolerate freezing, such as paper-white *Narcissus,* are grown as house plants. Cold-tender bulbs such as *Dahlias* and *Gladiolus* have to be dug in fall and stored in a protected location during the winter.

Cold Areas—Even in the coldest areas such as Zones 2 to 4, certain bulbs are easy to grow. Among those that are cold-hardy are: *Belamcanda, Bulbocodium, Camassia, Chionodoxa, Convallaria,* many *Crocus, Eranthis, Erythronium, Fritillaria, Galanthus* and *Tulipa.*

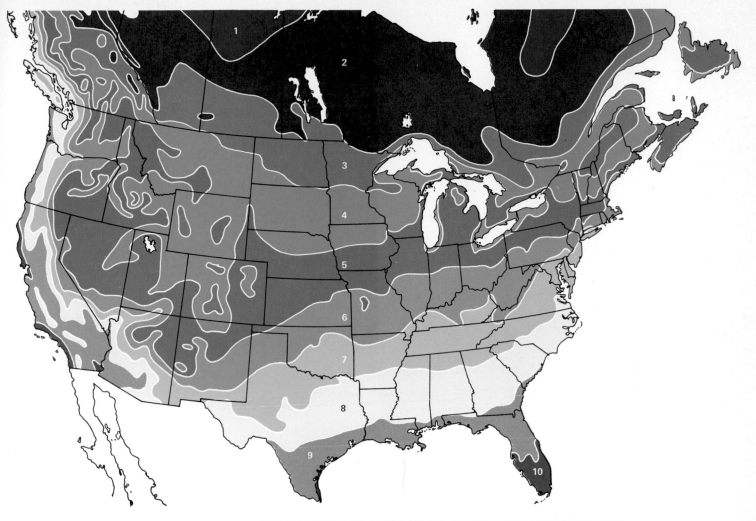

Hardiness Zones
of the United States and Canada

	Zone 1	Below −50F (−45C)
	Zone 2	−50 to −40F (−45 to −40C)
	Zone 3	−40 to −30F (−40 to −35C)
	Zone 4	−30 to −20F (−35 to −29C)
	Zone 5	−20 to −10F (−29 to −24C)
	Zone 6	−10 to 0F (−24 to −18C)
	Zone 7	0 to 10F (−18 to −12C)
	Zone 8	10 to 20F (−12 to −7C)
	Zone 9	20 to 30F (−7 to −1C)
	Zone 10	30 to 40F (−1 to 5C)

Each of the bulb descriptions in the following pages contains recommended zone adaptations based on the hardiness zone map shown above, developed by the United States Department of Agriculture. To find out if a bulb will grow in your area, note which climate zone you live in, then refer to the bulb descriptions for the zone recommendation.

Climate zones and maps are based on average temperatures, and many small climates exist within a general climate zone. Because of these variables, it is possible that you can grow plants not rated for your zone. For the best information on bulbs and climate adaptation, consult your local county extension agent or nurseryman.

Achimenes hybrid

Achimenes

Family: Gesneriaceae.
Native to: Central America, Mexico.
Bulb type: Scaly rhizome.
Bloom season & length: All summer.
Colors: Pink, rose, lavender, purple and yellow.
Height: Low, sometimes trailing.
Planting time: After frost.
Planting depth: Cover with 1/2 inch of soil.
Soil: Loose, fast-draining, house-plant soil mix.
Water: Keep moist.
Fertilizer: Monthly with a liquid formula at half the recommended dose.
Spacing: 1 inch.
Exposure: Light shade, humidity and warmth.
Propagation: Cuttings, seeds or small rhizome in leaf axils.
Pests & diseases: Few.
Storage: Store in regular pots or in vermiculite after drying.

Achimenes, a relative of *Gloxinia,* is best displayed in a hanging basket or planter. Flowers appear from early summer to fall. They come in shades of rose, pink, lavender, mauve, purple-blue and a rare yellow. Plants are somewhat fussy, growing best where *Fuchsias* and tuberose begonias thrive. Provide a temperature between 55F and 85F (13C and 30C) in semishade with moderate humidity. Rhizomes grow and multiply quickly, and produce great quantities of bloom.

Many species exist, but improved hybrids are usually grown. Some of the newer hybrids put out a 1- to 2-inch flower from the base of every leaf.

Plant 3 to 5 of the small, conelike rhizomes in an 8-inch pot. Cover with 1/2 to 1 inch of soil. Water moderately until growth begins. When the shoots are 3 inches long, make cuttings and stick them into the soil around the edge of the pot. They will form new plants, making the container planting full and attractive. Plant in pots outdoors after danger of frost has past, or indoors if you want to get a head start on the season. Fertilize once a month with a mild, liquid fertilizer at half the recommended dosage. When flowers cease to bloom in fall, gradually let the soil dry out. Because rhizomes are brittle and damage easily if exposed to air, keep bulbs in the pot during winter. If bulbs become crowded, divide in spring before growth begins. Adapted to most Zones but must be kept above 45F (7C).

Acidanthera bicolor

Family: Iridaceae.
Native to: Tropical and South Africa.
Bulb type: Corm.
Bloom season & length: Summer for 2 to 3 weeks.
Colors: White, with maroon or chocolate throat.
Height: 2 to 3 feet.
Planting time: After last frost.
Planting depth: Cover with 3 to 4 inches of soil.
Soil: Rich, well drained.
Water: Ample during growing season.
Fertilizer: Light application when leaves emerge, then again 1 month later.
Spacing: 6 inches.
Exposure: Full sun or light shade.
Propagation: Cormels that form at base of corm.
Pests & diseases: Occasionally bothered by thrips.
Storage: Dry peat moss, vermiculite or perlite.

Only one of the 33 species of *Acidanthera,* the Ethiopian *Acidanthera bicolor,* is grown in home gardens. Presently considered by some experts a species of *Gladiolus,* it is best known as *Acidanthera.* Plant grows to 3

Acidanthera bicolor

feet high. White, sweetly scented flowers are loosely spaced on slightly arching stems that reach 2 feet above spiky foliage. Flowers are 2 inches across and twice as deep. Each petal has a narrow, dark brown or chocolate-colored blotch at its base.

Fragrant and long lasting, *Acidanthera* is valued as a cut flower. It also has a delicate and graceful quality in the garden.

Culture is similar to *Gladiolus*. See page 99. Dig and store for winter, except in Zones 7 to 10, where it can remain in the ground.

Agapanthus
Lily-of-the-Nile

Family: Amaryllidaceae.
Native to: South Africa.
Bulb type: Rhizome.
Bloom season & length: Summer for 1 to 2 months. Longer in mild climates.
Colors: Blue, white and dark purple.
Height: 1 to 5 feet.
Planting time: Spring.
Planting depth: Cover rhizomes with 1/2 inch of soil.
Soil: No preference.
Water: Water well during active growth. Withstands some drought.
Fertilizer: In spring and summer, if grown in containers. Otherwise not necessary.
Spacing: 1 foot.
Exposure: Full sun or light shade.
Propagation: By division in spring.
Pests & diseases: Few, but occasional infestations of mealybugs at leaf bases.
Storage: Mulch plants to protect them from frost in mild-winter areas. In cold areas, bring plants indoors in containers as foliage plants.

Agapanthus is a handsome container plant in cold-winter climates, and a successful, low-maintenance landscape plant in temperate climates, such as Zones 9 and 10. Foliage is damaged by frost, but recovers quickly with warm weather. If the below-ground rhizome freezes, the plant is doomed to die. There are evergreen and deciduous species. Deciduous kinds are slightly hardier to cold.

Agapanthus is commonly called *Lily-of-the-Nile,* which is a misnomer, because it is native to the southern tip of Africa. The most common variety is *Agapanthus praecox* subspecies *orientalis,* an evergreen with handsome, strap-shaped leaves. Flower stems grow to 5 feet high topped with umbels of white or blue flowers. Dwarf forms are available that have 12- to 18-inch stems. Taller forms have stems that reach 5 feet high. *A. africanus* has deeper blue flowers and is slightly shorter than *A. praecox* subspecies *orientalis.* It is used in hybridizing to increase the depth of flower color.

Because *Agapanthus* hybridizes easily, many shades of blue and white are available. For this reason, it is often advisable to buy a named variety, or buy plants in bloom. 'Alba' is a fine variety with white flowers that grows 5 feet tall. *Agapanthus inapertus,* a deciduous species, has drooping, deep-purple flowers in small clusters.

Permanent outdoor plantings require little care. Mature, thick clumps may benefit from division. The

Agapanthus species

Agapanthus species

Allium neopolitanum

Allium species

best time to divide plants is in spring just before new growth begins. After they are divided, plants take some time to adjust and bloom well again.

The flowers are handsome in contrast to daylilies. *Agapanthus* is also an excellent cut flower. In pots, they are similar to *Clivia,* in that they bloom best when rootbound. They can remain in tubs until they look as if they will break the container. Fertilize container plants in spring and again in midsummer.

Allium

Family: Amaryllidaceae.
Native to: Northern Hemisphere.
Bulb type: True bulb.
Bloom season & length: Spring to summer for 1 month.
Colors: White, purple, mauve, pink, blue or yellow.
Height: 6 inches to 5 feet.
Planting time: Spring.
Planting depth: Three times depth of bulb.
Soil: Not particular, but good drainage is preferred.
Water: Regular during growth.
Fertilizer: Light applications.
Spacing: 6 to 12 inches.
Exposure: Usually full sun.
Propagation: Offsets at bulb base or seeds.
Pests & diseases: Few.
Storage: Usually not necessary.

People seem to either love or hate plants belonging to the onion and garlic group—the genus *Allium*. This genus is large, including more than 350 species. Some are noxious weeds and some are exceptionally beautiful. Their reputation for producing an unpleasant odor is largely overstated. All *Allium* species have an onion odor when leaves are bruised, but many have sweetly fragrant flowers.

Smaller species such as yellow *Allium moly,* blue *A. caeruleum,* white *A. neapolitanum* 'Grandiflorum', and white and green *A. triquetrum* are excellent for naturalizing and planting in drifts. Successful plantings multiply profusely. The spectacular, large-flowered species can grow 5 feet high, with flowers in shades of mauve, gray and lavender. Most grow successfully in Zones 4 to 10. Plant in sun to semishade.

The most important species include:

Allium aflatunense, a native of northern Iran. It bears large, round heads of lilac-mauve flowers in clusters on 3-foot-high stems.

Allium caeruleum, also known as *A. azureum,* is native to Siberia. It has small, compact, cornflower-blue flowers on 18-inch-high stems. It is easy to grow and often used in conjunction with yellow *A. moly,* which blooms at the same time and is similar in size and shape.

Allium christophii (Allium albopilosum), native to Iran, makes spherical umbels of star-shaped lilac flowers on 1-foot-high stems. 'Star of Persia' is a popular selection.

Allium giganteum is a rare and splendid species from Siberia. It is the tallest—up to 6 feet, with an umbel of lilac flowers 6 inches across. It is a valuable plant for background plantings. It also makes a long-lasting cut flower.

Allium karataviense, from Turkestan, has broad, crimson-tinted leaves, usually two, that lie on the ground. It produces large, 12-inch umbels of white or pink flowers on stems 12 inches high. It makes a handsome pot or border plant.

Allium moly, golden garlic, is from southern Europe. It is one of the best known *Alliums.* The golden-yellow umbel of flowers top a 1-foot-high stem. It is one of the best for growing in drifts, grouping plants in natural-looking plantings.

Allium neapolitanum is native to southern Italy and is slightly tender to frost. *A. neapolitanum* 'Grandiflorum' is a superior form and slightly more cold-hardy. It bears white flowers in loose umbels on top of 1-foot-high stems.

Allium triquetrum is from southern Europe. It prefers shade, and with ideal conditions, it naturalizes to the point of being invasive. The green and white pendulous flowers are borne at the top of a triangular-shaped, 1-foot stalk.

Alophia

Family: Iridaceae.
Native to: North and South America.
Bulb type: Bulb.
Bloom season & length: Spring to summer.
Colors: Lavender-blue.
Height: About 3 inches.
Planting time: Fall.
Planting depth: Cover with 1 inch of soil.
Soil: Sandy loam.
Water: Keep moist during growth.
Fertilizer: Little is necessary.
Spacing: 2 inches.
Exposure: Full sun to light shade.
Propagation: Seeds.
Pests & diseases: Few.
Storage: Keep in pots until spring. Allow to naturalize in warm climates.

The best and most commonly grown species is *Alophia pulchella (Herbertia pulchella),* a native of Chile, Argentina and southern Brazil.

A 2- to 3-inch stem holds the flower above grasslike leaves. Small, lavender-blue flowers resemble miniature *Tigridia* or *Morea* flowers. Like them, *Alophia* flowers last only one day. Flowers are composed of six petals. Three large petals have a white area spotted with purple near the base. Three recurved inner petals are much smaller.

Alophia is easy to grow in mild climates, but is rare and considered a collector's item. It shows off well in a bonsai pot. Use a planting mix of equal parts sand, peat moss and loam. Cover bulb with 1 inch of soil. Plant several in a 6-inch pot. Keep watered once plants begin growing.

The original bulb forms small bulblets and eventually fills the pot. Separate offsets as they become crowded. Seeds are easy to collect because they fall out when the stem is bent over. Seeds germinate easily and the plant often self-sows.

Allium neapolitanum 'Grandiflorum'

Alophia pulchella

Alstroemeria ligtu

Alstroemeria ligtu

Alstroemeria
Peruvian lily

Family: Alstroemeriaceae.
Native to: West coast of South America primarily.
Bulb type: Elongated, thickened roots.
Bloom season & length: Late spring for 5 weeks.
Colors: Orange, yellow, pink, red, lavender and white.
Height: 1 to 4 feet.
Planting time: Early spring.
Planting depth: Cover roots with 2 to 4 inches soil.
Soil: Rich, well-drained loam.
Water: Keep moist during growing season.
Fertilizer: Once with light application after shoots appear.
Spacing: 1 foot.
Exposure: Prefers filtered shade.
Propagation: Usually from seeds, but roots can be divided in spring.
Pests & diseases: Snails.
Storage: Leave in ground in Zones 6 to 10. In other zones grow in containers and bring inside during periods of cold weather.

This elegant and superior garden plant deserves wider recognition. It is adaptable to a number of climates, growing outdoors in Zones 6 to 10.

Alstroemeria produces thick, long, tuberous roots that look like fingers. Handle carefully because they are brittle. Plant in a rich, loamy, well-drained soil. Build a small cone in the planting hole and spread the roots gently out from the crown. Position the crown 2 inches below the soil surface. Planted in filtered shade, it grows and spreads indefinitely. The tall, stiff stems usually do not require staking.

Alstroemeria aurantiaca, A. ligtu and their hybrids are becoming staples of the florist trade. Each stem produces many flowers. They are pretty and among the longest-lasting cut flowers. Their common names Peruvian lily and lily-of-the-Incas refer to the lily shape of the 2-inch flowers.

Notable species are:

Alstroemeria ligtu and its hybrids are available in many colors. The color of the species is light pink with purple spots. White, dark pink, salmon, apricot and orange-red are also available. All have 2- to 3-foot-high stems and bloom over a long period. Those known as *Dutch hybrids* include some of the most popular kinds.

Alstroemeria pelegrina, lily-of-the-Incas, grows to 1 foot high. Its lilac flowers are splashed with purple, and are the same size as taller varieties.

Alstroemeria psittacina also grows low. Flowers are dark red tipped with green. Flowers are more tubular than other forms. Plant does well in light shade and spreads by seeds.

Amaryllis belladonna
Naked lady

Family: Amaryllidaceae.
Native to: South Africa.
Bulb type: Bulb.
Bloom season & length: Late summer to fall for about 3 weeks.
Colors: Usually pink, but some varieties range from white to dark red.
Height: 2 to 3 feet.
Planting time: Midsummer to late summer.
Planting depth: Cover bulb with 2 inches of soil. Plant slightly deeper in cold climates.
Soil: No preference.
Water: Keep moist when in foliage.
Fertilizer: Not necessary in most soils.
Spacing: About 10 inches.
Exposure: Full sun or filtered shade.
Propagation: Divide bulbs in late summer or start from seeds.
Pests & diseases: None.
Storage: Leave in ground.

Amaryllis belladonna has many close relatives. *Brunsvigia, Hippeastrum, Lycoris, Sprekelia* and *Vallota* species are similar and occasionally confused with *Amaryllis.* At one time, all were classified as *Amaryllis.*

In late summer or fall, when the garden is lacking in flowers, these large, 4-inch bulbs send up a bare stem from the earth. Although bulbs produce foliage, the leaves dry out before the blooming period—thus their common name, "naked ladies." The 2-foot-high stem is topped by a cluster of large, light pink, fragrant trumpets. Plants live for years in mild-climate regions, multiplying into large clumps. Large clusters of bulbs eventually push their way out of the soil.

Plant with *Agapanthus* or Shasta daisies to mask the bareness of the stems. *Amaryllis* are tough enough to push their way up through a ground cover of English ivy.

Hybrids are superior to the original species. Trumpet-shaped flowers go all the way around the stem to form a loose umbel. Colors range from wine-red through shades of pink and rose to white. Most hybrids have a yellow center.

Plant grows in Zones 9 and 10 without care. It can be planted with the bulb barely covered. In Zones 5 to 8, plant in a warm, sunny location. Cover with at least 5 or 6 inches of soil to protect bulbs from frost. Plant grows in any soil that is not overly wet. *Amaryllis* do not do well after they are moved. They may require three or four years to bloom if moved when roots or leaves are actively growing. The best time to divide is in summer or when they are in bloom, before growth of new roots and leaves begins.

Amaryllis belladonna

Amaryllis belladonna 'Hybrid White'

Anemone coronaria, de Caen group

Anemone

Family: Ranunculaceae.
Native to: Most from Mediterranean and Asia Minor. Some originate from North America and Japan.
Bulb type: Tuberous rhizome.
Bloom season & length: Spring and summer.
Colors: Blue, white, pink, rose, mauve and terra-cotta.
Height: 2 to 15 inches.
Planting time: Fall south of Zone 7. Spring in Zone 7 and north.
Planting depth: 1 inch deep.
Soil: Rich, sandy loam.
Water: Keep moist during growing season.
Fertilizer: Responds well to moderate applications of complete fertilizer.
Spacing: About 4 inches.
Exposure: Full sun or filtered shade.
Propagation: Seeds.
Pests & diseases: Few.
Storage: Keep dry.

Basically, two forms of *Anemone* grow from tubers. Because fibrous-rooted forms of *Anemone* are not types of bulbs, they are not discussed in this book.

One group of the tuberous form is similar to a low-growing ground cover, with daisy-shaped, pastel flowers. The best known, low-growing forms come from the mountains of southern Europe, and are at home in Zones 6 to 9. *Anemone apennina* from Italy and *A. blanda* from Greece are similar. Both have blue flowers. Both also have cultivars in pink, mauve and white. They are delightful when planted between steppingstones, under shrubbery or in drifts under flowering trees.

The other tuberous form grows 1 foot or more high with poppy-shaped or double flowers. These include *Anemone coronaria* and *A. fulgens.*

The small tubers of either form look like raisins or twigs. *Anemone coronaria* tubers grown in California have a flattish top and a cone-shaped bottom. Tubers from Europe look like dried raisins. Plant them as soon as they are received in the mail or after you bring them home from the nursery. Cover lightly with soil. They accept a variety of conditions but do best in lightly shaded, moist locations under tall trees. It takes them several years to become adapted and spread.

Anemone coronaria is best known for its de Caen hybrids. The single, 3- to 4-inch flowers are dark purple-blue, bright red, rose or white. Used by florists for spring bouquets, de Caen hybrids can be induced into a long period of bloom by successive plantings. The St. Brigid group of *A. coronaria* is double with slightly smaller flowers of less-intense color. The St. Bravo group from Holland has 2-inch flowers with a wider range of colors, including a rich terra-cotta.

Anemone x fulgens has dazzling, 2-inch scarlet flowers. This group should be planted in the fall as far north as Zone 7, but it is best to plant them in spring in areas farther north. In Zones 9 and 10, dig bulbs after the foliage dies to keep them dry during the summer. Farther north, dig in fall to protect them from cold. They do best with a 6-month dormant period.

Plant *Anemone x fulgens* in soil that is well drained. Cover with 1 to 2 inches of soil. Usually a circle on the tuber indicates where the foliage will appear. Plant with the circle facing upward, points facing down.

Anemone coronaria, de Caen group

Anemone coronaria, St. Brigid group

Anthericum liliago
St. Bernard's lily

Family: Liliaceae.
Native to: Southern Europe.
Bulb type: Tuberous root.
Bloom season & length: Spring and early summer for 4 weeks.
Colors: White.
Height: 2 to 3 feet.
Planting time: Spring or fall.
Planting depth: Cover bulb with 2 inches soil.
Soil: Light and well drained.
Water: Constant supply of moisture.
Fertilizer: Not necessary.
Spacing: About 6 inches.
Exposure: Medium sun.
Propagation: From fleshy roots in fall or with seeds.
Pests & diseases: Few.
Storage: Not usually necessary.

There are many species of *Anthericum,* but St. Bernard's lily is the only important garden species. It is best adapted to Zones 6 to 9. You should be aware, however, that St. Bernard's lily is a loose term applied to many plants. It is closely related to *Chlorophytum comosum,* the house plant known as *spider plant.*

Anthericum liliago bears 1-1/2-inch flowers along 2-foot-long stems. It has conspicuous yellow anthers and a snow-white, funnel-shaped flower that resembles a lily. The bloom period is from late spring through early summer.

Anthericum looks best grown as an edging or in front of a border. It requires moisture and a light, well-drained soil with partial or filtered sun. Plant in spring or fall. Spread out roots as if planting a bare-root rose. Cover with 2 inches of soil.

Anthericum species

Babiana rubrocyanea

Babiana
Baboon flower

Family: Iridaceae.
Native to: South Africa.
Bulb type: Corm.
Bloom season & length: Spring for 1 month.
Colors: Usually blue, lavender or white.
Height: 8 to 12 inches.
Planting time: Fall.
Planting depth: Cover with 1 inch soil.
Soil: Any well-drained soil.
Water: Necessary during growing season.
Fertilizer: Light, seasonal applications are helpful but not required.
Spacing: About 6 inches.
Exposure: Full sun or part sun.
Propagation: Remove small corms that form around base, or sow seeds.
Pests & diseases: Few.
Storage: Dry peat moss or in container.

Babiana, like many of the bulbs from South Africa, grows from a corm. The name is derived from the fact that baboons dig up the corms for food. There are more than 50 species, but *Babiana stricta* is most popular for gardens or in pots. It grows 1 foot high or more with flowers in various shades of blue, lavender, creamy white and occasionally crimson. Leaves are pleated and slightly hairy. Five or six cup-shaped flowers appear on each stem. 'Tubergen's Blue' has light-

Tuberous begonia

blue flowers on a tall stem. 'White King' is white with striking blue anthers.

Babiana rubrocyanea, considered by some to be the best species, has a sky-blue flower with a large crimson center. It is dwarf in size compared to other forms.

Babianas are easy to grow in Zones 8 to 10. Grow in containers in other zones. They like well-drained soil and at least a half-day of sun. Plant 7 or 8 corms to a 6-inch pot and place 1 inch of soil over the top. Some gardeners recommend a light application of a complete fertilizer when the shoots first emerge.

Babianas are well suited for flower borders, rock gardens, edgings and pots. Because leaves remain in an upright position, cut them off after they turn brown. Corms multiply rapidly and can be divided in two or three years.

Begonia

Family: Begoniaceae.
Native to: South America.
Bulb type: Tuber.
Bloom season & length: Early summer to frost.
Colors: White, pink, red, orange, apricot and yellow.
Height: 12 to 18 inches.
Planting time: Spring after frost, or indoors late winter.
Planting depth: Top of tuber level with soil.
Soil: Rich, organic loam.
Water: Keep moist.
Fertilizer: Liquid organic fertilizer at half the recommended strength, once each month.
Spacing: 1 foot.
Exposure: Light shade.
Propagation: Division.
Pests & diseases: Mildew.
Storage: Dry peat moss.

Tuberous begonias are the "prima donnas" of the summer shade garden. Because of their glorious performance, they deserve center stage. Other plants might play accompanying roles, but do little to draw attention away from the stars of the show.

Tuberous begonias are temperamental. They dislike wind, but must have air circulation. They don't do well in full sun or dense shade. They prefer humidity, but will not tolerate water on their foliage. They perform best in cool, summer weather with bright light and cool, circulating air. Flowers drop during warm weather.

Traditionally, they give a poor showing in the Southeast but are standouts in the Northwest. They grow to perfection in coastal gardens of the West. Despite the trouble, no other flower can surpass tuberous begonias. After you understand their idiosyncrasies, you'll love them.

Begonia x tuberhybrida grows upright. The 'Pendula' group drapes and trails so it is used for hanging baskets. Plant tubers two to three months before the outdoor planting date, in a location protected from frost. Plant in a flat of peat moss with a little sand mixed in for drainage. The depression in the tuber is where the leaves appear. The rounded part is where the roots show. The roots also appear around the sides, so bury the tuber almost to the rim. To prevent rot, the saucer area on top of the tuber should be kept clean and dry. Soon, fat, pink buds appear, followed by the leaves.

Babiana hybrid

Bright shade beneath this lath house provides ideal light for tuberous begonias. Strong light reaches leaves, but lath reduces heat.

Rose form *Begonia*

Camellia form *Begonia*

Ruffled form *Begonia*

Ruffled form *Begonia*

Tuberous begonias make excellent bedding plants.

At this time, transplant into pots or plant in the ground. Position plants at the same depth as in the flat. Plants prefer humus-rich soil with good drainage. Allow 2 inches between the tuber and the edge of containers. Some people prefer to use wooden tubs or long boxes. Leaves of tuberous begonias tend to grow in one direction. Take this into account when planting.

When watering, keep the water off the foliage as much as possible because it encourages mildew. Water also adds weight to the flowers, causeing them to droop. Irrigate by flooding plants or use a soaker hose. Do not use a sprinkler. Keep soil moist but not soggy.

Pale-green leaves indicate a need for nitrogen. Use a liquid, organic fertilizer at monthly intervals. Well-fed begonias have dark-green leaves that tend to turn down at the edges. Stop feeding in late summer and allow plants to go dormant gradually.

Plants can be kept in pots until the following spring, as long as they remain dry and protected from freezing. Plants in garden soil should be dug in the fall and stored in a dry place. Too much water and mold causes them to rot. Remove stems before storing. See page 27 for storage techniques.

Tuberous begonias are easy to grow from seeds, which are available from mail-order nurseries. Seeds started indoors in January often produce some blooms the first year. They are also easy to grow from cuttings taken in the spring. They will bloom and form a new tuber by the end of summer. Spray or dust at the first signs of mildew.

Varieties are available in many colors: white, pink, rose, yellow, salmon, apricot, scarlet and red. Some, such as 'Picotee' and 'Marginata', are bordered with another color. Flower forms create further distinctions. They are classified as *Rose, Camellia, Carnation, Single* and *Ruffled.*

In addition to varieties with large, 6-inch flowers, there are *Multifloras.* These have many, small, double flowers. *Begonia x intermedia* 'Bertini' have single, trumpet-shaped, pendulous blossoms, and are more tolerant of drier conditions.

Begonia grandis grows 2 to 3 feet high. It has pink or white flowers in drooping cymes that resemble bedding begonias. Leaves are red.

Rex begonias, *Begonia rex,* are so different from the tuberous kinds, you may assume they are not related. They are *rhizomatous,* meaning they are grown from rhizomes rather than tubers. Rex begonias are grown primarily for their attractive foliage. Many named varieties have leaf markings of silver, red, mauve, purple, black and light and dark green. Flowers of most varieties are inconsequential. Care is similar to tuberous begonias but plants are more robust. Because they usually remain in the same container for years, wash away salt deposits that build up by soaking the soil repeatedly.

Belamcanda chinensis

Belamcanda chinensis
Blackberry lily

Family: Iridaceae.
Native to: China and Japan.
Bulb type: Rhizome.
Bloom season & length: Midsummer for 4 to 5 weeks.
Colors: Orange and yellow.
Height: About 30 inches.
Planting time: Spring.
Planting depth: Just below soil surface.
Soil: No preference.
Water: Keep moist during growing season.
Fertilizer: Not necessary.
Spacing: About 6 inches.
Exposure: Full sun.
Propagation: Divide in spring or fall or plant seeds.
Pests & diseases: Few.
Storage: Not usually required. Mulch north of Zone 6.

The blackberry lily is a little-known bulb from the Orient. It is related to the rhizomatous iris but resembles it only in foliage. It earned its common name from the clusters of shiny black seeds that form after flowering. Showy, 2-inch flowers appear on 2- to 3-foot-high stems during summer. Flower colors include pure yellow, orange and yellow, and orange and crimson. New hybrids and crosses are being developed that will increase the range of colors. Most important is the hybrid genus, *x Pardancanda,* which is available in a wide range of colors, including stripes and polka dots.

Blackberry lily grows as far north as Ohio, farther if plants are protected with a mulch during winter. Heat and drought tolerance are excellent.

Bessera elegans

Bessera elegans
Coral-drops

Family: Amaryllidaceae.
Native to: Mexico.
Bulb type: Corm.
Bloom season & length: Midsummer for several weeks.
Colors: Coral, red and purple.
Height: About 2 feet.
Planting time: Whenever available, usually in fall.
Planting depth: Cover with 4 inches of soil.
Soil: Rich and gritty.
Water: Regular during growing season.
Fertilizer: Light applications.
Spacing: About 10 inches.
Exposure: Full sun.
Propagation: Divide after leaves die to ground.
Pests & diseases: Snails and slugs.
Storage: Dig and store in regions where the ground freezes.

Coral-drops is an unusual bulb that produces drooping, scarlet buds on top of 2-foot-high stems. When buds open, they reveal a white center with conspicuous purple anthers. Each stem has 10 to 15 buds. The bulbs are attractive in groups and make interesting cut flowers.

Coral-drops is cold-hardy as far north as Zone 7. Use it as an attractive container plant that can be taken outdoors in late spring in colder areas.

Give plants a rich, gritty soil in full sun. Cover with 4 inches of soil. Keep well watered until foliage dies down. At that time dig, divide and replant.

Bletilla striata
Chinese ground orchid

Family: Orchidaceae.
Native to: Asia.
Bulb type: Tuberous rhizome.
Bloom season & length: Late spring for about 2 weeks.
Colors: Lavender or white.
Height: 2 feet.
Planting time: Early spring.
Planting depth: Cover with 1 inch soil.
Soil: Prefers loose, well-drained loam.
Water: Regular during growing season.
Fertilizer: Little is necessary.
Spacing: 1 foot.
Exposure: Full sun but with afternoon shade.
Propagation: Divide in spring.
Pests & diseases: Snails and slugs.
Storage: Dry peat moss or leave in ground.

Bletilla striata, Chinese ground orchid, is an easy-to-grow orchid that should be grown more often. Fleshy roots are completely dormant in winter and available from nurseries at this time.

Bletilla striata grows best in a loose, loam soil with good drainage. Because it accepts temperatures to 20F (−7C) and lower if mulched, it is often called the *hardy orchid.* As soon as the weather warms in spring, pleated leaves appear. They are followed by a 1- to 2-foot-high spike covered with several, small, orchid flowers. The purple and lavender flowers resemble small cattleya orchids. 'Alba' is a choice variety with pure-white flowers.

Chinese ground orchid grows well in Zones 9 to 10, but needs a mulch in winter north of Zone 8. Transplant only when dormant in winter. Eventually, a planting forms a large clump. This can be divided, but the longer it is left to establish, the better the blooms.

Bletilla striata

Brodiaea

Family: Amaryllidaceae.
Native to: Western North America.
Bulb type: Corm.
Bloom season & length: Late spring for several weeks.
Colors: Lavender, purple and gold.
Height: 18 inches.
Planting time: Fall.
Planting depth: 2 to 3 inches.
Soil: Adaptable.
Water: During growing season.
Fertilizer: Not necessary.
Spacing: 2 inches.
Exposure: Full sun.
Propagation: Small cormels that form around base of corm.
Pests & diseases: Few.
Storage: Leave in ground.

Brodiaea pulchella (Dichelostemma pulchellum) is native to the dry hills of California. Its small, tight umbels of papery, lavender flowers bloom in great quantities on 18-inch-high stems. *B. ixioides (Triteleia ixiodes)* has larger, gold, star-shaped flowers with brown rays on the exterior. It is more cold-tender than the others. The best variety for the garden is *Brodiaea laxa (Triteleia laxa)* and its superior form, 'Queen Fabiola'. The purple flowers appear in a spreading umbel on 1-foot-high stems. *Triteleia, Ipheion* and *Dichelostemma* are related to *Brodiaea.* All grow in Zones 6 to 10.

Brodiaea laxa

Brunsvigia josephinae

Bulbinella floribunda

Brunsvigia josephinae
Josephine's lily

Family: Amaryllidaceae.
Native to: South Africa.
Bulb type: True bulb.
Bloom season & length: Late summer for 2 weeks.
Colors: Dark pink, dark red.
Height: 18 inches.
Planting time: Fall after flowering has finished.
Planting depth: Cover with 1 inch soil.
Soil: Sandy loam.
Water: Regular during growing season.
Fertilizer: Not necessary.
Spacing: 1 foot.
Exposure: Full sun or filtered sun.
Propagation: Seeds, occasionally from offsets.
Pests & diseases: Few.
Storage: Cool, dry location.

This native to South Africa is a dramatic-looking member of the *Amaryllis* family. Rose-red flowers appear in an umbel on 18-inch-high stems in late summer. From 30 to 60, 3-inch-long, funnel-shaped flowers are separated from the stem by 6-inch *pedicels,* the stalks of individual flowers. Bulbs are huge—8 inches in diameter—and more in depth.

Brunsvigia josephinae grows in California in Zones 9 and 10, and in other areas where summers are not too wet. It prefers rich soil that has excellent drainage. When planting, position the neck of bulb at soil level. Plants need at least a half-day of sun. After the foliage dies back in early summer, keep fairly dry until naked stem appears in late summer.

Plants seldom produce offsets, so they are usually grown from seeds. But be prepared for a long wait: It takes 12 *years* or more for them to bloom!

Bulbinella floribunda

Family: Liliaceae.
Native to: South Africa and New Zealand.
Bulb type: Rhizome.
Bloom season & length: Early spring for several weeks.
Colors: Yellow, cream and orange.
Height: 2 feet.
Planting time: Fall.
Planting depth: Cover with 1 inch or less of soil.
Soil: Any well-drained soil.
Water: Regular during growing season.
Fertilizer: Not necessary.
Spacing: 1 foot.
Exposure: Full sun.
Propagation: Divide clumps in fall.
Pests & diseases: Few.
Storage: Keep dry.

A pretty bulb with pure, sulfur-yellow flowers, *Bulbinella floribunda* resembles a dainty version of the common red-hot poker plant, *Kniphofia.* Stems are slender, growing more than 2 feet tall, topped by a dense cluster of flowers. Colors are variable, generally in shades of yellow and orange-red. Cut flowers are excellent and long lasting.

Bulbinella is a native of South Africa, but grows outdoors in southern England. It has not been tested for cold hardiness in the United States. Plant multiplies rapidly. Division is possible after the second year. If not divided, it forms a large, beautiful clump with many flower spikes. The rhizomes can withstand dry periods during summer months.

Bulbocodium vernum
Spring meadow saffron

Family: Liliaceae.
Native to: Europe.
Bulb type: Corm.
Bloom season & length: Early spring for 2 to 3 weeks.
Colors: Lavender-pink.
Height: 4 inches.
Planting time: Early fall.
Planting depth: Cover with 3 inches of soil.
Soil: Well drained.
Water: Regular during growing season.
Fertilizer: Light dose at planting time.
Spacing: About 4 inches.
Exposure: Full sun.
Propagation: Cormels that form at base.
Pests & diseases: Few.
Storage: Not required.

This is one of the most reliable and useful bulbs in cold climates. It can be grown successfully as far north as Zone 3 in Canada. It adds its lavender-pink color in early spring. Flowers look like those of *Crocus*. When fully open, flowers look like stars.

Culture is simple. Plant about 3 inches deep and 4 inches apart in a sunny location. Soil should have good drainage. Dig every 2 to 3 years to separate and replant.

Caladium x hortulanum
Fancy-leafed caladium

Family: Araceae.
Native to: Tropical South America.
Bulb type: Tuber.
Bloom season & length: Attractive leaves are displayed all summer.
Colors: Leaves in combinations of green, white, pink and red.
Height: 12 to 15 inches.
Planting time: After last frost or start indoors.
Planting depth: Cover with 1 inch soil.
Soil: Rich loam is best.
Water: Ample supply at all times.
Fertilizer: Once per month with complete liquid fertilizer.
Spacing: 8 inches.
Exposure: Filtered shade.
Propagation: Divide tuber.
Pests & diseases: Snails and slugs.
Storage: Allow bulb to dry gradually, then store in warm, dry area.

These tubers from the tropical part of South America are a boon to gardeners in warm, humid climates. In Louisiana, they have naturalized on the levees, but *Caladiums* are grown throughout the United States and Canada for the brilliant leaf colors. In most areas, tubers must be dug in fall and kept dry and warm during the winter. As house plants, they need at least 75% humidity, warmth and bright light.

Their combinations of leaf colors—green, white, red and pink—seem endless. Some, such as the popular 'Candidum', are white with thin, green veins. At the other extreme is 'Postman Joyner', with dark-red leaves with a wide, green border. In between are 'Pink Cloud', and 'Miss Chicago', which has pink and white with green speckles clustered around the border.

Although these are shade plants, they need lots of bright, indirect light. Indoor locations are usually too dark. After a week or two, they begin to lose their color intensity, especially the pink and red kinds.

Caladium x hortulanum

Caladium x hortulanum

A month before the last frost, start tubers indoors by pressing them into damp peat. When rooted, transfer to 4-inch pots. After soil warms in spring, set out as bedding plants or transplant into larger pots for the terrace or house. Rich, organic, well-drained soil is best. Feed once a month with liquid, organic fertilizer. Flowers resemble small calla lilies. Remove them because they sap strength from the plant. Leaves are fragile. They are damaged if whipped by wind and burn in direct, intense sun. Bait for snails and slugs.

In fall, allow tubers to dry, then dig and store in a warm, dry place. Don't stack tubers on top of one another. Store in a box filled with perlite or vermiculite. Tubers in containers can be stored dry during winter.

Calochortus venustus

Calochortus venustus

Calochortus

Family: Liliaceae.
Native to: Pacific Coast of North America, Mexico.
Bulb type: True bulb.
Bloom season & length: Late spring into summer for 3 weeks.
Colors: White, pink, lavender, yellow and red.
Height: 6 to 24 inches.
Planting time: Fall.
Planting depth: Cover with 2 inches of soil.
Soil: Fast draining and gritty.
Water: Regular while actively growing.
Fertilizer: Not required.
Spacing: 6 inches.
Exposure: Full sun or light shade.
Propagation: Separate small bulbs that form around base.
Pests & diseases: Few.
Storage: Dry peat moss or vermiculite.

These attractive natives of the Pacific Coast and Mexico include many varieties and colors. The species most often seen in gardens is *Calochortus venustus,* the Mariposa lily. Several, cup-shaped flowers 3 to 4 inches long grow on an 18-inch-high stem. Flowers may be white, pink, lavender, yellow or reddish brown. A blotch of contrasting color appears at the base of each petal.

Mariposa lily requires excellent drainage and prefers dry summers. Cover bulbs with 3 to 4 inches of soil. Under favorable conditions, bulbs multiply rapidly from offsets.

Most spectacular is *Calochortus kennedyi,* a desert native. It is also the most difficult to grow. It has sparse foliage and showy, scarlet flowers with a purple blotch.

Calochortus albus, fairy-lantern, produces several white flowers and prefers to grow in shade.

Calochortus coeruleus, cat's-ear, has 1-inch, bluish flowers with furry insides. They grow on top of a 5-inch stem.

All *Calochortus* are cold-hardy as far north as Zone 6. Because they do best if dry during the summer, dig them after bloom if you live in an area receiving summer rains. Store and replant after the first fall frost.

Camassia
Quamash

Family: Liliaceae.
Native to: North America.
Bulb type: True bulb.
Bloom season & length: Spring for 1 month.
Colors: Lavender, blue or white.
Height: 2 to 3 feet.
Planting time: Fall.
Planting depth: Cover with 3 inches soil.
Soil: Organic and moist.
Water: Ample.
Fertilizer: Not required.
Spacing: 6 inches.
Exposure: Full sun to light shade.
Propagation: Offsets or seeds.
Pests & diseases: Few.
Storage: Leave in ground.

Northwest Indians gave this bulb the name *quamash.* Although it is a small, 2-foot-high plant with many small flowers, quamash is striking in a group planting. It is often considered the North-American counterpart of England's bluebells.

Plants thrive in moist, woodland conditions. The most common *Camassia* species, *C. quamash,* has blue or white flower spikes. *C. leichtlinii* is also popular, producing 20 to 40, dark blue, cream or white flowers per spike. Bright-yellow anthers add to the overall attractiveness.

Plant the large, soft bulbs 6 inches apart in fall, and cover with 3 inches of soil. Keep soil moist while bulbs are growing. Both species are easy to grow from seeds, but it takes four years before they bloom. Plants can also be multiplied by offsets. Bulbs are cold-hardy and grow as far north as Zone 3.

Camassia leichtlinii

Canna

Family: Cannaceae.
Native to: Tropics and subtropics.
Bulb type: Rhizome.
Bloom season & length: Continually through warm weather.
Colors: Red, orange, yellow, cream, pink and coral.
Height: 2 to 7 feet.
Planting time: Spring.
Planting depth: Cover with 1 inch soil.
Soil: Rich.
Water: Ample.
Fertilizer: Not necessary if planted in rich soil.
Spacing: 1 foot.
Exposure: Full sun to light shade.
Propagation: Divide rhizomes in spring.
Pests & diseases: Snails and slugs.
Storage: Dry peat moss or vermiculite.

Cannas are the lazy gardener's delight. They start blooming with the first warm days of spring and do not stop until frost. The original species grown in home gardens were popular because of their dark bronze or variegated tropical foliage. Now, after hybridizing, the showy flowers are more important.

Cannas are traditionally grown in straight rows, but they are probably more attractive combined with lush, tropical foliage plants. Their brilliant flowers are reminiscent of a Gauguin painting. Dwarf forms are often

Canna 'President'

used to provide color in a perennial border. Flowers come in pastel shades of cream, rose, pink and coral, and clear, brilliant shades of red, yellow and orange. Some have variegated flowers.

Tall varieties grow over 6 feet high. Plants in the Opera Series grow 4 feet high. Those in the newer Pfitzer Series seldom exceed 3 feet. Dwarf kinds can be grown in pots.

Cannas can be left in the ground permanently in areas where the soil does not freeze. Because they grow from rhizomes, *Cannas* grown in mild-winter areas spread considerably. In areas where the soil freezes, they must be dug and stored during winter. When dividing rhizomes in the spring, allow the cut portions to dry and heal before planting them. Cover with 1 inch of soil.

All *Cannas* thrive in rich, moist soil but accept poor soil. They survive dry periods but flowers are not as attractive. As soon as a stalk has finished blooming, remove it and a new one will take its place.

Canna 'Wyoming'

Chasmanthe aethiopica

Chasmanthe

Family: Iridaceae.
Native to: South Africa.
Bulb type: Corm.
Bloom season & length: Spring for 1 month.
Colors: Orange-red.
Height: 4 feet.
Planting time: Fall.
Planting depth: 2 inches.
Soil: No special requirements.
Water: Regular during growing season.
Fertilizer: Not necessary.
Spacing: 6 inches.
Exposure: Full sun or part shade.
Propagation: Collect and plant cormels from base.
Pests & diseases: Few.
Storage: If planted in spring, keep dry during winter.

Chasmanthe is common in established gardens in California. In fall or early spring, it sends up gladiolus-like foliage and spikes 4 feet high, topped with orange-red and yellow, tubular flowers. It rapidly forms large clumps. It is native to South Africa and so well adapted to dry summers that it grows in abandoned gardens. *Chasmanthe* is rarely seen in nurseries. More often than not, it is passed over the backyard fence.

The biggest problem is confusion over its name. It has been called *Montbretia, Tritonia, Crocosmia* and, at one time, was labeled botanically as *Antholyza,* from which it got its common name, "Aunt Eliza." The correct botanical name is *Chasmanthe aethiopica.*

Chasmanthe is easy to grow in mild climates such as Zones 9 and 10 if given at least a couple of hours of sun a day. Outside of these areas, it should be dug and stored during winter like *Gladiolus.* Cover corms with 1 or 2 inches of soil. Divide after the foliage dies down.

Chionodoxa
Glory-of-the-snow

Family: Liliaceae.
Native to: Eastern Mediterranean.
Bulb type: True bulb.
Bloom season & length: Early spring for 1 month.
Colors: Blue and white.
Height: 6 inches.
Planting time: Fall.
Planting depth: Cover with 2 inches soil.
Soil: Must be well drained.
Water: Regular during growing season.
Fertilizer: Not necessary.
Spacing: 1 to 3 inches.
Exposure: Full sun to light shade.
Propagation: Primarily by offsets. Sometimes self-sows.
Pests & diseases: Few.
Storage: Best left in ground to naturalize.

As the name implies, glory-of-the-snow is best adapted to cold areas. In Asia Minor and the mountains of Crete, they appear in early spring just as the snow recedes. Flowers are brilliant blue, 6 to 10 in number, appearing on a 6-inch spike. They are excellent in contrast to *Azaleas* and *Forsythias*.

Chionodoxa luciliae is the most common variety, with blue flowers and white centers. *C. sardensis* is rich, bright blue with a small, white eye. Because they are inexpensive, consider planting them in drifts and allow them to multiply.

Chionodoxa is well adapted to Zones 3 to 8. Cover the small bulbs with 2 inches of rich, moist, well-drained soil improved with organic matter. Although they bloom at the same time as snow drops, *Galanthus* species, *Chionodoxa* need more sun. In warm areas, provide filtered shade and plant deeper than usual so they will produce more extensive root systems.

Chionodoxa luciliae

Chlidanthus fragrans
Perfumed fairy lily

Family: Amaryllidaceae.
Native to: Andes Mountains.
Bulb type: True bulb.
Bloom season & length: Intermittent through summer.
Colors: Yellow.
Height: 10 inches.
Planting time: Spring.
Planting depth: Cover with 1 to 2 inches soil.
Soil: Any fast-draining soil.
Water: Regular during growing season.
Fertilizer: Light applications of 5-10-5 fertilizer after flowering.
Spacing: 6 inches.
Exposure: Full sun.
Propagation: Separate small bulbs that form at base.
Pests & diseases: Few.
Storage: Pack in dry peat moss or vermiculite after bulbs are fully dry.

Chlidanthus is a summer-blooming native of the tropical Andes. Its leaf shape resembles those of daffodil. The 4-inch flowers are shaped like lilies and appear in a cluster at the top of the stem. *Chlidanthus fragrans* is the most common species. It has a pleasing, lilylike fragrance and is an excellent cut flower.

Chlidanthus fragrans

North of Zone 8, grow *Chlidanthus* in pots and move indoors before the first frost arrives. After foliage dies, keep soil dry until spring. Plant three bulbs in a 6-inch pot, leaving the neck exposed. Plant outdoors in mild areas with top of the neck exposed. Leave in ground during winter. In cold areas, plant in the ground but dig in fall and store in a dry, frost-free location.

Clivia miniata

Clivia
Kaffir lily

Family: Amaryllidaceae.
Native to: South Africa.
Bulb type: Fleshy, rhizomelike roots.
Bloom season & length: Spring for one month or more.
Colors: Orange, red and yellow.
Height: 2 feet.
Planting time: Any time.
Planting depth: Just under the soil surface.
Soil: Rich loam.
Water: Regular during growing season.
Fertilizer: Feed container plants with light dose once per month during spring and summer.
Spacing: 6 inches.
Exposure: Shade.
Propagation: Separate clumps, but flowers best when crowded.
Pests & diseases: Few.
Storage: Leave in ground in mild-winter areas. Grow in containers indoors during winter in cold areas.

One could not ask for a more spectacular flower than *Clivia.* Sometimes called *Kaffir lily,* this beautiful plant was named for Lord Clive of India. Although it originally came from South Africa, Kaffir lily first bloomed in England in the conservatory of Lord Clive's wife. Handsome, dark-green leaves are strap-shaped. They serve as a perfect backdrop for the umbels of brilliant, salmon-orange, yellow-centered flowers.

Clivia miniata hybrids have flowers varying between yellow and dark orange-red. Leaves of hybrids are wider and flowers larger. *C. nobilis,* a rarer species, has more numerous but smaller flowers in each umbel. The flowers are scarlet tipped with green and hang down.

Clivia is a superb container plant that blooms best when rootbound. Repotting is not necessary until it looks as though the plant will break the pot. Divide in spring after flowering. Allow it to go slightly dry in the fall to encourage flower production. Plants grown in the ground do not require fertilizer. Potted plants, however, should be fed in spring and summer. *Clivia* is not particular about soil as long as it is well drained and not acid.

It excels outdoors in Zones 9 and 10 when given filtered shade. Although it will tolerate some frost, *Clivia* is best grown in pots in cold areas so it can be given protection during freezing weather. Move to protected location if temperatures below 28F (−2C) are expected.

Clivia miniata

Colchicum

Family: Liliaceae.
Native to: Europe and North Africa.
Bulb type: Corm.
Bloom season & length: Fall for several weeks.
Colors: Lavender, white and yellow.
Height: 6 to 7 inches.
Planting time: Fall.
Planting depth: Cover with 3 inches soil.
Soil: Adapts to any soil that is well drained.
Water: Regular during growing season.
Fertilizer: Not necessary.
Spacing: 8 inches.
Exposure: Full sun to part shade.
Propagation: Collect and plant cormels that form around base.
Pests & diseases: Few.
Storage: Best if left undisturbed.

There are many species of *Colchicum,* including a yellow, spring-blooming variety. Those most readily available are the hybrids of *C. byzantinum, C. speciosum* and *C. autumnale.* All of these are called *autumn crocus.* The only relationship to true *Crocus* is the flower shape and the low growth habit.

The most remarkable aspect of some *Colchicum* is their ability to bloom without soil or water. Because of this trait, they make marvelous gifts for people without gardens. Place bulbs on a windowsill or desk, and the plants bloom with absolutely no care. Avoid placing bulbs in direct sunlight or they will burn.

Colchicum do well in the outdoor garden. They are usually relegated to informal plantings because their foliage turns an unattractive yellow and then brown. Lavender and white *Colchicum* do well in all but the coldest parts of the United States. Plant in a sunny location in soil that does not dry out in summer. Cover with about 3 inches of soil.

Colchicum species

Colocasia esculenta
Elephant's ear

Family: Araceae.
Native to: East Indies, tropical Asia.
Bulb type: Tuber.
Bloom season & length: Large, dramatic leaves all season.
Colors: Green.
Height: 3 to 6 feet.
Planting time: Spring.
Planting depth: Cover with 2 inches soil.
Soil: Rich loam.
Water: Abundant—will grow in water.
Fertilizer: Feed with complete fertilizer once each month during growing season.
Spacing: 18 inches.
Exposure: Full sun to light shade.
Propagation: Divide tubers in spring.
Pests & diseases: Few.
Storage: Dig and store like *Caladium.*

Colocasia esculenta has large, heart-shaped leaves. It grows to 3 feet long and almost as wide. The common name, elephant's ears, refers to its size and shape. Dasheen is another name used for the plant. Poi, a common tropical food, is made from the tubers. In the United States the plant is used in the landscape for its bold, tropical appearance. Flowers are insignificant.

Colchicum autumnale

Colocasia does well in Zones 9 and 10. It can grow in sun or shade, and requires plenty of water. Plant tubers 3 feet apart and cover with 3 inches of soil. In colder areas, grow them in large pots.

For landscape use in cold climates, start them indoors one or two months before the last frost. Plant tubers after all danger of frost has passed. Dig and store tubers after the first frost in fall.

Colocasia esculenta

Convallaria majalis

Convallaria majalis
Lily-of-the-valley

Family: Liliaceae.
Native to: Europe.
Bulb type: Rhizome.
Bloom season & length: Spring for 3 weeks.
Colors: White, light pink.
Height: 10 inches.
Planting time: Spring.
Planting depth: Cover with 1 inch soil.
Soil: Rich, slightly acid soil.
Water: Regular during growing season.
Fertilizer: Mulch with manure in fall.
Spacing: 5 inches.
Exposure: Partial shade.
Propagation: Separate in fall after foliage dies.
Pests & diseases: Snails and slugs.
Storage: Rhizomes sprout with warmth. Keep in cold storage.

Lily-of-the-valley is popular for its white, sweet-scented flowers that appear in spring. Round, bell-shaped flowers hang on 9-inch stems. Foliage is attractive bright green. Plants are often used to make a ground cover in shade or semishade. Flowers are a standard for florists and popular for bridal bouquets. They are forced into bloom for most of the year by keeping the rhizome in cold storage. A small bouquet brings a fresh, sweet scent to a room. A double form and a pink variety are available.

Lily-of-the-valley is easy to grow in Zones 3 to 7. It likes shade and a rich, moist, highly organic soil that is slightly acid. Plant rhizomatous roots 1 to 2 inches below the surface. As long as plants bloom well, don't divide them. They bloom best left undisturbed.

Because lily-of-the-valley needs exposure to cold, it is normally not recommended for mild climates. There are always exceptions for the gardener who gives individual plants special consideration, such as covering them with ice cubes to simulate cold.

Note: All plant parts are poisonous. Plant with care if there are young children around.

Crinum

Family: Amaryllidaceae.
Native to: South Africa and tropical areas.
Bulb type: True bulb.
Bloom season & length: Late summer for several months.
Colors: White, pink and rose.
Height: Up to 4 feet.
Planting time: Spring and fall.
Planting depth: Place neck of bulb at soil surface.
Soil: Loam.
Water: During growing season.
Fertilizer: Light doses of complete fertilizer.
Spacing: 2 feet.
Exposure: Sun to part sun.
Propagation: Separate bulbs that form at base.
Pests & diseases: Few. Occasionally mealybugs and snails.
Storage: Replant after digging. Does best when rootbound.

Crinum is a large genus, with members originating from Africa, Asia, Australia and North and South America. All are natives of mild climates, but some can be grown as far north as Zone 7. They are large plants, similar to shrubs in appearance. Almost 100 species are known, with others probably remaining to be discovered. All are similar bulbs, large in size. They produce flowers in an umbel on top of tall stems. Rose, pink or white flowers are shaped like stars or lilies. They have a strong, sweet fragrance. Plants are evergreen or almost so with long, strap-shaped leaves.

Crinum x powellii is by far the best known. It is a cross between *C. bulbispermum* and *C. moorei*. Its trumpet-shaped flowers are 4 inches long and 3 inches wide. Up to 10 flowers appear at the end of each 2-foot-high stem, which rises above the foliage. Flowers are white to deep rose. A mature bulb is 5 inches wide.

In the North, locate plants where they will receive as much heat as possible. In the South, provide with a rich soil and fertilize regularly. In hot areas, they appreciate some afternoon shade.

Deep rooted and somewhat drought resistant, they dislike being disturbed and multiply rapidly. Plant with the neck just beneath the soil surface.

Crinum x Amarcrinum and *x Crinodonna* are names for the same cross of *Crinum moorei* and *Amaryllis belladonna*. The *Amaryllis* side produces shell-pink flowers. The *Crinum* side produces the normally evergreen foliage. Many fragrant flowers open over several months. *x Amarcrinum* was developed in California by Fred Howard. During the same period, *x Crinodonna* was developed in northern Italy. Because the name *Crinodonna* was published first, it is botanically most correct. Bulbs can be planted in the ground as far north as Zone 6, but should be protected with a mulch in winter.

Crinum 'Cape Dawn'

x Amarcrinum howardii

Dutch hybrid *Crocus*

Crocosmia

Family: Iridaceae.
Native to: South Africa.
Bulb type: Corm.
Bloom season & length: Summer for several weeks.
Colors: Orange to yellow.
Height: 2 to 4 feet.
Planting time: Spring.
Planting depth: 2 inches of soil over corm.
Soil: Sandy loam.
Water: Regular during the growing season.
Fertilizer: Apply complete fertilizer after foliage appears.
Spacing: 1 inch.
Exposure: Full sun.
Propagation: From cormlets that form at base.
Pests & diseases: Few.
Storage: In dry peat or vermiculite during winter in cold areas.

Crocosmia is a small group of corms originally from South Africa. Leaves are swordlike. Flowers appear in shades of yellow, orange and red, with several on each stem. The garden types, known botanically as *Crocosmia x crocosmiiflora,* are hybrids between *Crocosmia aurea* and *C. pottsii.* The somewhat star-shaped flowers appear in summer on stems that are noticeably branched. *C. masoniorum* is distinguished by flower spikes that bend at a sharp, horizontal angle, covered with tight racemes of regularly spaced, tubular flowers. These flower spikes make attractive, long-lasting cut flowers. Plants resemble *Chasmanthe,* page 76, but their culture is different. They bloom in summer and must have water until foliage turns brown.

    Crocosmia grows in the ground as far north as Zone 6. Plants are rapid multipliers but do not need to be divided for years. Plant them in the spring in average garden soil. Space 3 inches apart and cover with 2 inches of soil. Fertilize lightly when shoots appear. They need several hours of sun a day and regular moisture while growing. In Zones 6 and 7, provide with a mulch in winter. In cooler areas, corms are dug and stored like *Gladiolus.* Unlike *Gladiolus,* corms shrivel if allowed to dry completely. Store in slightly moistened sand or peat moss. *Crocosmia* can also be propagated from seeds started in flats of sandy compost. It is generally better to buy new corms of improved varieties.

Crocosmia x crocosmiiflora

Crocus species

Crocus

Family: Iridaceae.
Native to: Mediterranean region.
Bulb type: Corm.
Bloom season & length: Fall to spring.
Colors: Lavender, purple, white, yellow and orange.
Height: 3 to 5 inches.
Planting time: Fall.
Planting depth: 2 to 4 inches of soil over corm.
Soil: Sandy loam.
Water: Regular during growing season.
Fertilizer: Little.
Spacing: 4 to 6 inches.
Exposure: Full sun.
Propagation: From corms that form at base, or from seeds.
Pests & diseases: Few.
Storage: Not necessary.

For most gardeners, *Crocus* bring to mind the large spring blooms of Dutch hybrid *Crocus,* native of high alpine regions. But other forms are equally valuable in

Crocus goulimyi

Tiny pot is home for purple and white Crocus.

the garden. There is no doubt the Dutch hybrids of *Crocus vernus* are splendid and showy. Their colors are clear and brilliant, and they make a great show in containers or in the ground. Many excellent hybrids are available in white, pale mauve with stripes, mauve without stripes, purple and yellow.

The smaller relatives of Dutch hybrids are from the Mediterranean region. Most others come from mountainous areas and require cold. Plants have tremendous charm, and are usually planted in drifts, between steppingstones, in rock gardens, beneath shrubbery or in containers. They bloom in fall, winter or spring.

Crocus close up to protect themselves when weather is cloudy or stormy. They reopen with sunlight, but it is not light that causes them to open, but warmth. Thus, plants grown indoors often stay open late into the evening. If you want to grow them in water in *crocus* jars, try the purple Dutch hybrids. See page 33 for more on growing bulbs in jars indoors.

Crocus do not require deep planting. Cover with an amount of soil equal to the bulb depth. Well-drained soil is important, or bulbs will rot. Because they have contractile roots, they adjust themselves to the proper depth. New corms form each year on top of the old ones, and cormels form around the base.

Species *Crocus* are available in white, yellow, orange, purple, lavender, and striped and feathered combinations. The following lists some of the most popular *Crocus*.

FALL FLOWERING

Crocus goulimyi and *C. niveus,* although rare, are popular in southern California. Both originate from southern Greece. *C. goulimyi* has handsome, lavender flowers. *C. niveus* flowers are white with yellow in the throat. Both plants require excellent soil drainage.

Crocus kotschyanus, better known as *C. zonatus,* blooms early. Flowers are rosy lilac with a yellow throat. It is native to Asia Minor and Lebanon.

Crocus longiflorus has a large, globular flower. It is purple-lilac on the outside and pale inside with an orange throat. Even though it is from southern Italy, it is hardy to cold.

Crocus sativus is the famous saffron *Crocus* from which the spice and dye are made, derived from the small, orange-red style branches of the flower's stigma. This explains their high cost when you think of the time involved in harvesting adequate quantities. Flowers vary from rosy lilac to a purple-mauve. It is native to Italy and Turkey.

Crocus speciosus, from eastern Europe and Asia Minor, is one of the best and easiest to grow. In September, it brightens the garden with its lavender-blue chalices. Flowers are unusually large for a species. It is a rapid multiplier from seeds or by division.

WINTER AND EARLY SPRING FLOWERING

Crocus chrysanthus is one of the most popular species, and rightly so. Its many hybrids range from orange through yellow to cream and from purple to lavender-blue. Many named varieties are available on the market. It blooms in early spring. It originally grew in Greece and Asia Minor.

Crocus flavus is an early blooming, yellow-orange variety. It is often planted with purple *C. tomasinianus.*

Crocus imperati is from southern Italy. Flowers are lilac-mauve with a yellow center, and bloom in winter.

It does not need cold to do well and multiplies freely where it is dry during the summer.

Crocus tomasinianus is a free-flowering, early spring variety from Dalmatia. Many named varieties are available in shades of purple. They are often planted with *C. chrysanthus.*

SPRING FLOWERING

Crocus angustifolius, 'Cloth of Gold', has medium-size, deep-orange flowers with a mahogany color feathered on the outside. When grown close together, it looks like a golden cloak spread over the ground.

Crocus biflorus, 'Cloth of Silver', is striped lilac-purple on the outside and white on the inside. Native to Italy and Asia Minor..

Crocus olivieri is brilliant, deep orange marked with purple on the outside. Native to Greece, Bulgaria and Romania. Not as large as other varieties.

Crocus sieberi is one of the best species. It is mauve with an orange-yellow throat, but variations include a white form.

Crocus vernus is best known as the parent of the showy Dutch hybrids. It blooms at the snowline in the Alps and Pyrenees.

Cyclamen

Family: Primulaceae.
Native to: Mediterranean region.
Bulb type: Tuber.
Bloom season & length: Spring or fall for many weeks.
Colors: Pink, red, white and lavender.
Height: 3 to 12 inches.
Planting time: Fall.
Planting depth: Near soil surface.
Soil: Loam with excellent drainage.
Water: Regular during growing season.
Fertilizer: Weak solution of liquid fertilizer every 2 weeks.
Spacing: 2 to 12 inches.
Exposure: Filtered shade.
Propagation: Usually from seeds. Corms can be divided.
Pests & diseases: Cyclamen mite.
Storage: In cool location for florist type. Others can remain in the ground.

There are two distinct types of *Cyclamen,* each having different cultural requirements. One type, large florist cyclamen, is a hybrid of *Cyclamen persicum.* Large flowers come in clear colors of pink, scarlet, salmon, white, lavender, wine and some bicolors and ruffled forms. Plants are cold-tender. They are commonly used as house plants, blooming from Thanksgiving to Easter if given the right conditions. They like cool temperatures—63F (17C) is ideal. Keep this in mind when growing them indoors. An east-facing bay window is the perfect location. This provides plenty of light, which they need in order to bloom.

The dwarf florist's cyclamen, sometimes labeled as 'Swiss' or 'Puck', is not as temperamental as the species. It is a fragrant, heavy bloomer, which more than makes up for its smaller size. In mild areas of the West, florist's cyclamen are grown as bedding plants.

Although plants require regular moisture, overly soggy soil suffocates roots and causes leaves to yellow. Don't keep the plant in florist-wrap, commonly foil or

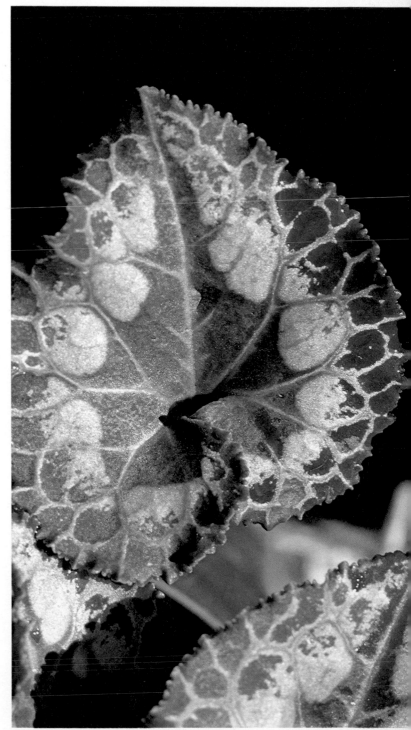

Cyclamen persicum

Cyclamen persicum

plastic, or allow it to sit in a saucer of water. Apply water until it runs out from the bottom of the pot. Don't water again until the top of the soil is almost dry. Regular feeding is important to keep plants in good health. Fertilize every two weeks with a diluted solution of liquid fertilizer. Remove faded flowers or leaves with a twist to separate them from the corm.

If you buy a plant in a 4-inch pot in the fall, transplant it immediately into a 6-inch pot. It may stop blooming for a while as new roots grow. But when plants bloom again, flowers will be more profuse than ever.

Cyclamen become almost dormant in summer with only one to two leaves. At this time, keep them cool and allow the soil to stay almost dry. Plants decline during the heat of August and September. When the weather cools and growth begins, begin to water and feed again.

The second type are the species *Cyclamen*. They are easy to grow as shade plants from Zone 5 southward, although parts of Florida may be too warm and humid. They are noted for growing in unlikely places such as among tree roots and rocks.

Cyclamen coum subspecies *coum* differs from others in that it sends out roots from the bottom of the corm. Plant begins to bloom the first of the year with purple-red or white flowers, which last until March. Leaves are usually reddish on the underside. *C. repandum* is the last to bloom, beginning in March with flowers of crimson, pink or white. It is more cold-tender than *C. hederifolium*.

Cyclamen hederifolium (*C. neapolitanum*) is the best known species. It blooms in late summer and early fall. Pink or white flowers appear first, followed by varicolored leaves. Flowers of *Cyclamen* species are typically 3/4 to 1 inch across. When flowers fade and seeds start to form, stems coil up like a spring.

In the ground, *Cyclamen hederifolium* can form a corm 12 inches across, so be sure plants have room to spread. Plant corms with the flat side facing down. Both roots and leaves come from the top of corms. Be careful not to damage the small, twiggy protuberances because they produce the flowers. Plant the corm no deeper than 2 inches.

Cyclamen are almost always grown from seeds. It takes about 18 months before plants produce flowers, although some hybrids are faster. Sow seeds in a mixture of screened compost or potting soil mixed with sand. Cover with 1/2 inch of soil and keep cool. Avoid overwatering. When they get their second leaf, transplant seedlings into individual 4-inch pots. *Cyclamen* have shallow roots so be careful when cultivating around plants.

Cyclamen species

Cyclamen in a unique container.

Formal decorative *Dahlia*

Informal decorative *Dahlia*

Formal decorative *Dahlia*

Bicolor decorative *Dahlia*

Dahlia

Family: Compositae.
Native to: Central America, Mexico, Colombia.
Bulb type: Tuberous root.
Bloom season & length: Summer over a long period.
Colors: Red, pink, white, lavender, purple, orange and yellow.
Height: 1 to 8 feet, rarely to 20 feet.
Planting time: Spring.
Planting depth: 2 to 3 inches.
Soil: Rich, sandy loam.
Water: Regular during growing season.
Fertilizer: Diluted liquid fertilizer during growth. Too much nitrogen reduces bloom.
Spacing: 1 to 3 feet.
Exposure: Full sun to light, filtered shade.
Propagation: Seeds or by division. Separate tuberous roots so each has a bud from the main stem.
Pests & diseases: Mildew, *Diabrotica* beetle and corn borer.
Storage: Store in frost-free area in dry peat moss or vermiculite. Can leave in ground in Zones 9 and 10.

Dahlias are probably the most versatile of all bulbs. They are available as 1-foot-high border plants or as shrubby trees 20 feet high. Because of their long bloom period, variety of flower sizes and shapes, and wide range of color—everything except blue—*Dahlias* have a place in every summer garden. In areas with mild climates, treat them like herbaceous perennials and leave them in the ground until they need dividing. Even in mild-climate areas, *Dahlia* fanciers dig and divide the roots and replant them in new soil to attain superior flowers. In cold areas where frost permeates the ground, they must be dug and stored away from freezing temperatures. They can then be replanted after the last frost.

Because of the numerous varieties of *Dahlias,* it is almost impossible to determine their ancestry. The American Dahlia Society recognizes these 12 groups of cultivars:

Single Dahlias—Fewer than two complete rows of *ray flowers,* flowers with a strap-shaped petal, the center being small, disc flowers.

Anemone Dahlias—One or more rows of ray flowers, with the central disc flowers that look like elongated pincushions.

Colarette Dahlias—Fewer than two complete rows of ray flowers, then one or more rows of ray flowers of a different color. Flat disc center.

Peony Dahlias—Open centers surrounded by two or three rows of petals that are often twisted or curled.

Formal Decorative Dahlias—Ray flowers only, arranged regularly about the center, with rounded or pointed tips.

Informal Decorative Dahlias—Same as above, with ray flowers arranged irregularly.

Ball Dahlias—Globose, slightly flattened, with ray flowers only.

Pompon Dahlias—Globose of miniature-size ray flowers only.

Incurved Cactus Dahlias—Ray flowers only with pointed tips incurving toward the center.

Straight Cactus Dahlias—Ray flowers only, with pointed tips that are straight.

Semicactus Dahlias—Ray flowers only, with pointed tips that have a broad base.

Miscellaneous Dahlias—Those that do not fit into any of the other groups.

Dahlia 'Jean Thompson'

Above and below: *Dahlias* make colorful bedding plants.

One species that always receives special attention is the tree dahlia, *D. imperialis,* which grows up to 20 feet high. It makes a spectacular perennial with its large leaves and white, lavender or rose-pink flowers that are 6 inches in diameter. Tree dahlias produce as many as 300 flowers in one season. It is not deciduous and is grown in Zone 10 only.

Dahlias generally do best in full sun protected from strong winds. In warm, dry areas, some protection from midday sun helps.

Planting requires a certain procedure. The tubers, which look like sweet potatoes, must have a section of the stem with a bud to grow. First dig a hole about the size of a 2-gallon bucket. Work in a handful of complete fertilizer such as 2-10-10 or 2-20-12. Place a 2-inch layer of soil or sand on top of the fertilizer and place the tuber on top of this. The top of the tuber should be 5 to 6 inches below the soil surface. The sand makes it easier to dig the tuber in the fall and supplies drainage while the tuber is beginning to grow.

If planting a tall variety, stake when you plant to provide for future support. Place the stake close to the bud end of the tuber at planting time, so you avoid the possibility of driving the stake through the tuber after it is planted. Cover the tuber with 2 inches of soil. As it grows, continue to cover with soil. For bushy plants with more flowers, pinch out the center when there are four or six leaves. Repeat this practice again for the next four or six leaves, then again one more time. By pinching out the center, side shoots will form.

Bedding dahlias do not need stakes, but should be pinched to make them bushy. To get exhibition-size blooms with large-flowered types, pinch out tips when shoots have three pairs of leaves. Two shoots form at each joint. When six shoots have formed, remove the top two, leaving four stems to produce huge flowers.

Plants grow rapidly and need a regular supply of water. Feed during the growing season with a diluted liquid fertilizer every other week or work a dry fertilizer into the soil twice during the season. Apply dry fertilizers several inches away from the plant stem. Avoid high-nitrogen fertilizers because they reduce bloom.

When digging tubers, use a spading fork to avoid damaging them. Separate clumps for new plants the next year. Make sure each tuber has a part of the stem with a bud. Many gardeners prefer to separate them in the spring when the buds are more apparent. To avoid mixing up the different varieties, label the tuber with an indelible pen at the time of digging.

When using *Dahlias* as cut flowers, wait until flowers are almost fully open before cutting. Water plants deeply the day before. Cut the stems in the early evening and immerse the stem completely in water. Leave in water overnight. Another method is to seal the cut ends of stems by burning them with a candle, or put them in boiling water.

Although not common, certain specific viruses infect *Dahlias.* Mosaic causes spindly shoots and crinkled, off-color leaves. Ring spot produces round, pale-green spots with zig-zag edges on lower leaves. These diseases are transmitted by insects and are impossible to control. If your plants become infected, dig them up and throw them away.

Endymion
Bluebells

Family: Liliaceae.
Native to: Western Europe, northern Africa.
Bulb type: True bulb.
Bloom season & length: Spring for several weeks.
Colors: Blue, white and mauve-pink.
Height: 18 inches.
Planting time: Fall.
Planting depth: One inch or more over bulb.
Soil: Loam.
Water: Regular during the growing season.
Fertilizer: Not necessary.
Spacing: 6 inches.
Exposure: Filtered shade to full sun.
Propagation: From small bulbs that form around bulb.
Pests & diseases: Few.
Storage: Not necessary.

Two species of bluebells are grown in home gardens: English bluebells, *Endymion non-scriptus;* and Spanish bluebells, *Endymion hispanicus.* Their former botanical names, *Scilla non-scripta* and *Scilla campanulata,* are still used in some bulb catalogs. From a distance, English and Spanish bluebells look similar. But with close inspection, you will notice that the Spanish *Endymion hispanicus* are taller, to 18 inches, and more erect. The stems of the English *E. non-scriptus* arch slightly. English bluebells are fragrant. The Spanish type is not. Both are superb for informal drifts under trees. Blue is the most popular color, but white and mauve-pink forms are available.

Endymion hispanicus is more robust and widely grown in Zones 4 to 10. *E. non-scriptus,* although a rampant grower in meadows in England, is a little fussier. It can be grown in Zone 5, but is seldom seen in Zones 9 or 10 except in the coastal Northwest.

Bulbs can be left in the ground for years before requiring division. Plantings increase rapidly, so they are seldom raised from seeds. In addition, it takes three to four years before plants bloom when they are grown from seeds.

Endymion hispanicus

Eranthis
Winter aconite

Family: Ranunculaceae.
Native to: Europe and Asia.
Bulb type: Tuber.
Bloom season & length: Early spring for 2 months.
Colors: Normally yellow or gold.
Height: 4 inches.
Planting time: Late summer.
Planting depth: 2 inches of soil over tuber.
Soil: Loam with good drainage.
Water: Regular when growing and during summer.
Fertilizer: Not required.
Spacing: 4 inches.
Exposure: Full sun to light shade.
Propagation: Self-sows.
Storage: Best left undisturbed.

The golden flowers of the low-growing winter aconite are special because they appear in early spring, when the garden lacks color and the soil is bare. Plant them up close, such as near a window or entrance, where the blooms can be appreciated the most.

Eranthis species

Winter aconite appears in the garden the same time as snowdrops and *Iris reticulata*. They frequently push up through snow to bloom. The effect is striking, especially when they are planted in drifts around trees and shrubs. They can also be used in the crevices of a rock garden or between steppingstones.

Winter aconite is cold-hardy and grows well in Zones 4 to 8. Moisture is necessary all year. Do not allow bulbs to dry out in summer. Provide soil that is rich and gritty. It should be fast draining with plenty of humus. Plant tubers 3 inches deep and 6 inches apart. Where adapted, winter aconite multiplies and makes a blanket of sunny, golden flowers. You can grow them from seeds, but wait for three years before expecting flowers in late winter or early spring. Because it takes a year or more to establish, the longer tubers are left in the ground without moving, the better.

Eremurus robustus

Eremurus robustus

Eremurus
Foxtail lily

Family: Liliaceae.
Native to: Western and Central Asia.
Bulb type: Tuberous root.
Bloom season & length: Spring for several weeks.
Colors: White, pink, yellow and orange.
Height: 3 to 7 feet.
Planting time: Fall.
Planting depth: 5 to 6 inches of soil over tuber.
Soil: Rich, sandy loam.
Water: During the growing season.
Fertilizer: Not required.
Spacing: 1 to 2 feet.
Exposure: Full sun.
Propagation: Seeds or divide tuberous roots.
Pests & diseases: Few.
Storage: Best left undisturbed.

A group of foxtail lilies in the garden is a spectacular sight. Tall kinds grow over 7 feet high. Half the stem is covered with hundreds of small flowers that start opening at the bottom of the stem. *Eremurus robustus* grows 7 feet high with peach-pink flowers. *E. stenophyllus* grows to 3 feet high and has golden orange flowers. *E. elwesii* grows 6 to 9 feet high and has white flowers.

Foxtail lilies known as *Shelford hybrids* are the most common garden varieties. They grow to 4 feet high. A wide range of colors is available, including pink, salmon, yellow, apricot and coppery orange. All are attractive and long lasting as cut flowers.

Foxtail lilies are cold-hardy in northern areas if given winter protection, and are recommended for Zones 5 to 8. The tuberous roots have a crown with roots shooting out to sides. Plant as you would a bare-root rose. Build a cone in the planting hole and carefully spread the roots over the cone. Handle roots carefully, because they are brittle and easily damaged.

Foxtail lily is long-lived and content to grow many years in the same location. Because of this, prepare the soil well before planting. Plants prefer a sandy soil improved with compost and a handful of bone meal. Soil should also be well draining. Roots die in waterlogged soil.

Erythronium
Dog-tooth violet, Trout lily

Family: Liliaceae.
Native to: Europe, Asia, North America.
Bulb type: Corm.
Bloom season & length: Spring for several weeks.
Colors: White, yellow, lilac, pink and purple.
Height: 6 to 24 inches.
Planting time: Fall.
Planting depth: 2 to 3 inches over corm.
Soil: Well-prepared soil with plenty of organic matter.
Water: When plants are growing. Do not allow corms to dry out completely in summer.
Fertilizer: Not necessary.
Spacing: 6 to 12 inches.
Exposure: Medium shade to light shade.
Propagation: From small bulbs around bulb, or seeds.
Pests & diseases: Few.
Storage: After digging, replant as soon as possible. If climate allows, leave them in the ground.

Erythronium americanum

Erythroniums are among the most graceful and charming spring flowers for a woodsy setting. The flower is similar to a lily. Flowers are available in several shades of purple, lilac, pink, white and yellow. Leaves can be bright green or an attractive mottled green, depending on the particular species.

Erythroniums have many interesting and descriptive common names. The dog-tooth violet grows from Europe through Asia to Japan. The name *dens-canis* or *dog-tooth* comes from the long, shiny, white tuberous root that resembles a canine tooth. Flowers are low growing in shades of purple, lilac, pink or white. Rounded leaves are heavily mottled with brown.

Erythronium americanum grows in damp woods from Nova Scotia as far south as Florida. The common name, trout lily, refers to the mottled foliage that resembles the marking on a trout. Another common name is adder's tongue. It has pale yellow, nodding flowers on a 9-inch stem.

Erythronium californicum is also named trout lily or fawn lily because of its foliage. It is one of the easiest American species to grow. Creamy white flowers with a small ring of orange at the throat are produced on a 1-inch stem.

Erythronium dens-canis is the easiest species to grow. This dainty plant, with its lilylike flowers, is charming in a group, rock garden or wooded glen.

Erythronium hendersonii has dark, heavily mottled leaves and several lilac flowers on each 6-inch stem.

Erythronium montanum, the avalanche lily, grows profusely on high slopes in California and Oregon. As the snow melts, white flowers with golden anthers emerge from the ground. It is considered difficult to grow in most gardens.

Erythronium oregonum has cream-colored flowers up to 3 inches across on a 15-inch stem. 'White Beauty' is more vigorous than most hybrids.

Erythronium revolutum grows in the forests of northern California. The green leaves are mottled with brown and white. White or pink flowers are 3 inches across.

Erythronium tuolumnense has light green, unmarked foliage. The golden-yellow flowers on a 1-foot stem open wide into a star. 'Pagoda', a hybrid, is easier to grow.

Erythroniums are grown from Zones 3 to 9 as long as their exacting requirements of coolness and moisture

Eucharis grandiflora

are met. All need a soil with good drainage. Soil should be cool and moist, improved with organic matter such as leaf mold, peat moss or compost. In most cases, roots can be planted about 2 inches under the soil surface. Roots dry out quickly when out of the ground. Growing them in the dry-summer regions of Zones 9 and 10 should be attempted only by dedicated gardeners.

Eucharis
Amazon lily

Family: Amarylliaceae.
Native to: Amazon.
Bulb type: True bulb.
Bloom season & length: Winter, but can bloom any time.
Colors: White.
Height: 18 inches.
Planting time: Usually spring.
Planting depth: Tip of bulb at soil surface.
Soil: House-plant type.
Water: Keep soil damp, but occasional drying out encourages bloom. Water less frequently in winter.
Fertilizer: Every two weeks with house-plant fertilizer.
Spacing: 3 to 4 inches.
Exposure: Bright light but not direct sun.
Propagation: Separate small bulbs from mother bulb.
Pests & diseases: Snails and slugs.
Storage: Keep in pot all year. Blooms best when rootbound.

The name *Eucharis* comes from a Greek word for *pleasant,* which refers to this bulb's fragrance. However, all plant parts are attractive. From a distance, the shiny foliage could easily be mistaken for *Aspidistra,* a house plant grown for its leaves. The 3-inch, pure white, waxy flowers resemble the Triandrus daffodil and appear in small clusters above the foliage. Flowers are popular with florists for bridal bouquets.

Eucharis makes a beautiful house plant. It is a native of the upper Amazon forests, so it prefers moisture, high humidity and bright light without direct sun.

Eucharis is grown outdoors in warm regions. It should be brought indoors if the temperature threatens to drop below 45F (7C). Because it is native to the tropics near the equator, seasonal changes do not affect it much. It can bloom almost any time of year. Coax it into bloom two or three times a year by letting the soil get fairly dry for about a month after blooming. The plant will form a new flower bud. Resume watering and fertilizing at that time.

Plant four or five bulbs in an 6-inch pot. Like *Amaryllis,* bulbs bloom best if rootbound. Bulb tips should be placed at the soil surface. Use a house-plant type of potting soil. After growth begins, feed once a week with a diluted liquid fertilizer. Water regularly, keeping soil moist. More bulbs can be obtained by separating the small bulbs from the mother bulb. This is not necessary until the pot is crowded.

Eucomis bicolor

Eucomis
Pineapple lily

Family: Liliaceae.
Native to: South Africa.
Bulb type: True bulb.
Bloom season & length: Late summer for 2 to 3 months.
Colors: White, pale green and pink.
Height: 2 feet.
Planting time: Spring.
Planting depth: 4 inches over bulb.
Soil: Sandy loam.
Water: During the growing season.
Fertilizer: When growth appears.
Spacing: 1 foot.
Exposure: Full sun to light shade.
Propagation: From small bulbs beside mother bulb.
Pests & diseases: Few.
Storage: Leave in container and protect from frost.

Pineapple lily is an attractive plant in the garden, but even more interesting in a container. Because of the unique appearance of its flower, pineapple lily always attracts attention. The 2-foot-high flower spike opens in late summer from a rosette of leaves. The top half is filled solidly with small flowers, on top of which is a tuft of *bracts,* modified leaves. Viewed as a whole, the flower resembles a pineapple.

Eucomis comosa has yellow-green flowers, sometimes tipped with lavender or pink. *E. bicolor* has 1-foot spikes. Flowers are more widely spaced. Flowers last about two months in the garden, and a week or more after they are cut.

Eucomis does well outdoors in Zones 8 to 10. It prefers a rich soil and responds to fertilizer. When actively growing it needs regular amounts of water. During winter it can go almost dry. To plant directly in the garden, cover bulbs with 4 or 5 inches of soil. Plant bulbs in containers close to the surface to allow maximum room for root growth.

Freesia 'Reynold's Golden Yellow'

Freesia hybrid

Freesia

Family: Iridaceae.
Native to: South Africa.
Bulb type: Corm.
Bloom season & length: Spring for several weeks.
Colors: White, yellow, orange, lavender-blue, red and pink.
Height: 12 to 18 inches.
Planting time: Fall.
Planting depth: 2 to 4 inches of soil over corm.
Soil: Sandy loam.
Water: When in growth.
Fertilizer: Light feeding once a month is usually beneficial.
Spacing: 2 inches.
Exposure: Full sun or light, filtered shade.
Propagation: Many cormels are formed at base, or by seeds.
Pests & diseases: Few.
Storage: Store in pots or in cool, dry peat moss or vermiculite.

Freesia is often grown solely for its fresh, sweet fragrance. Indeed, some say it is the finest scent of any flower. But its attraction does not stop there. The original *Freesia refracta* from South Africa has been hybridized to produce larger flowers and longer stems to please florists. Many colors are available, including white through cream, yellow, gold, orange, pink, crim-

son and lavender-blue. Some mixed colors are also available. The first pink and blue hybrids did not have as much fragrance as the others but hybridizers are taking care of that. Because European florists use them so extensively, a ready market is available for new developments such as double-flowered *Freesias*.

Freesias are easy to grow and tolerate a little frost. Plant in sandy loam with one inch of soil over the top of corms. They are excellent under a low-growing ground cover such as *Iberis* or *Ajuga*. The ground cover also protects the heavy flower from falling over into soil muddy from rain or irrigation.

Freesias grow equally well in sun or partial shade. Buy them early in the season—before the corms start to shrivel. Gardeners in cold-winter areas can grow plants in a greenhouse or indoors where they get plenty of bright sunlight. The temperature should be moderate—in the 65F to 75F (19C to 24C) range.

Like many spring bulbs, *Freesia* likes cool temperatures—35F to 65F (2C to 19C). Put 6 in a 6-inch pot, 12 in an 8-inch pot or 24 in a 10-inch pot. Plant them 4 inches below the collar of the pot to provide support for the top-heavy flowers. Bulbs can stay in the same pot for three to four years, then become crowded enough to divide.

Freesia, double-flower form

Fritillaria imperialis

Fritillaria
Fritillary, Crown imperial

Family: Liliaceae.
Native to: North America, Europe, Asia.
Bulb type: True bulb.
Bloom season & length: Spring for several weeks.
Colors: Yellow or orange, white or checkered.
Height: Crown imperial 3 to 4 feet. Checkered lily 6 to 12 inches.
Planting time: Fall.
Planting depth: 6 inches of soil over tall-growing bulbs; 3 inches of soil over short-growing bulbs.
Soil: Slightly acid, organic soil with drainage.
Water: During growing season.
Fertilizer: When new growth appears.
Spacing: 10 inches.
Exposure: Shade at midday.
Propagation: Separate in fall and replant.
Pests & diseases: Few.
Storage: Best left undisturbed.

These members of the lily family have some of the most spectacular flowers, as well as some of the smallest and daintiest. Showiest is crown imperial, *Fritillaria imperialis*. It has drooping flowers of yellow, orange or red under a topknot of bright-green *bracts,* modified leaves that serve to protect the flowers. It has been cultivated for centuries, and is often seen in Renaissance flower paintings. It lasts well as a cut flower, but emits a musky odor some find unpleasant.

Crown imperial grows 3 to 4 feet tall, and is best planted at the back of a border or among shrubbery. It prefers a deep rich soil and needs moisture all year. It does not transplant well. Crown imperial has the reputation of not doing well in warm-summer areas of the South or in dry areas of the Southwest.

Bulbs are fragile, so handle them carefully. Cover with 6 to 8 inches of soil. Plant them on their sides.

This way water does not fill the hole left by the stem from the previous year, which can cause the bulb to rot.

Another common species is the checkered lily, *Fritillaria meleagris*. It is different from crown imperial. It grows less than 1 foot high and has dainty, single or multiple flowers. Flowers are checked purple and white or are sometimes completely white. They are charming in a shady rock garden. Plant the small bulbs 3 inches deep.

Give checkered lily and crown imperial moist, organic soil and light, filtered shade. If conditions are right for good growth, they are long-lived and multiply well.

Many other species are available. Some are native to Asia, Europe and the western United States. Most are temperamental and are pets of devoted specialists.

Galanthus
Snowdrops

Family: Amaryllidaceae.
Native to: Asia Minor.
Bulb type: True bulb.
Bloom season & length: Early spring for several weeks.
Colors: White.
Height: 4 to 9 inches.
Planting time: Fall.
Planting depth: 2 to 3 inches of soil over bulb.
Soil: Loam with drainage.
Water: During the growing season.
Fertilizer: None required.
Spacing: 3 inches.
Exposure: Light shade.
Propagation: Separate and replant immediately. Often self-sows.
Pests & diseases: Few.
Storage: Not necessary.

Snowdrops are popular in cold-climate areas. Their dainty blossoms arrive early in spring. When planted in quantity, flowers resemble drops of snow sitting on top of their low foliage. Flowers can be covered by snowfall. When the snow melts, they reappear, unharmed.

Snowdrops have a single, 6-petal flower per stem. They consist of 3 long petals on the outside and 3 short petals on the inside, which almost always have touches of green. There are at least 20 species and subspecies. All are similar, varying mostly in size, foliage color, and the amount of green in the short petals. The somewhat small flowers are most effective in groups, as a drift between trees or along the bottom of a wall. Sometimes they are grown in pots and brought indoors, but these hardy little bulbs prefer cold conditions.

The two most popular snowdrops are *Galanthus nivalis,* the common snowdrop of English gardens, and *G. elwesii,* a fine species adapted to milder climates. It has larger flowers and a 6-inch stem. Other forms include those with double flowers and at least one with a pure-white flower. Snowdrops are quite different from their close relative, *Leucojum,* which has stems over 1-1/2 feet tall with several flowers at the top.

Galanthus nivalis

Snowdrops combine well with *Iris reticulata* and *Eranthis* species.

Snowdrops accept all but the coldest temperatures, and grow as far north as Zone 3. They are not fussy about soil but do need moisture and good drainage. Light, filtered shade is preferred. Fertilizer is not recommended. Plant bulbs 3 inches apart and cover with 2 inches of soil. The best time to divide is just after blooming while the foliage is still green. Replant as soon as possible so bulbs do not dry out. Plants self-sow and spread, but take three to four years before blooming. They can be grown as far south as Zone 9, but are a challenge because of the lack of necessary cold. Gardeners in these areas will have more success with *Galanthus elwesii*.

Galtonia
Summer hyacinth

Family: Liliaceae.
Native to: South Africa.
Bulb type: True bulb.
Bloom season & length: Summer for several weeks.
Colors: White.
Height: 4 feet.
Planting time: Spring and fall.
Planting depth: 6 inches of soil over bulb.
Soil: Loose loam.
Water: During the growing season.
Fertilizer: Not required in good soil.
Spacing: 1 foot.
Exposure: Full sun.
Propagation: From small bulbs around base, or seeds.
Pests & diseases: Few.
Storage: Better to leave in place. If digging is necessary, store where they get air circulation.

Galtonia is often called *summer hyacinth.* Although it is related to hyacinth, it could never be mistaken for one. It lacks the fragrance of hyacinth, and grows 3 to 4 feet high, much taller than true hyacinth. It is a handsome plant in the background of the summer border. Tall stems carry many white, pendant-shaped flowers faintly tinged with green at the base. Gray-green leaves are long and strap-shaped. *Galtonia candicans* from South Africa is the best species and the most common. *Galtonia* also makes an excellent cut flower.

In Zones 8 to 10, plant in fall in a sunny location. Cover bulbs with 5 to 6 inches of soil. Keep moist while in growth. In Zones 5 to 8, plant in spring and cover with a mulch in winter. Some gardeners dig bulbs in the fall and store them during winter, but it is better to leave them in the ground. Protect against slugs and snails.

Galtonia species

Gladiolus

Family: Iridacaeae.
Native to: South Africa primarily.
Bulb type: Corm.
Bloom season & length: Spring and summer for 2 weeks.
Colors: All except true blue.
Height: 1 to 5 feet.
Planting time: Fall or spring depending on growing season.
Planting depth: 4 to 6 inches over corm.
Soil: Sandy loam.
Water: Ample supply during the growing season.
Fertilizer: Light dose when flower spikes appear.
Spacing: 4 to 6 inches.
Exposure: Full sun.
Propagation: From cormels formed at base.
Pests & diseases: Thrips can be a problem during warm weather and may infest corms stored during winter.
Storage: Dig when foliage dies down. Air circulation is necessary, so store in net bags or nylon stockings. Dust with insecticide and fungicide.

The name *Gladiolus* comes from the Latin word *gladius,* meaning sword, and refers to the plant's sword-shaped leaves. The word gladiator is from the same root word.

Gladiolus is a florist's delight. Flowers are available in a spectrum of colors that includes all but the richest delphinium-blue. If you are planning a garden of complementing hues and tints, look to *Gladiolus* for choice colors. By staggering planting times, flowers can be brought into bloom over a long period. Flowers last well when cut, and ship easily.

Plants are available in a variety of sizes and shapes, but they generally have a narrow, upright growth habit. Because of the vertical growth, it is difficult to make *Gladiolus* look natural in a flower border. For the most natural effect, do not plant singly, in rows or toward the front of the border. Instead, plant a single color in groups of 8 or 10 behind bushy perennials such as marguerites. In Zones 8 to 10, leave them in the ground from year to year.

Most *Gladiolus* currently available are hybrids of mixed parentage. It is difficult to identify and count original species, but some botanists believe there are close to 300. Most are from the southern part of Africa. However, others are natives of the Canary Islands, England and Turkey. *Gladiolus* is easy to hybridize, so new plants appear every year as old ones decline in popularity.

Hybrids are quite variable. Some are full with overlapping petals. Others have individual flowers separated from each other along the stem. Flower size and spike length also differ. It is pointless to explain the complicated classification of hybrid *Gladiolus* used for show. The United States, England and New Zealand each have a different set of rules. Eventually, rules will become uniform and more meaningful.

Don't overlook *Gladiolus* species. Some are hard to find but most are easy to grow. They definitely have charm. The following include some of the best for home gardens.

Gladiolus alatus grows 4 to 10 inches high. Red and yellow flowers are most common. It does well in a rock garden where it is given good drainage.

Gladiolus byzantinus, from Turkey, is hardier than most, and does well as far north as Zone 5. Its 2-foot stem has magenta-red flowers. The pure-white form is desirable and popular in Europe as a cut flower.

'Majesty', a late, midseason, large-flowered *Gladiolus*.

Gladiolus hybrid

A selection of *Gladiolus* demonstrates variety of color and range of flower size.

Gladiolus x colvillei, hardy to Zone 7. Hybrids are often sold as "baby glads." They are short—to 2 feet tall—and informal in appearance compared with the taller hybrids. Named varieties include 'The Bride', pure white; 'Spitfire', scarlet with violet flakes; 'Peach Blossom', delicate pink; and 'Amanda Mahy', bright salmon.

Gladiolus natalensis, the parent of many large-flowered hybrids, does well in mild climates. This species was discovered around 1900 near Victoria Falls on the Zambesi River in South Africa. Large flowers are orange-red and yellow on 5-foot-high stems. The upper petal is hooded, bending over flower parts to protect them.

Gladiolus tristis, hardy to Zone 7, has creamy white-yellow flowers sometimes striped with purple, on 2-foot-high stems. Flowers are fragrant in the evenings. Where adapted, it self-sows to cover large areas.

When choosing corms at the nursery, judge quality more by *depth* rather than width. *Gladiolus* prefer sandy, rich soil in full sun but are adaptable. When planting, it is beneficial to mix a small amount of complete fertilizer into the soil under the bulb. Put a layer of soil on top of the fertilizer so it does not touch the corm. Cover corms with 2 to 6 inches of soil, depending on corm size and soil type. Plant tall varieties deeply so that stem is better able to support stalks.

Florists can closely determine the blooming times of *Gladiolus.* Most start their bloom 100 days after planting, depending on weather conditions. The warmer the temperatures, the sooner the blooms appear. Begin planting corms after frost has passed. With proper timing and a little luck, you can have blooms for special occasions such as Mother's Day, Memorial Day, June Weddings or the Fourth of July.

In the past, it was believed that *Gladiolus* should complete bloom before the Fourth of July to prevent potential problems with *thrips,* tiny insects that feed on the blossoms. It's true that thrips are big enemies of late-blooming *Gladiolus.* They can be detected by pale streaks on the foliage and badly distorted flowers. If you pull flowers apart, you can see the tiny insects. They are so tiny it is hard to believe that they can be so damaging. Spray with a systemic insecticide such as Orthene. It is especially important to eliminate thrips before storing for winter because they hibernate under the cover of the corms. Use a bulb dust or napthalene flakes around stored corms if thrips were a problem during summer.

When picking blooms for cut flowers, leave four or five leaves on the plant. They are necessary to produce food for the next year's growth.

Gloriosa
Gloriosa lily, Climbing lily

Family: Liliaceae.
Native to: Africa.
Bulb type: Elongated tuber.
Bloom season & length: Summer.
Colors: Yellow and red.
Height: Climbing to 6 feet.
Planting time: Spring after frost.
Planting depth: 4 inches on top of tuber.
Soil: Rich loam with good drainage.
Water: Keep moist during growing season.
Fertilizer: Monthly with complete fertilizer.
Spacing: 10 inches, but usually planted singly as a specimen.
Exposure: Prefers to have its roots cool and shaded with foliage in sun.
Propagation: Divide tubers in spring, but each must have a bud.
Pests & diseases: Few. Watch for snails when shoots first appear.
Storage: Dig after foliage dies and store in dry peat or vermiculite.

Gloriosa is one of the most exotic plants you can grow. Although it is a lily, its leaves end in tendrils, which support the plant as it climbs, sometimes over 6 feet high. Given the proper conditions, plant blooms over a long period in summer. Flowers are produced from the leaf axils at the top of the plant—striking 3- to 4-inch flowers resembling a Turk's-cap lily. Undulating petals are strongly reflexed with protruding stamens.

There is some variation of species color, but *Gloriosa rothschildiana* from Africa and *G. superba* from India are similar. Their petals are yellow at the center, changing to orange-red at the tops. *G. rothschildiana* is slightly darker yellow and tips are darker red. Both are excellent cut flowers for bouquets and corsages.

Gloriosa is grown outdoors in Zones 8 to 10. It prefers a rich, fertile soil and good drainage. Plants grow in sandy loam in the wild. Plant the long tuber horizontally and cover with 2 to 3 inches of soil. Plant in sun or where plant can climb toward sunlight. Keep the soil moist when plant is growing. Fertilize once a month with a light dose of dry fertilizer. North of Zone 8, start indoors in the early spring for an extended bloom period. In the fall, dig and store. See page 27. They can be divided when they are dug, but each tuber must have an "eye" to grow. Eyes are easiest to see in the early spring. If growing from seeds, allow three to four years before expecting bloom. *Gloriosa* makes a good house plant in a container if exposed to a window with plenty of bright sunlight.

Gloriosa rothschildiana

Gloriosa rothschildiana

Habranthus robustus

Habranthus

Family: Amaryllidaceae.
Native to: North to South America.
Bulb type: True bulb.
Bloom season & length: Flowers appear after summer rains.
Colors: Red, pink and yellow.
Height: 6 to 9 inches.
Planting time: Spring.
Planting depth: 1/2 inch of soil over bulb.
Soil: Sandy loam.
Water: Periodically.
Fertilizer: Not necessary.
Spacing: 2 to 4 inches.
Exposure: Full sun to light shade.
Propagation: From offshoots and seeds.
Pests & diseases: Few. Watch for snails.
Storage: Store in pots until crowded.

Habranthus is a small group of true bulbs. Most species bloom in summer and fall. They are similar to *Zephyranthes,* but most have larger flowers. *Habranthus* can also be distinguished by its stamens, which are four distinctly different lengths. Upward or outfacing, solitary, funnel-shaped flowers appear on a short stem. Some kinds bloom with the foliage, some without. Often, first flowers appear before leaves. Later flowers appear after leaves have grown. Most are natives of South America. One, *Habranthus* var. *andersonii texanus,* is native to Texas. There it is called *rain lily* because it often blooms soon after a rain.

Habranthus andersonii has gold-yellow flowers on 6-inch stems. A coppery brown tint flushes the outside. Variety *texanus* is yellow on the outside and petals are more rounded. *H. robustus* has large, 3-inch, pale-pink flowers with deeper-colored veins and a green throat. Flowers appear in late summer before leaves appear.

In Zones 9 and 10, *Habranthus* is grown in a sunny location outdoors in well-drained soil. Plant with the neck of the bulb at soil surface, and leave it undisturbed to multiply. In other areas, *Habranthus* is an interesting pot plant, similar to *Amaryllis,* to which it is related. Plants do not need large pots. Plant a dozen bulbs in a 6-inch container.

Haemanthus
Blood lily

Family: Amaryllidaceae.
Native to: Africa.
Bulb type: True bulb.
Bloom season & length: Summer or fall.
Colors: Red, coral or white.
Height: 6 inches to 2-1/2 feet.
Planting time: Spring after frost.
Planting depth: Just under soil surface.
Soil: Loamy with fast drainage.
Water: Ample during the growing season.
Fertilizer: Light application with a complete fertilizer when growth starts.
Spacing: 1 foot.
Exposure: Light, filtered shade.
Propagation: By offsets in spring.
Pests & diseases: Snails and mealybugs.
Storage: Store dry bulbs in their pots.

At least four dozen species of *Haemanthus* grow wild in central and southern Africa. Some are called *blood lilies* because of the red spots on the bulb. Others are called *paint brush* or *shaving brush* from the thickly set stamens in the flowers. Presently, three species are commonly available for home gardeners. They are quite distinct from one another.

Haemanthus albiflos is easiest to grow. It is evergreen and multiplies prolifically. Strap-shaped leaves are leathery and bordered with tiny, white hairs. Flowers appear in late summer, held above the foliage on 8- to 10-inch stems. Bracts around the flower are white, and the center is filled with many golden stamens. Grown closely together in a large low tub, they look similar to an exotic water lily.

Haemanthus coccineus is the most unusual species. Its flower appears in late summer without foliage on a 6-inch stem. The 3-inch-wide flowerheads are coral-red with typical, upright-protruding stamens. The scarlet bract underneath is wider than the umbel. After the flower dies, two leathery leaves grow from the bulb, spreading over the ground. The leaves grow to 6 inches wide and 2 feet long.

Haemanthus katharinae is the most beautiful of the group. It develops a large, completely round umbel of small, salmon-red, sometimes scarlet or pink flowers with bright yellow, protruding stamens on a 2-foot stem. Leaves are generally evergreen, but not leathery as with most *Haemanthus*. It is often grown in pots in cold areas, then brought inside during winter. A pot twice the size of the bulb is adequate.

All *Haemanthus* can be grown outdoors in Zones 9 and 10. They need fast drainage and a winter rest period. Most prefer filtered shade or optimum light indoors. A light application of fertilizer when plants are growing is beneficial. Plant bulbs with the neck at the soil surface. Watch for slugs and snails. Protect from frost.

Haemanthus katharinae

Haemanthus albiflos

Hemerocallis 'Blue Jay'

Hemerocallis hybrid

Hemerocallis 'Jean George'

Hemerocallis 'Victoria Elizabeth Barnes'

Hemerocallis 'Persian Market'

Hemerocallis 'Lucille Guidry'

Hemerocallis
Daylily

Family: Liliaceae.
Native to: Japan and Europe.
Bulb type: Tuberous roots.
Bloom season & length: Summer for several months.
Colors: Yellow, orange, red, cream, pink and maroon.
Height: 1 to 3-1/2 feet.
Planting time: Spring or fall.
Planting depth: 1/2 inch below soil surface.
Soil: Adaptable.
Water: During the growing season.
Fertilizer: Not required in fertile soil.
Spacing: 2 feet.
Exposure: Full sun to light shade.
Propagation: By separation when crowded.
Pests & diseases: Few.
Storage: Best left in ground.

Daylilies have long been popular, and have gained many new admirers recently due in part to new hybrids. All are easy to grow, and have naturalized in some areas. Colors range from cream-white through lemon, gold, apricot, melon, orange, pink, salmon, red, dark mahogany and the purples and lavenders. Some flowers have stripes, petals of different colors or a contrasting color in the center.

New varieties grow from 1 to 4 feet high, sometimes higher. They are hybrids and clones of a few species: *Hemerocallis fulva*, orange-red; *H. aurantiaca*, orange with a lavender blush; *H. citrina*, lemon-yellow; *H. thunbergii*, sulfur-apricot; and dwarf *H. nana*, orange and reddish brown.

Daylilies grow almost anywhere. The beauty, neat appearance and ease of maintenance is demonstrated by their popularity with commercial and municipal landscapers.

Evergreen varieties do best in mild climates. They require little maintenance and are a boon for the home gardener. They combine beautifully with the blues of *Delphinium, Veronica* and *Agapanthus*. Consider planting early blooming bulbs such as daffodils around deciduous daylilies. Their fading foliage will be covered by the new leaves of the daylilies as they shoot up.

Daylilies grow in all zones but need a mulch in winter north of Zone 5. They bloom best with full sun, but most do suprisingly well with two hours of sun a day. They grow in any soil from sand to clay, but a rich, moist soil is ideal. Daylilies can go up to five years without being divided. Divide them any time if new starts are desired. Plant the tuberous roots 2 or more feet apart, depending on ultimate height and spread.

Hemerocallis make permanent, low-maintenance garden plants. Flowers are available in a wide range of colors.

Hippeastrum
Dutch amaryllis

Family: Amaryllidaceae.
Native to: Mostly tropical America.
Bulb type: True bulb.
Bloom season & length: April to May for in-ground planting.
Colors: Red, pink, orange, salmon, white and striped.
Height: 2 feet.
Planting time: Fall, spring.
Planting depth: Just under soil surface.
Soil: Sandy loam.
Water: Frequently during growing season.
Fertilizer: Light applications of a house-plant fertilizer.
Spacing: 1 foot.
Exposure: Full sun or light shade.
Propagation: From offsets removed in fall before new growth appears.
Pests & diseases: Snails, mealybugs, narcissus fly and cutworm.
Storage: Dry, directly in their pots. Start watering about 5 weeks before flowering.

Common *Hippeastrum* is usually sold as Dutch hybrid amaryllis. It was developed from crosses of *Hippeastrum reginae, H. vittatum* and the hybrid *H. x johnsonii.* From these beginnings, outstanding varieties were developed.

Hippeastrum are sold by the tens of thousands before Thanksgiving—potted and ready to bloom indoors for Christmas and New Year. Colors are white, pink, orange, salmon, scarlet and dark red, including many variations and combinations. They grow 2 feet high and develop showy, 6-inch flowers.

Plant bulbs in pots 1 inch wider than the bulb. The top of the bulb should protrude out of the soil. Hold the bulb in the container with the roots pointing down. Add soil carefully. Soil should be loose with lots of humus and good drainage. Push soil down to firm it and eliminate air pockets. Keep soil slightly damp until growth begins. As it grows, gradually increase amount of water. Rotate pot so the stem does not lean toward light.

After blooming, Christmas bulbs can be saved for the following year. Cut off faded flowers and seed pods after bloom. Put the plant in filtered shade after danger of frost has passed. Apply a light dose of fertilizer and water regularly. Let it begin to dry out and rest by the first of August. Stalk and leaves eventually wither and disappear. This supplies a necessary dormant period. Begin the watering cycle again in the second week of November to have plants bloom again at Christmas time.

Hippeastrum are easy to grow outdoors in Zones 9 and 10. Bulbs grown in the ground generally bloom in May. Snails can be a serious problem, and will even eat the bulb.

Of the 70-odd species, only a few are commercially available, primarily because most people grow the immensely popular Dutch hybrids.

Hippeastrum Dutch hybrid

Hippeastrum

Hippeastrum Dutch hybrid

Homeria

Family: Iridaceae.
Native to: South Africa.
Bulb type: Corm.
Bloom season & length: Summer for 6 weeks.
Height: 18 inches.
Planting time: Spring.
Planting depth: 2 inches.
Soil: Sandy loam.
Water: During the growing season.
Fertilizer: Not required.
Spacing: 10 inches.
Exposure: Full sun.
Propagation: Seeds and cormlets.
Pests & diseases: Few.
Storage: In dry peat moss or vermiculite.

This South-African bulb is related to *Moraea, Ixia* and *Tigridia* species. Like them, the 2-inch, cup-shape flowers have spreading petals that last only a day. However, *Homeria* stems carry many buds, which open in succession, providing continuous color over several weeks.

There are two common forms, the important difference being color. *Homeria breyniana* 'Aurantiaca' has apricot-color flowers while *H. ochroleuca* has yellow flowers. Both grow about 2 feet tall. With the right conditions, plants spread from their own seeds. *H. lilacina* is a rare but obtainable form. Flowers are lilac with purple veins and have yellow-speckled, purple basal blotch.

Homeria are easy to grow in Zones 9 and 10. Plant them in soil with excellent drainage and in full sun. Cover corms with 2 to 3 inches of soil. In areas where they are not cold-hardy, grow them like *Gladiolus,* digging and storing corms in fall.

Hyacinthus
Hyacinth

Family: Liliaceae.
Native to: Mediterranean region, Asia Minor.
Bulb type: True bulb.
Bloom season & length: Spring for several weeks.
Colors: White, pink, blue, mauve, rose, red, purple and tawny orange.
Height: 8 to 12 inches.
Planting time: Fall.
Planting depth: 5 inches over bulb.
Soil: Sandy loam.
Water: Generous during growing season.
Fertilizer: Not required.
Spacing: 6 inches.
Exposure: Full sun to light shade.
Propagation: Slow to multiply. Cut bulbs 1/2 inch deep in criss-cross fashion through basal plate. Bulblets form along edges.
Pests & diseases: Few.
Storage: Leave undisturbed, but flowers become smaller in time.

Hyacinths are grown for their sweet, pervasive fragrance and full, formal spires of flowers. The fragrance has always been a trait of *Hyacinthus orientalis,* but the thickly set flowers are the result of extensive Dutch hybridizing and culture over the past 200 years.

Dutch hyacinths are the most expensive of all spring bulbs. This is due to the amount of work and time involved in propagating each bulb and growing it to size.

Hippeastrum Dutch hybrid

Homeria breyniana 'Aurantiaca'

Homeria ochroleuca

Dutch hybrid hyacinth

Pink Dutch hybrid hyacinths in container are showcased with white *Freesias* and blue *Anemone.*

Part of the process is removing all the flowers from the spike the first year the bulb blooms. Watching this being done in the fields of Holland and seeing the huge piles of hyacinth flowers can be quite a surprise for the person viewing it for the first time. By removing the flowers, all the strength is put back into the bulb. This in turn produces thickly set stems of flowers the following year.

When you see the blooms of your bulbs the second year, you may think that your bulbs have deteriorated. But they are simply returning to their natural state with looser, more informal flowers. You may prefer them that way. If this is the case, buy the blue, white or pink French or Roman hyacinths. They are a variety of *Hyacinthus orientalis* from the Mediterranean region. They are cold-hardy as far north as Zone 6. Dutch hybrids are cold-hardy to Zone 4.

Dutch hybrids are available in a wide range of colors: white, creamy yellow, pale pink, dark rose, light blue, dark blue and shades of salmon and red. Salmon and red flowers are not as large and fine as the other colors, but continued hybridizing will result in further improvements.

Hyacinthus azureus, technically *Pseudomuscari azureum,* is a less common species. It is a native of Asia Minor and looks like a grape hyacinth. Flowers are sky-blue and sweetly scented.

Plant hyacinth in fall as soon as possible so roots develop in warm soil. In mild climates, store bulbs like tulips in a cool place until Thanksgiving. This still gives them enough time to produce roots before spring. Plant 5 inches apart and cover with 4 inches of soil.

Hyacinths are excellent for growing in pots. Plant them close together with their sides barely touching. Place them near the surface to provide adequate root space. Bulbs must be kept covered in a cool, dark place while the roots are forming. This may take two to three months. As the spike emerges, you will be able to see the flower buds under the leaves, white from lack of exposure to light. Expose the potted bulbs to filtered light until they green up. After they have turned green, they can be moved to full sun. Exposing them to too much light too soon may cause the flowers to bloom on too-short stems.

Plants can be grown in special jars that hold the bulb just above a reservoir of water—a popular and simple method. Keep the jars in a cool, dark closet until they fill with roots, and then slowly expose them to increasing amounts of light. See photo, page 29.

Hyacinths are expensive bulbs, so they are rarely planted in large, formal beds. If you want to try them this way, remove all soil from bed and level soil at planting depth.

Hymenocallis narcissiflora

Pancratium canariense

Hymenocallis and Pancratium
Spider lily, Sea daffodil

Family: Amaryllidaceae.
Native to: Caribbean, North to South America.
Bulb type: True bulb.
Bloom season & length: Summer for several weeks.
Colors: White or yellow.
Height: To 3 feet.
Planting time: Spring.
Planting depth: Bury bulbs so tip of neck is at soil surface.
Soil: Sandy loam.
Water: During growing season.
Fertilizer: Light applications during growing season.
Spacing: 6 to 18 inches.
Exposure: Light, filtered shade to full sun.
Propagation: By offsets, but they do not need to be separated.
Pests & diseases: Snails, mealybugs and narcissus fly.
Storage: Indoors in pots in lighted area with occasional water.

Hymenocallis is a group of bulbs native to the Western Hemisphere. The common name spider lily refers to their long, thin, recurving petals. Another common name, Peruvian daffodil, was given because the flower resembles a daffodil. The bulb produces strap-shaped foliage and fragrant, white flowers. Exceptions are *H. amancaes* and its hybrids, whose flowers are shades of yellow.

Hymenocallis caroliniana is a native of the southeastern United States. It has fragrant white flowers on 1-1/2- to 2-foot-high stems.

Hymenocallis x festalis has several white flowers on a 2-foot-high stem and a widespread *staminal cup,* formed when the stamens unite below the pollen-bearing anthers.

Hymenocallis narcissiflora is the most widely grown species. It is a native of Peru, the so-called Peruvian daffodil. It has a pronounced staminal cup. 'Sulphur Queen' is a cross between *H. narcissiflora* and *H. amancaes.* The flower is light yellow and has green bands on the staminal cup.

Hymenocallis tolerate some cold, growing as far north as Zone 8. They prefer full sun or light, filtered shade. Plant in rich, well-drained soil. In the North, dig immediately after the first frost and store indoors in winter. They make interesting and handsome container plants.

Pancratium is so similar to *Hymenocallis* that they are difficult to distinguish. Positive identification is determined by the placement of the ovules and seed type. Most bulb gardeners look at the leaves for characteristic features. *Hymenocallis* usually have bright-green leaves. *Pancratium* leaves are usually dull green with a dusty covering. Flowers are also slightly different. For *Pancratium,* the teeth at the edge of the flower cup are triangular. If the teeth are fringed, it is *Hymenocallis.*

Pancratium is well adapted to Mediterranean climates. In California and Florida, it grows like a native, thriving on normal rainfall. *P. maritimum* is the most common species. Flowers are white with a sweet scent. Each flower has a long staminal cup that resembles a trumpet daffodil.

Ipheion uniflorum
Spring star flower

Family: Amaryllidaceae.
Native to: Argentina and Uruguay.
Bulb type: True bulb.
Bloom season & length: Spring over a long period.
Colors: Pale to dark blue.
Height: 6 inches.
Planting time: Fall.
Planting depth: 1 inch of soil over bulb.
Soil: Not fussy.
Water: During the growing season.
Fertilizer: Not necessary.
Spacing: 1 inch.
Exposure: Full sun to light shade.
Propagation: Seeds and offsets.
Pests & diseases: None.
Storage: Not necessary. Can be grown in the same pot up to four years.

Ipheion uniflorum is a pretty but surprisingly tough bulb from South America. Because of its low growth habit, *Ipheion* is especially well suited for rock gardens, between steppingstones and as edgings. It has been previously classed as a *Brodiaea, Triteleia* and *Milla.*

The plant carries 1-inch, star-shaped flowers on a 6-inch stem above grasslike foliage. It blooms for months. Leaves smell like onions when bruised.

Ipheion can remain undisturbed for years in a container. Bulbs should be planted fairly close together for the best effect when plants are in bloom. The most-common variety has pale-blue flowers. The dark-blue variety was discovered mixed with other *Ipheion* in the Wisley Gardens outside London. It is named 'Wisley Blue', and is worth looking for.

Grow *Ipheion* outdoors in Zones 6 to 10. Plant with 1 to 2 inches of soil over the top of bulbs in almost any soil, except soggy soil. In cold, Northern areas, plant bulbs deeper than normal for frost protection. Bulbs are splendid indoors, and bloom a month earlier than those planted outdoors. Provide them with an exposure to a sunny window.

Ipheion uniflorum

'Odyssey' bearded iris

'Kilt Lilt' bearded iris

'Ship Shape' bearded iris

'Tsuzure Nishki' Japanese iris

'Nemuri Sishi' Japanese iris

Louisiana iris

Dutch iris

Spuria iris

Pacific Coast iris

Iris

Family: Iridaceae.
Native to: Northern Hemisphere.
Bulb type: Rhizome or bulb.
Bloom season & length: Early spring through summer, depending on variety.
Colors: All except true red.
Height: 3 inches to 4 feet.
Planting time: Fall and spring.
Planting depth: Rhizomes near surface. Bulbs 1 to 3 inches under soil.
Soil: No special requirements.
Water: Regular during the growing season.
Fertilizer: Sparingly.
Spacing: 2 to 12 inches.
Exposure: Full sun or light shade.
Propagation: Bulbs by separation; rhizomes by division.
Pests & diseases: Snails, rhizome rot and iris borer.
Storage: Usually not stored, but can be stored where necessary.

Irises are well named. The name comes from Iris, Goddess of the Rainbow, reflecting the fact that every color of the spectrum—except true red—can be found in their flowers.

Irises are a varied group, with forms native to most areas of the Northern Hemisphere. Of more than 300 species, most, such as the bearded varieties, are adaptable to various climates. There are two basic types: those that grow from bulbs and those that grow from rhizomes.

BULB TYPES

The most widely grown bulb types are the Dutch iris. They are not from Holland, but were hybridized there with species from North Africa, Spain and England. 'Wedgewood' is a popular, early blooming Dutch iris, with wedgewood-blue flowers. It blooms at the same time as golden daffodils, and complements them wonderfully. Other Dutch iris bloom three weeks to a month later. Flowers come in shades of white, lemon, gold, light blue, dark blue, purple, rich brown and many color combinations.

Cover Dutch iris bulbs with 2 inches of soil. Average garden soil is satisfactory. Plant in a sunny location. They look best planted in groups.

Iris danfordiae has golden-yellow flowers speckled with brown. It grows 4 inches high. Flowers appear almost before the leaves. Cover bulbs with 1 inch of soil. Cool climates are preferred.

Iris douglasiana and *I. innominata* are natives of the West Coast. These two species have generated much interest and have been crossed to form a fine, new group. *I. innominata* is a good example. It quickly forms a large, 2-foot-wide, 2-foot-high clump covered with many flowers. Flower colors are lovely shades of cream, yellow, apricot, lavender, purple, blue and white. Many are bicolored and some have contrasting veins. They prefer light shade except in coastal areas, where they should be given more sun.

RHIZOME TYPES

Rhizomatous irises are a large and diversified group. Most are easy to grow. In general, rhizomes grow along the surface of the ground with the roots appearing from the bottom. Most prefer full sun and good soil drainage.

Iris cristata is known as *dwarf crested iris*. It is native to the East Coast, from Maryland to Georgia. Flowers

Iris sibirica

Iris reticulata

Iris cristata 'Alba'

are white, light blue or lilac with golden crests. Crested iris is beautiful in rock gardens and effective as a ground cover. It blooms best in full sun but also blooms in shade.

Iris foetidissima is grown solely for its scarlet, pea-size seeds that appear when the blue-green seed pods open. It prefers some shade.

Bearded iris, *I. x germanica,* is a show-stopper in late spring. If you are planning for interesting color combinations, bearded irises are available in many colors. Categorized as *tall, 4-foot, medium* and *dwarf,* all bearded irises should stay in the ground until they become crowded. The best time to divide them is after the blooming period. Because they grow from a surface rhizome, plant them pointing the direction you want them to grow.

Remontant, reblooming iris, are desirable in mild-winter areas. In California, some bloom around Christmas time. Additional water and fertilizer encourages this second bloom.

Iris kaempferi, the beautiful Japanese iris, has large, almost flat flowers—up to 10 inches wide. It prefers boggy conditions when actively growing, but tolerates dry conditions after the growth period. Hundreds of named varieties in white, blue, lavender, pink and purple are available. Some are bicolored and many have veins. All are spectacular in the landscape or as cut flowers.

Louisiana irises grow naturally where the soil is damp and acid but are adaptable to other conditions. These are mostly hybrids of *Iris fulva* and *I. giganticaerulea,* and to a lesser extent, *I. brevicaulis.* They produce flowers on tall stems in shades of light and dark blue, yellow, pink and terra-cotta.

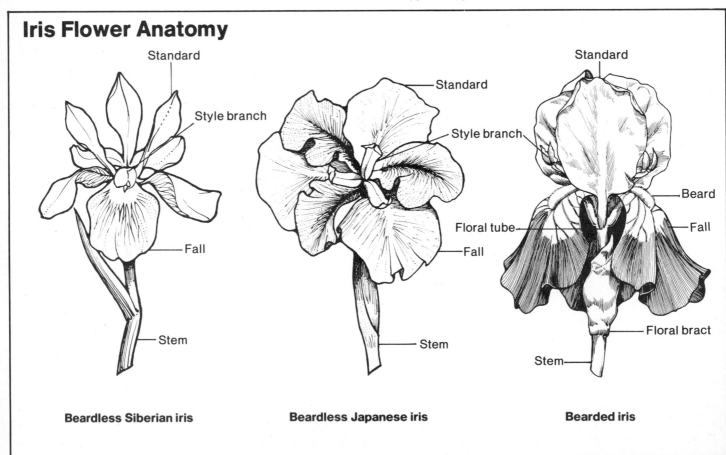

Iris Flower Anatomy

Standard
Style branch
Fall
Stem

Beardless Siberian iris

Standard
Style branch
Fall
Stem

Beardless Japanese iris

Standard
Beard
Floral tube
Fall
Floral bract
Stem

Bearded iris

Iris orientalis, formerly *I. ochroleuca,* is commonly known as *Spuria iris.* A strong-growing, cold-hardy species from Asia Minor, its tall stems are topped with yellow and white or all-yellow flowers. It goes to seed and spreads around the garden. This can be a virtue or a problem, depending on the situation. They prefer hot summers and exist on little moisture.

Iris reticulata, sold commercially, is a bright, violet-blue. It is early blooming and grows best in a cool climates. The species is a reddish purple. Grown from seeds, it reverts to the color of the species.

Regeliocyclus hybrids were developed in Holland from Asia Minor species. They accept cold and need good soil drainage and a long, dry, dormant period. Flowers are usually heavily veined. Colors are muted. Some flowers are fragrant.

Iris sibirica is a small, slender and delicate species. Flowers resemble thin Dutch iris growing on a 2-foot-high stem. Colors are purple, light blue, dark blue, white and sometimes mixed. It is easy to grow and adapted to different climates. Plantings eventually form tight clumps that produce many flowers.

Iris tectorum is known mainly as the *Iris* that grows on the thatched roofs of Japan. The 15-inch-high stems have lilac-blue flowers. It requires fast drainage and tolerates dry summer conditions.

Iris unguicularis is an eastern Mediterranean native. Easy to grow in warm areas of the South and West, it has the advantage of blooming in midwinter. Unfortunately, the lilac-blue flowers are sometimes hidden down in the foliage. Compensate by cutting back foliage to 4 inches in the fall before buds develop. This does not hurt the plant and enables flowers to be viewed in all their beauty.

Iris xiphioides, English iris, grows best in cooler areas, such as parts of Oregon and Washington. The flowers, which appear late in the season, resemble Dutch iris, but the foliage bends over.

AWARD-WINNING IRIS

Almost every year, the breeder of the top *Iris* variety is awarded the Dykes Medal by The American Iris Society. Winning the Dykes Medal is not necessarily the only criteria for selecting *Iris.* New gardeners may find the following bulbs good choices to begin with. Prize-winning *Irises* are selected on the basis of form, substance, branching, bud spacing, color, size, length of bloom, period of bloom, vigor and resistance to pests and diseases. All *Iris* classes are eligible for the Dykes Medal. Recent winners are:

1967	'Winter Olympics'	38" ruffled white
1968	'Stepping Out'	38" white-edged pansy violet
1970	'Skywatch'	38" pale blue
1971	'Debby Rairdon'	34" light-yellow standard, falls white-yellow edge
1972	'Babbling Brook'	38" French blue
1973	'New Moon'	36" lemon-yellow
1974	'Shipshape'	38" medium blue, yellow beard
1975	'Pink Taffeta'	32" ruffled rose-pink
1976	'Kilt Lilt'	38" standard apricot, falls maroon on gold
1977	'Dream Lover'	38" standard ice-blue, falls purple
1978	'Bride's Halo'	38" white ruffled yellow edge
1979	'Mary Frances'	38" blue orchid, white centered, falls
1980	'Mystique'	36" violet-purple
1981	'Brown Lasso'	(short) caramel and violet, a short border iris
1982	'Vanity'	36" light coral-red beard

Categories of Bearded Iris

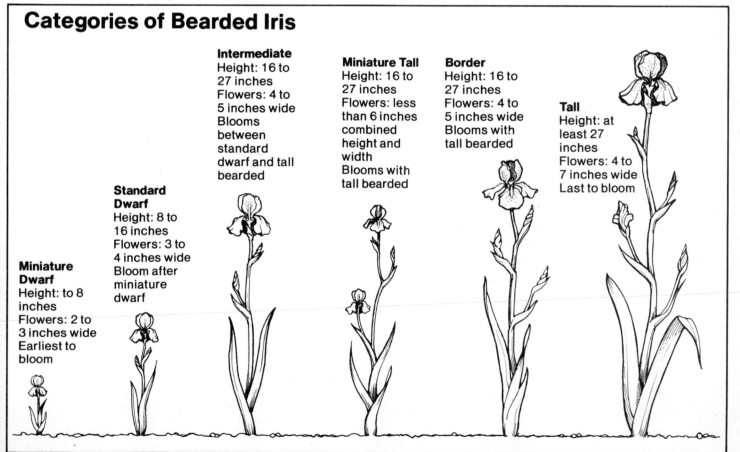

Miniature Dwarf
Height: to 8 inches
Flowers: 2 to 3 inches wide
Earliest to bloom

Standard Dwarf
Height: 8 to 16 inches
Flowers: 3 to 4 inches wide
Bloom after miniature dwarf

Intermediate
Height: 16 to 27 inches
Flowers: 4 to 5 inches wide
Blooms between standard dwarf and tall bearded

Miniature Tall
Height: 16 to 27 inches
Flowers: less than 6 inches combined height and width
Blooms with tall bearded

Border
Height: 16 to 27 inches
Flowers: 4 to 5 inches wide
Blooms with tall bearded

Tall
Height: at least 27 inches
Flowers: 4 to 7 inches wide
Last to bloom

Ixia maculata

Ixia hybrid

Ixia
African corn lily

Family: Iridaceae.
Native to: South Africa.
Bulb type: Corm.
Bloom season & length: Spring for several weeks.
Colors: Rose, red, orange, cream, yellow and blue-green.
Height: 2 feet.
Planting time: Fall.
Planting depth: 2 inches over corm.
Soil: Fast drainage.
Water: During growing season.
Fertilizer: Not necessary in regular soil.
Spacing: 2 to 3 inches.
Exposure: Full sun.
Propagation: By cormlets that form at base. Self-sows.
Pests & diseases: Few.
Storage: In cold areas dig in fall and store in above-freezing temperatures in a dry location.

In Europe, *Ixia* is a florist's delight. Flowers are long lasting, usually for more than a week. They are frequently used in mixed bouquets. Don't pick flowers until they start to open, and immediately submerge in water. If out of water too long, flowers will not reopen.

Flowers develop along ends of long, thin, 18- to 20-inch stems. They are as colorful in bud as when the 1- to 2-inch flowers open in the warmth of the sun. Usual colors are rose, red, orange, yellow or cream with darker centers.

Ixia viridiflora is a fascinating species with metallic, blue-green flowers and a purple center. But it is not recommended unless you have grown other *Ixia* species successfully. It requires exceedingly well-drained soil.

Ixia grows well in Zones 8 to 10. In other areas, it is an attractive container plant or is grown in the same way as *Gladiolus*. It prefers dry conditions in the summer. In the Southeast, it needs sandy, well-drained soil. Cover corm with 2 to 3 inches of soil. In pots, planting 1-1/2 inches deep permits better root growth. Indoors, it needs at least a half-day of full sun.

Ixiolirion

Family: Amaryllidaceae.
Native to: Siberia.
Bulb type: True bulb.
Bloom season & length: Late spring for 6 weeks.
Colors: Blue.
Height: 1 foot.
Planting time: Fall.
Planting depth: 3 inches soil over bulb.
Soil: Good drainage is essential.
Water: During the growing season.
Fertilizer: When shoots appear.
Spacing: 3 inches.
Exposure: Full sun.
Propagation: Remove and plant small bulbs from mother bulb.
Pests & diseases: Few.
Storage: From Zone 6 north, dig bulbs and store in dry peat moss or vermiculite.

The several species of *Ixiolirion* are similar. The most common is *I. tataricum* var. *pallasii*. It has several, violet-blue, star-shaped flowers in a loose umbel at the top of a 1-foot stem. It makes a good cutting flower and is grown commercially. Because foliage is grasslike and disappears quickly, *Ixiolirion* are excellent bulbs to plant under ground covers.

Even though *Ixiolirion* are native to Siberia, plants are not cold-hardy north of Zone 6. Plant in a sunny area in well-drained soil. Cover with 3 inches of soil. Plant 2 to 3 inches apart for best display. Moderate applications of fertilizer are beneficial. Culture is similar to *Alstroemeria*. See page 62. Bulbs are available for planting in the fall. North of Zone 6, dig and store in fall. Plant when weather warms in spring.

Lachenalia
Cape cowslip

Family: Liliaceae.
Native to: South Africa.
Bulb type: True bulb.
Bloom season & length: Winter, spring.
Colors: Red, yellow, orange, light blue, lavender, pale green and white.
Height: 7 to 15 inches.
Planting time: Fall.
Planting depth: 1 inch soil over bulb.
Soil: Sandy.
Water: During the growing season.
Fertilizer: Liquid fertilizer once a month during growing season.
Spacing: 2 inches.
Exposure: Full sun to light shade.
Propagation: By offsets and seeds.
Pests & diseases: Slugs and snails.
Storage: Store dry in their pots until fall.

Lachenalia species

Showy yellow, orange, red, white or blue-shaded flowers of *Lachenalia* appear over a long period in spring. Pendulous flowers are thickly set on short stems. Leaves are plain green or mottled.

Of the 35 species that grow in South Africa, only a few are available commercially. *L. glaucina,* a somewhat rare species, is smaller than the others and resembles *Muscari*. See page 125. Its 6-inch spike is a beautiful combination of colors—light blue, mauve, lavender and pale green.

Lachenalia aloides has a 12-inch flower spike with yellow flowers, each with a green base and a tip edged in red. Leaves and stems are heavily spotted with purple-brown. Subspecies *L. aloides aurea* has golden-orange flowers and *L. aloides* 'Nelsonii' has yellow flowers tipped with green.

Lachenalia bulbiferum (L. pendula) is first to bloom. It can sometimes be forced for Christmas bloom. After it is established in a container, move to a warm window for an earlier bloom. Its 7-inch spike carries 20 or more tubular red flowers, each edged with green at the tip. The green leaves are unspotted.

Lachenalia pearsonii, a hybrid, has two heavily spotted leaves from which a 15-inch flower spike develops. Flowers are yellow edged with red at the tip.

In Zones 9 and 10, plant *Lachenalia* outdoors in September. Prefers a sandy soil. They are inclined to rot if allowed to get soggy during hot weather. Allow container plantings to go dry until September. When planting in the ground, put 1 inch of soil over the soft bulb. In pots, plant bulbs just under the soil surface. Water lightly until growth appears. Use a diluted solution of liquid fertilizer every other week. All *Lachenalia* species are rapid multipliers and make distinctive container plants. Watch for infestations of snails or slugs.

Lachenalia aloides

Lapeirousia laxa

Lapeirousia laxa

Lapeirousia

Family: Iridaceae.
Native to: South Africa.
Bulb type: Corm.
Bloom season & length: Spring for several weeks.
Colors: Salmon, red and pale lavender.
Height: 6 to 9 inches.
Planting time: Fall.
Planting depth: 1 inch.
Soil: Undemanding.
Water: During growing season.
Fertilizer: Not necessary.
Spacing: 2 inches.
Exposure: Full sun to light shade.
Propagation: Easy from seeds, or separate and replant corms.
Pests & diseases: Few.
Storage: Store in pots dry through summer.

In many ways, *Lapeirousia laxa,* formerly *L. cruenta,* resembles a miniature, 6- to 9-inch-high species *Gladiolus.* When planted in a mass in a flower border or rock garden they give a lovely drift of color. *Lapeirousia* produces beautiful little flowers that are best viewed up close.

Star-shaped flowers open at the end of a 1-inch tube called a *perianth.* Flowers are bright salmon-red with a dark spot on lower segments. All flowers face the same direction. Leaves are sword-shaped. Flowers are good for cutting.

Despite its size, *Lapeirousia* is a tough corm that grows well among tree roots, in semishade or full sun. It is easy to grow, often blooming the same year when planted from seeds. Left alone, it self-sows over a large area.

Lapeirousia laxa is native to South Africa and does well in Zones 7 to 10. Further north, the small corms are dug in fall and stored for winter. Not fussy about soil as long as it is well drained. Cover the small corm with 1 to 4 inches of soil. Plant as close as 1/2 inch apart. *L. laxa* grows well in small containers.

Leucocoryne
Glory-of-the-sun

Family: Amaryllidaceae.
Native to: Chile.
Bulb type: True bulb.
Bloom season & length: Spring for several weeks.
Colors: Bright blue.
Height: 1 foot.
Planting time: Fall in mild climates. Spring in cold climates.
Planting depth: 2 inches.
Soil: Sandy loam.
Water: During growing season.
Fertilizer: Small doses of complete fertilizer during growing season.
Spacing: 3 inches.
Exposure: Full sun.
Propagation: Seeds only.
Pests & diseases: Few.
Storage: Dig in fall and store in frost-proof area, or store planted in pots.

Leucocoryne, glory-of-the-sun, grows wild in the foothills of the Andes along the entire length of Chile. At one time, this bulb was readily available, but it is now rare. It was propagated by only one man in the United

States, and when he retired, it practically disappeared from the market.

Leucocoryne has 6 to 9 sky-blue flowers on an 18-inch stem. Each fragrant, saucer-shaped flower is over 1 inch across. The flowers are often compared with *Freesia* because they are similar in size, make good cut flowers and are equally fragrant. Culture is also similar. Both grow outdoors in Zones 9 and 10.

Provide rich soil with excellent drainage. Plant bulbs under 3 inches of soil. Bulbs pull themselves down deeper into the soil each year. Eventually, they finally go too deep to grow. Bulbs in the wild have been found 10 inches underground. To prevent this, place a wire screen or similar barrier under the bulb at planting time. *Leucocoryne* is grown from seeds only because it does not increase by division.

Leucocoryne species

Leucojum

Family: Amaryllidaceae.
Native to: Southern Europe and the Mediterranean.
Bulb type: True bulb.
Bloom season & length: Spring, fall.
Colors: White or pale pink.
Height: 4 to 18 inches.
Planting time: Fall.
Planting depth: 1 to 4 inches.
Soil: Rich, sandy loam is best, but generally not that fussy.
Water: During the growing season.
Fertilizer: Regular applications of a complete fertilizer.
Spacing: 2 to 4 inches.
Exposure: Light shade.
Propagation: From offsets.
Pests & diseases: Few.
Storage: Usually left in the ground.

Three species of *Leucojum* are commonly grown, but *Leucojum aestivum,* spring or summer snowflake, is the most widely planted. It is also tallest, with a 2-foot-tall flower stem. Clusters of pendulous white flowers appear along the stems. Each petal of the 3/4-inch flowers has a green spot near the tip. Strap-shaped leaves are lush, bright green. From Zones 4 to 10, it is one of the most adaptable and easiest bulbs to grow. It prefers a shady location, but adapts to full sun if watered regularly.

In England, it grows wild along the banks of the River Loddon. In California, it grows in light shade and can exist solely on winter rainfall. If given regular water, blooms appear a month earlier. Plant bulbs 4 inches apart and cover with 2 inches of soil. They multiply fast but do not require division for years.

Leucojum autumnale, as its species name implies, blooms in autumn. It has small flowers that are lightly shaded with mauve-pink and tipped with green. There is usually one flower on each 6-inch stem. Grasslike foliage appears after the flowers. The small bulb should be covered with 1 to 2 inches of soil. It does well in a warm, sunny location in Zones 6 to 10.

Leucojum vernum has much larger flowers than *L. aestivum* but usually only one flower on each 9-inch stem. The small, round bulb has a green skin. It grows well only in Zones 4 to 8.

Leucojum vernum

Lilium 'Enchantment' with tulips in foreground

Lilium
Lily

Family: Liliaceae.
Native to: North temperate zones.
Bulb type: True bulb.
Bloom season & length: Varieties vary from spring to fall.
Colors: White, yellow, pink, orange, red and maroon.
Height: 1 to 7 feet.
Planting time: Fall to spring.
Planting depth: Usually twice the depth of bulb. Plant *Lilium candidum* near soil surface.
Soil: Sandy loam—good drainage is important.
Water: Keep moist while actively growing. Do not allow to dry out completely during dormant period.
Fertilizer: Light doses when shoots appear with 0-10-10 or 2-10-10 fertilizer.
Spacing: 1 foot.
Exposure: Some sun, but not full sun.
Propagation: Bulbs that form at base, bulbils that form on stem above ground, or on stem below ground, or from seeds.
Pests & diseases: Watch for lily mosaic transmitted by aphids. New hybrid lilies less subject to diseases.
Storage: If necessary to dig, do not allow to dry out. Best stored in damp peat moss.

To many, lilies are the ultimate plants in any garden. Of almost 80 species—all from the Northern Hemisphere—you can find one that meets a special situation. Some like sun and some prefer shade. Some like acid soil and some grow best in alkaline soil. Some dry out in summer but most do not. Some like a warm climate and some like it cool. Perhaps lilies have the unfair reputation of being difficult to grow because their requirements from species to species are so variable.

All lilies require good drainage and plenty of organic material in the soil. If your soil does not have these two attributes, you will have greater success planting in containers filled with potting mix.

Unlike many bulbs, lilies are never completely dormant. In fact, the bulbs you purchase may have actively growing roots, which should *not* be removed before planting. Bulbs have no outer protective covering like tulips or daffodils, so handle them carefully. Keep bulbs undisturbed in slightly damp peat moss until planting time.

Plant lilies of different varieties and maturity dates, and you can have blooms from late spring to fall. As a bonus, their perfume fills the garden in the evening.

The Royal Horticultural Society and the North American Lily Society have classified lilies as follows:

Division 1—Asiatic hybrids. Plant in late spring, 4 to 5 inches deep. Roots develop along stem. Compact habit, 2-1/2 to 3 feet high. These are mid-century hybrids raised by Jan de Graaff in Oregon. Mr. de Graaff spent most of his life working with lilies and is the best-known lily hybridizer in the world. One of his goals was to make lilies easy to grow for the amateur. 'Enchantment' is in this group of upright-flowered lilies. The flowers of 'Fire King' face outward. Others have *pendant,* or hanging flowers. See illustration, page 122.

Division 2—Turk's cap. Hybrids of *Lilium martagon* and *L. hansonii* raised in Holland by Van Tubergen. Turk's cap lilies are woodland plants. They like neutral or acid soil and light shade. Stems root.

Division 3—Includes hybrids of *L. candidum,* the madonna lily. Plant bulbs close to the surface in early

Lilium auratum 'Yellow Ribbon'

Lilium speciosum 'Rubrum'

Aurelian hybrid lily

fall. Soon after planting they send out a rosette of leaves. Flowers appear in early summer.

Division 4—Hybrids of native North American lilies, mostly progeny of tall-growing *L. parryi* and *L. pardalinum*. These may reach up to 7 feet tall with many pendant flowers on a stem. Flowers are *reflexed,* meaning the petals curve back. They appear in shades of yellow, orange and red. Most flowers are two colors and spotted. Plant 4 inches deep in well-drained compost. Bellingham hybrids exemplify this group.

Division 5—*Lilium longiflorum* hybrids—the white Easter lilies commonly forced for spring bloom. Natural blooming time is midsummer.

Division 6—Trumpet lilies derived from Asiatic species. The flower umbel appears in July on stems 5 to 6 feet high. Aurelian and Olympic hybrids are a part of this group. Colors are shades of white, gold, greenish white, pink, apricot and white with a yellow center. Their stems root, so plant with 4 inches of soil over bulb. Mulch to keep roots cool. Some have pendant flowers.

Division 7—Oriental hybrids derived mostly from *L. auratum* and *L. speciosum.* Flowers are usually large and shaped like bowls, but some are recurved like *L. speciosum.* All root from their stems, so they require 4 inches of soil over bulbs when they are planted.

Division 8—Includes all other hybrids.

Division 9—All lily species. They are too numerous to list. Many are commonly available.

Lily Flowers and Bulbs

Pendulous or Nodding with Recurved Petals
Example is *Lilium martagon.*

Erect Facing
Example is mid-century hybrid.

Out Facing
Example is *Lilium auratum.*

Trumpet or Funnel Shaped
Example is *Lilium regale.*

Lily Bulbs
Bulbs usually have conspicuous scales. Because bulbs are never fully dormant, keep bulbs moist and plant them as soon as possible when they are out of the ground.

Cross-section of lily bulb shows emerging shoot. Young shoots are brittle. Be careful when working with them.

Lycoris
Spider lily

Family: Amaryllidaceae.
Native to: China, Japan.
Bulb type: True bulb.
Bloom season & length: Fall for several weeks.
Colors: Red, pink, white and yellow.
Height: 1 to 2 feet.
Planting time: Fall.
Planting depth: Bury in soil to tip of neck.
Soil: Sandy loam.
Water: During the growing season.
Fertilizer: Not required.
Spacing: 10 inches.
Exposure: Full sun.
Propagation: From offsets. Crowding not a problem.
Pests & diseases: Snails.
Storage: Because they produce foliage in winter, bulbs are not stored during the cold season. After foliage dies down in early summer, they can be dug and stored.

Lycoris species and their exotic flowers are easily confused with the similar *Nerine* species. Both bloom in fall, producing umbels of spidery or funnel-shaped flowers on a bare stem. Narrow, strap-shaped leaves appear after bloom. *Lycoris* are from China and Japan. *Nerine* are from South Africa.

Lycoris radiata, Japanese spider lily, is one of the most attractive varieties. Beautiful, coral-red flowers have extremely long stamens curving upward. It blooms on a 15-inch stem in September. 'Alba' has cream-white flowers. 'Carnea' flowers are tinted pink. These grow outdoors in Zones 8 to 10.

Lycoris squamigera is the hardiest variety. It grows as far north as Zone 6. Wide, funnel-shaped, pink flowers resemble a small *Amaryllis belladonna*. See page 63. Flowers grow on a 15-inch stem.

Plant *Lycoris* where they will remain dry during summer. Like many of the *Amaryllis* family, they are best left undisturbed after they are planted. Blooms best when crowded. Plant so that the top of the dark bulb is just under the surface. Adapted to all but soggy soils.

Milla biflora
Mexican star

Family: Amaryllidaceae.
Native to: Southwest United States and Mexico.
Bulb type: Corm.
Bloom season & length: Spring to fall.
Colors: White.
Height: 10 to 15 inches.
Planting time: Late spring.
Planting depth: Under 2 inches of soil.
Soil: Sandy loam.
Water: During the growing season.
Fertilizer: Light applications of a complete fertilizer.
Spacing: 2 inches.
Exposure: Half to full sun.
Propagation: Separate small corms from mother corm in the fall.
Pests & diseases: Few.
Storage: Keep in pot until corms become crowded.

Milla biflora and *Ipheion uniflora* have the same common name, Mexican star. Adding to the confusion, *Ipheion uniflora* was once called *Milla uniflora*. Both have grasslike foliage and star-shaped

Lycoris radiata

Milla biflora

Moraea villosa

Dietes vegeta

flowers, but are otherwise quite different. *M. biflora* has two or more white flowers on a 1-foot stem, each with a green vein. *I. uniflora* has a single blue flower on a 4-inch stem.

Milla biflora is a native of Arizona and Mexico, and easy to grow in Zones 8 to 10. It likes sun and responds to light applications of fertilizer. Cover with 2 inches of soil. In colder areas, it makes a sweetly fragrant pot plant. Divide clumps and replant in two or three years. Flowers appear over a period of several months. It is well suited for an edging or for the front of a border.

Moraea and Dietes
Peacock iris, Fortnight lily

Family: Iridaceae.
Native to: South Africa.
Bulb type: *Moraea*—corm; *Dietes*—rhizome.
Bloom season & length: *Moraea*—summer, for 7 weeks; *Dietes*—intermittent spring to fall.
Colors: *Moraea*—lavender, yellow and white; *Dietes*—white and creamy yellow.
Height: *Moraea*—3 inches to 5 feet; *Dietes*—3 feet.
Planting time: *Moraea*—spring; *Dietes*—any time.
Planting depth: 1 inch.
Soil: Sandy loam.
Water: *Moraea* blooms better if not overwatered. *Dietes* is drought tolerant and tolerant of regular watering.
Fertilizer: Little.
Spacing: *Moraea*—3 inches; *Dietes*—1 foot.
Exposure: *Moraea*—full sun; *Dietes*—full sun or filtered shade.
Propagation: *Moraea*—separation of small corms from mother bulb. Easy from seeds, often self-sows. *Dietes*—divide rhizome any time.
Pests & diseases: None.
Storage: Usually left in ground, but both can be stored.

Moraea and *Dietes* belong to the *Iris* family. Their flowers resemble those of wild *Iris*. Each flower lasts only one day, but there are many to replace it. Do not cut flowering stems—one stem will produce flowers for several years.

At one time, both were considered to be *Moraea*. Recently, the rhizomatous evergreen species have been placed in their own genus, *Dietes*. The popular landscape plant, *Moraea iridoides,* is properly called *Dietes vegeta*. Popular forms have pure white, 3- to 4-inch-wide flowers with blue and gold markings at the center. The smaller flower of *Dietes bicolor* is creamy yellow and the leaves are narrower.

These *Iris* relatives accept almost any growing condition except dense shade in Zones 8 to 10. They are planted extensively in mild areas as accents in low-maintenance gardens.

True *Moraeas* are usually hybrid varieties available in many colors—orange, red, yellow, slate-blue, mauve, cream and white. The 15-inch-high stems carry 2-inch flowers.

Moraea neopavonia earned the common name peacock iris because of its blue-black or dark-green basal spots. The species has orange flowers, but hybrids of many colors are available. Plant grows 1 to 2 feet high. It is a native of South Africa, often growing in damp locations beneath trees.

Moraea polystachya begins growth after the first rains of late summer or early fall. It blooms over a long period with several, 1-1/2-inch lavender flowers on branching stems. Plant grows 1-1/2 feet high. It self-sows, eventually forming large colonies. Cover the corm with 1 inch of soil.

Moraea villosa is occasionally available. It has 2-inch, lilac flowers, each with a half-circle of greenish blue bordered with a black spot. Hybrids may be white, scarlet, orange or bronze, but all have the distinctive "peacock" mark. Plant grows 1 to 2 feet high.

Moraeas are fussier than *Dietes*. In the wild in South Africa, *Moraeas* grow in damp meadows. Plant corms 2 inches deep in sandy compost where they will receive adequate moisture and sun.

Muscari
Grape hyacinth

Family: Liliaceae.
Native to: Mediterranean region and Asia Minor.
Bulb type: True bulb.
Bloom season & length: Spring for a month.
Colors: Blue and white.
Height: 6 to 9 inches.
Planting time: Fall.
Planting depth: 2 to 3 inches over bulb.
Soil: Not too fussy.
Water: During the growing season.
Fertilizer: Not necessary.
Spacing: 3 inches.
Exposure: Full sun to part shade.
Propagation: From many small bulbs that form around mother bulb, and from seeds.
Pests & diseases: Few.
Storage: Not necessary.

Nothing can create a blanket of blue in the spring garden quite like *Muscari*—grape hyacinths. Although related to hyacinths, they are quite different in appearance. Grape hyacinths have little fragrance, and flowers are blue or white. They are inexpensive, and multiply rapidly. Their small flowers appear in grape-like clusters and are especially attractive under deciduous trees or flowering trees. For closer viewing, they can be planted between steppingstones or in pots. Plants are also attractive massed as a border in the spring rose garden.

Many varieties are available. *Muscari armeniacum* is the most commonly grown. It has cobalt-blue flowers, each with a narrow rim of white. Flower spikes grow 8 inches high.

Muscari botryoides, similar in shape and color, comes from southern France. It grows about 6 inches tall, and is available in a white form, 'Pearls of Spain'.

Muscari comosum is different in appearance, and was recently categorized into its own genus, *Leopoldia*. It has sterile, purple flowers on top of 12-inch stems and green, fertile flowers below. Its cultivar 'Monstrosum' produces sterile, purple flowers, and is sold as feather hyacinth.

Muscari tubergenianum is a pretty little species that grows 6 to 7 inches high. Sky-blue flowers appear at the top of the spike and navy-blue flowers appear below.

Muscari grow anywhere from Zones 2 to 10. Plant bulbs in sun or partial shade and cover with an inch or more of soil. They like well-drained garden soil and do well without fertilizer. Do not remove the foliage until it turns brown. The leaves manufacture food that is stored in the bulb for growth the following year.

Muscari armeniacum

Muscari armeniacum with white candytuft.

Daffodil 'Smiling Maestro'

Narcissus
Daffodil

Family: Amaryllidaceae.
Native to: Europe to China.
Bulb type: True bulb.
Bloom season & length: Spring for more than two months.
Colors: Yellow, gold, white, orange, red and pink.
Height: 2 to 18 inches.
Planting time: Fall.
Planting depth: Twice the depth of bulb.
Soil: Sandy loam.
Water: Ample during the growing season.
Fertilizer: Little is necessary.
Spacing: Approximately 6 inches, but depends on bulb size.
Exposure: Full sun or part sun. Flowers face toward light source.
Propagation: Separate new bulbs that form beside old one or by seeds.
Pests & diseases: Narcissus fly, snails and basal rot.
Storage: In cool, dry area with air circulation.

If tulips are the *best known* of all bulbs, daffodils must be the *most loved*. Tulips please one year and are usually gone the next. But daffodils are as reliable as old friends. Daffodil beds planted during colonial times in Virginia still bloom each spring. In California, paperwhites bloom where houses and gardens have long been abandoned. Daffodil societies exist in many countries of the world, with many hundreds of members eagerly anticipating the newly released varieties.

Many gardeners are confused by the words "daffodil," "narcissus" and "jonquil." To set the record straight, you can use daffodil and *Narcissus* interchangeably—they refer to the same group of bulbs. *Narcissus* is the botanical name and daffodil is the common English name. Jonquils are a distinct group of *Narcissus*. Generally, they are late-blooming bulbs that produce clusters of flowers that are usually yellow and fragrant.

Daffodils are native to the Northern Hemisphere. The greatest number come from Spain and Portugal. They grow wild in Europe, northern Africa and around the Mediterranean. Some varieties of *Narcissus tazetta* grow as far east as Japan. Almost 100 years ago, the stage was set for the development and improvement of daffodils. An English clergyman produced 'King Alfred', perhaps the best known daffodil variety of all time. A large "trumpet" daffodil such as 'King Alfred' was unknown at that time. It became popular even though it was expensive to purchase. Because of its demand, it was an inspiration for other hobbyists to try their hand at hybridizing.

In 1950, the Royal Horticultural Society Daffodil Committee decided to reclassify daffodils, hoping to avoid confusion between the new developments. Of the 11 divisions, only one division includes species or wild daffodils. The other divisions are for hybrids or daffodils of garden origin. The divisions are:

Division I—Trumpet. The trumpet is as long or longer than the flat *perianth segment*—the six petals that form a circle at the back of the flower.
Division II—Large-cupped trumpets. The cup is more than one third, but less than the length, of the perianth segment.
Division III—Small-cupped trumpets. The cup is less than one-third the length of the perianth segment.
Division IV—Doubles. Double flowers.

Daffodils are excellent flowers for cutting.

Rows of daffodils are striking as border plants.

Division V—Triandrus. More than one flower to a stem and often hanging down. Practically no fragrance compared to Tazettas.

Division VI—Cyclamineus. Perianth is reflexed like a cyclamen.

Division VII—Jonquilla. Usually fragrant with more than one flower to a stem. Foliage is often reedlike.

Division VIII—Tazetta. Many strongly fragrant flowers in a cluster. They come from the Mediterranean region through Asia to Japan. Tazettas come up early in the year and are often killed by frost. Gardeners in the North should avoid growing them outdoors.

Division IX—Poeticus. A large, white perianth and a small cup. Late blooming.

Division X—Species and wild forms, plus their close hybrids.

Division XI—All others, such as 'Split Cups', that are not included in any of preceding.

When buying daffodils, pick up each bulb to be sure it is firm and heavy. A lightweight or soft bulb probably indicates the presence of basal rot. It is usually caused by overly warm temperatures or damage from grubs of narcissus flies.

Daffodils, especially single-flowered varieties, love the sun and turn their open flowers toward sunlight. Take this into account when planting bulbs. If you don't, you may find your flowers turning their "backs" on you at bloom time.

Because daffodil bulbs vary in size, the best rule is to plant them twice the depth of the bulb. Sandy loam soil is ideal, but daffodils are adaptable as long as there is adequate drainage. They are not heavy feeders. Work a complete fertilizer into the soil when they first break ground, and it will see them through the growing season. Overfeeding with nitrogen will make the foliage floppy and frail.

Except in mild-winter areas, such as portions of the South and southern California, plant bulbs as soon as they become available. This gives them plenty of time to form roots. In these mild areas, wait until the soil has cooled, usually about the end of October, before planting.

Daffodils are particularly adapted to growing under deciduous trees. Such a location is also good for the bulbs. The shade provided by trees help cool the soil during summer.

Daffodils look best planted informally in drifts or groups, and are excellent in containers. Plantings are long-lived and do not need to be divided until they become crowded and begin to produce small flowers. When and if you decide to thin and divide the bulbs, don't pull the side bulbs off until they have a piece of basal plate. Without it, the bulb will not form roots.

SPECIES DAFFODILS

The names of species and subspecies of *Narcissus* can fill a book of their own. Many are of interest only to hybridizers or collectors. The following includes some of the most charming and interesting.

Autumn-Flowering Group—These sweet-scented species bloom in the wild in September and October near the Mediterranean Sea. Because of their olive-green flowers they are more interesting than beautiful. *Narcissus viridiflorus* grows on and near Gibraltar. It produces up to 4 rather inconspicuous but fragrant flowers on its 8-inch stem.

Bulbocodium Group—These are known as *hoop petticoats*. They are a dwarf species growing 4 to 6

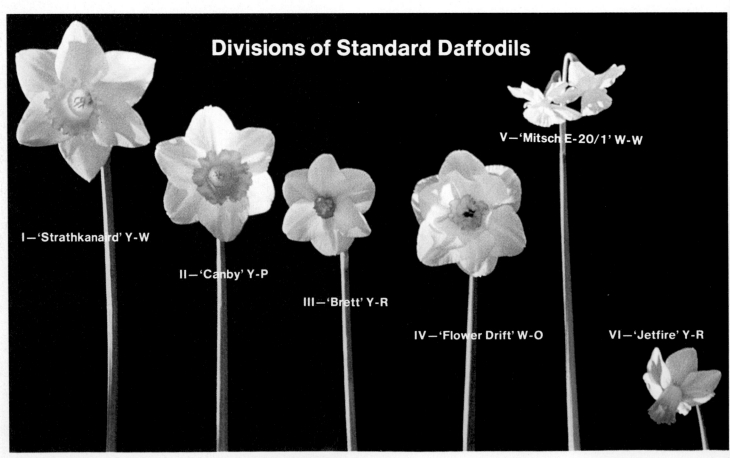

Divisions of Standard Daffodils

I—'Strathkanaird' Y-W

II—'Canby' Y-P

III—'Brett' Y-R

IV—'Flower Drift' W-O

V—'Mitsch E-20/1' W-W

VI—'Jetfire' Y-R

inches tall. Single flowers open horizontally on the stem and resemble a hoop petticoat. The perianth at the back is small compared with other *Narcissus*. *N. b. conspicuous* has deep-yellow flowers and is the most common variety. *N. bulbocodium obesus* is the largest, also producing deep-yellow flowers. *N. bulbocodium* var. *citrinus* has pale, lemon-yellow flowers.

With the best conditions, bulbocodium daffodils reseed freely to form large stands. Most prefer a moist planting site. Exceptions are two hard-to-find species from North Africa that prefer dry conditions in the summer. These are *Narcissus bulbocodium* subspecies *romieuxii*, with large, pale-lemon flowers, and *N. cantabricus* var. *petunioides,* with flat flowers similar to small, white petunias. Because they do not grow outdoors in England and Holland, bulbs are available in a limited supply.

Cyclamineus Group—*Narcissus cyclamineus* produces a bright, golden-yellow flower 4 to 8 inches tall. It has a long trumpet and the perianth lies back flat. Originally from Spain and Portugal, it prefers damp areas. A cross between it and a trumpet species produced 'February Gold', one of the most reliable of all daffodils.

Jonquila Group—Most members of *Narcissus jonquilla* are known for their fragrance. Characteristically, the golden flowers are short cupped and appear on a 1-foot-high stem. Leaves are round like reeds. The best known garden variety is the late-blooming 'Trevithian'. *N. watieri* has a single, large, white flower on a 6-inch stem. It tolerates moderately dry soil in the summer. It comes from the Atlas Mountains so it also tolerates cold. It is not fragrant.

Poeticus Group—These are the most cold-hardy

Narcissus. *N. poeticus* is different from the usual *Narcissus* in that it has a large, pure-white perianth and a small cup, or eye with a red rim. It is widely distributed from Spain to Greece. Flowers are sweet scented, and are often used for hybridizing. The garden variety 'Actea' is best known.

Tazetta Group—*Narcissus tazetta* is more widely distributed than any other variety. It grows from Spain and Portugal, around the Mediterranean, through Iran to China and Japan. Flowers appear in bunches and are sweet scented. Plants are popular as indoor plants where climate restricts outdoor culture. The bicolors have a white perianth and a small cup of orange or gold. Best known of these is the Chinese sacred lily, *N. t. orientalis*. *N. albae* are pure white. The most popular is paper-white. *N. luteae* has a yellow perianth and a yellow cup, frequently a different shade of yellow. 'Soleil d 'Or' is the best known of this type.

Triandrus Group—*Narcissus triandrus*, Angel's tears, has several pure-white flowers on a 12-inch stem. In the wild, *N. triandrus* is variable in color—flowers are cream or pale yellow. It is a graceful species. 'Thalia' and 'Tresemble' are among the best known of the hybrids.

Dwarf Trumpet Group—*Narcissus asturiensis* is a miniature copy of the large, hybrid trumpet daffodils. At one time, it was classified as *N. minimus*. It is a deep, golden yellow with the mouth of the trumpet almost frilled. An early bloomer, it is a good choice for the rock garden, where it will receive the drainage it requires. *N. minor* is a tall, bicolor trumpet, up to 8 inches. *N. pseudonarcissus* is the native daffodil of England. 'W. P. Milner' is a well-known garden hybrid. Yellow flowers appear on 8- to 10-inch stems.

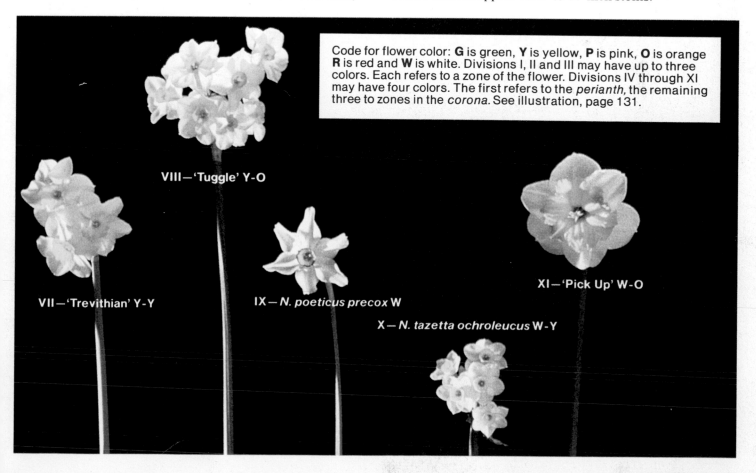

Code for flower color: **G** is green, **Y** is yellow, **P** is pink, **O** is orange **R** is red and **W** is white. Divisions I, II and III may have up to three colors. Each refers to a zone of the flower. Divisions IV through XI may have four colors. The first refers to the *perianth,* the remaining three to zones in the *corona.* See illustration, page 131.

VIII—'Tuggle' Y-O

VII—'Trevithian' Y-Y

IX—*N. poeticus precox* W

XI—'Pick Up' W-O

X—*N. tazetta ochroleucus* W-Y

Daffodil Bulbs

Triple-nose means 3 flowers

Double-nose means 2 flowers

Cross-section of
double-nose daffodil bulb

Single-nose means 1 flower

Narcissus poeticus

Narcissus tazetta acticolor

Bulbs of miniature
daffodils

Divisions of Miniature Daffodils

V—'Hawera' Y-Y

X—N. jonquilla Y-Y

VI—'Tête à Tête' Y-O

XI—'Kennelis' W-Y

X—N. bulbocodium
var. conspicuus Y-Y

V—'Silver Bells'
x triandrus W-W

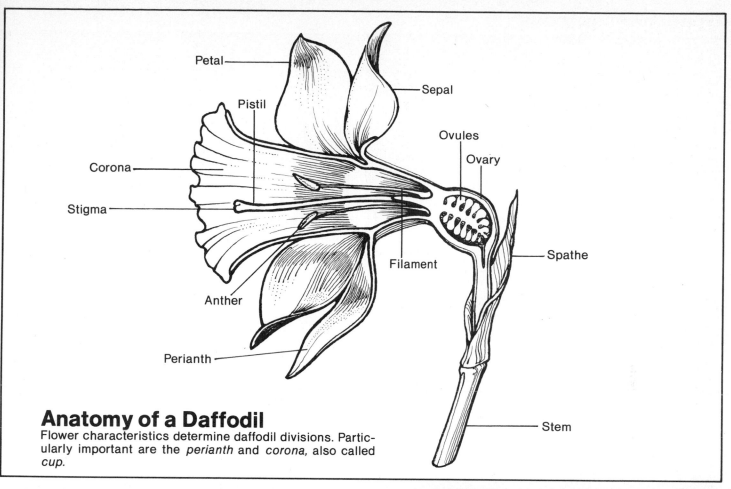

Petal

Sepal

Pistil

Ovules

Ovary

Corona

Stigma

Filament

Spathe

Anther

Perianth

Stem

Anatomy of a Daffodil

Flower characteristics determine daffodil divisions. Particularly important are the *perianth* and *corona*, also called *cup*.

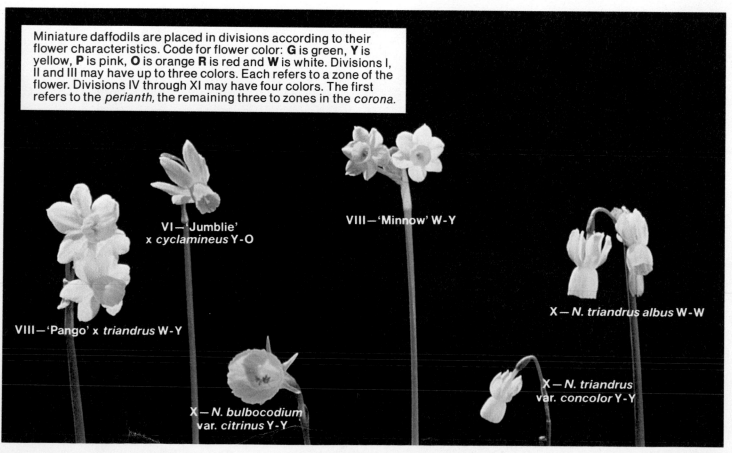

Miniature daffodils are placed in divisions according to their flower characteristics. Code for flower color: **G** is green, **Y** is yellow, **P** is pink, **O** is orange **R** is red and **W** is white. Divisions I, II and III may have up to three colors. Each refers to a zone of the flower. Divisions IV through XI may have four colors. The first refers to the *perianth,* the remaining three to zones in the *corona*.

VI—'Jumblie'
x *cyclamineus* Y-O

VIII—'Minnow' W-Y

VIII—'Pango' x *triandrus* W-Y

X — *N. triandrus albus* W-W

X — *N. bulbocodium*
var. *citrinus* Y-Y

X — *N. triandrus*
var. *concolor* Y-Y

Gallery of Daffodils

'Allurement' II—W-P

'Apricot Distinction' III—Y-O

'Confuco' II—Y-R

'Daydream' II—Y-W

'Highfield Beauty' VIII—Y-GYO

'Joy Bell' VI—W-Y

'Kissproof' II—Y-R

'La Paloma' III—W-GYR

'Peace Pipe' I—W-Y

'Pink Plume' II—W-P

'Professor Einstein' II—W-O

'Pueblo' VII—W-W

'Soleil D'Or' VIII—Y-O

'Tahiti' IV—Y-R

N. tazetta ochroleucus X—W-Y

'Thalia' V—W-W

Code for flower color: G = green, Y = yellow, P = pink, O = orange, R = red and W = white.

'Duke of Windsor' II—W-Y

'Esperan' II—Y-R

'Flying Saucer' II—W-Y

'Gaily Clad' II—W-P

'Mondragon' XI—Y-O

'Orangery' XI—W-POY

Paper-white X—W-W

'Pasteline' II—W-P

'Quail' VII—Y-Y

'Replete' IV—W-P

'Scarlet Gem' VIII—Y-R

'Smiling Maestro' II—Y-YRR

'Unsurpassable' I—Y-Y

'Vigil' I—W-W

'White Lion' IV—W-Y

'Willet' VI—Y-Y

Nerine

Family: Amaryllidaceae.
Native to: South Africa.
Bulb type: True bulb.
Bloom season & length: Fall for several weeks.
Colors: Red, scarlet, pink, rose, mauve and white.
Height: 20 inches, but variable.
Planting time: Early fall.
Planting depth: Tip of neck at soil surface.
Soil: Fast drainage.
Water: Keep on dry side when dormant.
Fertilizer: Not necessary.
Spacing: 1 foot.
Exposure: Full sun or light shade.
Propagation: Bulbs form dense clumps and force their way out of the soil. Blooms best when crowded.
Pests & diseases: Few.
Storage: Store in pots.

Although *Nerine* species are rare, they are bound to become better known. One reason is the excellent keeping-quality of their flowers. Another reason is the cross-breeding work done by Edmund de Rothschild in England. There are many species and hybrids, but this book deals only with the two most important species.

Nerine bowdenii comes from the mountains of South Africa. It can be grown as far north as Zone 8. In its native habitat, it is watered heavily by summer rains and remains comparatively dry in winter. The home gardener should follow suit and water the same way. The pink flower cluster is borne on 15-inch stems.

Nerine sarniensis is from the lowlands of South Africa where it rains during winter and is dry during summer. It received its common name guernsey lily when the first bulbs shipped from Africa were cast adrift in a storm onto the isle of Guernsey. There they rooted and bloomed, and soon gained the attention of horticulturists.

It is less cold-hardy and grows only in Zones 9 and 10. It is the more exciting of the two species. Flowerheads are fuller with more protruding stamens. Petals are covered with an iridescent sheen that makes the flower look as though it had been sprinkled with gold or silver dust. Indoors, under artificial light, this quality is even more pronounced. Most of the hybridizing has been done with this species, resulting in shades of pink, orange, salmon, red, scarlet, mauve and white. Some have two-toned flowers.

According to some authorities, *Nerine* grows wild in some of the poorest soils in the world. For best results, soil should be sandy with good drainage. Plant bulbs with the top of the neck exposed. A small amount of fertilizer may be beneficial, but too much nitrogen keeps them from blooming. It used to be thought that they needed high summer heat to produce flowers, but this has been proven to be untrue.

Nerine blooms best when rootbound, so they make excellent pot plants. Divide or move them to a larger pot if overcrowded. In the ground, they form large clumps with exposed bulbs. They do not have to be separated except to increase plantings.

Nerine hybrid

Ornithogalum

Family: Liliaceae.
Native to: Africa, Europe, Asia Minor.
Bulb type: True bulb.
Bloom season & length: Spring for several weeks.
Colors: White, rarely yellow or orange.
Height: 12 to 30 inches.
Planting time: Fall.
Planting depth: 1 to 2 inches of soil over bulb.
Soil: Adaptable.
Water: During the growing season.
Fertilizer: Not required.
Spacing: 3 to 4 inches.
Exposure: Full sun to part shade.
Propagation: Remove new bulbs from bulb in fall. Seeds.
Pests & diseases: Few.
Storage: Usually left in ground or pot except when separating bulbs.

Of the more than 150 species of *Ornithogalum,* only a few are grown in home gardens. *O. caudatum,* the pregnant onion, is not grown for its flowers but for its curious, light-green bulb. To show it off, plant with three-quarters of the bulb above-ground in a semishaded location. Full sun can burn the bulb. Because of its unusual reproductive cycle, it makes a fascinating house plant or patio plant. The cycle begins with a small swelling under the skin of the bulb. In time, the skin peels back, revealing a baby bulb ready to plant, sometimes with the beginning of a green leaf. The unusual, but not overly attractive flowers are white and grow along the end of a 2- to 3-foot-long stem.

Other *Ornithogalum* species are grown for their glistening white flowers. *O. arabicum* is adapted to grow in Zones 7 to 10. It makes an excellent, long-lasting cut flower. In the center of each pure white, 2-inch flower is a shiny, black, beadlike ovary.

Ornithogalum balansae produces a short, 6-inch spike with white, star-shaped flowers striped green on the outside. It is interesting in rock gardens or planted as an edging.

Ornithogalum thyrsoides, Zones 7 to 10, is from South Africa, where it is called *chincherinchee.* It is an exceptional cut flower. Flowers are shipped from South Africa to Europe in bud, with blooms lasting up to three weeks. Flowers are dense, white buds, opening to reveal a brown center with yellow stamens.

Ornithogalum umbellatum, Zones 5 to 10, has 1-inch, star-shaped, rather flat flowers. It comes from Bethlehem and the Middle East so it truthfully deserves its common name, star of Bethlehem. Flowers are held far out on a 1-foot stem. Because it opens late in morning and closes in evening, it is not a particularly good cut flower. It is also apt to spread rampantly once planted.

All *Ornithogalum* species prefer well-drained soil with plenty of organic material. Plant in fall and cover bulbs with 2 inches of soil. They like sun or part shade. When bulbs become too crowded, dig and replant in late summer. For the most part, they bloom in late spring.

Ornithogalum arabicum

Oxalis purpurea 'Grand Duchess'

Oxalis deppei

Oxalis

Family: Oxalidaceae.
Native to: South Africa, South America.
Bulb type: True bulb.
Bloom season & length: Spring for a long period.
Colors: White, pink, lavender, rose and yellow.
Height: 4 to 12 inches.
Planting time: Fall.
Planting depth: 1 inch of soil over bulb.
Soil: Adaptable.
Water: During the growing season.
Fertilizer: Little.
Spacing: 2 to 6 inches.
Exposure: Full sun.
Propagation: From numerous bulbs that develop around the mother bulb.
Pests & diseases: Few.
Storage: Can be left in pots. If dug, put in dry peat moss.

There are over 800 species of *Oxalis*. Some are choice garden plants, others are noxious weeds. If you are familiar only with the weedy ones, don't turn up your nose until you've seen some of the attractive members such as 'Irish Shamrock' and 'Lucky Clover'.

Oxalis adenophylla is from the Chilean Andes and grows farther north than most—Zones 6 to 10. It has fan-shaped, gray-green foliage and pink flowers with maroon eyes. It is low growing, and looks attractive in rock gardens or as an edging. It blooms in late spring.

Oxalis bowiei, adapted to Zones 7 to 10, is from South Africa. It has downy, clover-shaped leaves and rose-purple flowers in the summer.

Oxalis deppei, lucky clover, is grown more for its striking foliage than its red flowers. The four leaf segments look like a four-leaf clover at the top of the stem. Each leaf has a large, almost black blotch at the base.

Oxalis hirta, for Zones 9 and 10, has *sessile* leaves, meaning they are crowded at the end of the stem. Flowers are violet, purple or white and appear in winter.

Oxalis pes-caprae, also known as *Bermuda buttercup,* is cold-hardy in Zones 9 and 10. Showy, bright-yellow flowers appear in spring and fall. It multiplies rapidly by seeds and underground runners, so consider its placement carefully. It is much too aggressive for a mixed border.

Oxalis purpurea, Zones 9 and 10, is one of the prettier types. 'Grand Duchess' is one of its best cultivars. The large, shamrocklike foliage is a rich green with large, open flowers in shades of bright, clear, pink, lilac or white with yellow throats. Showy blooms start in December and continue for several months. It makes a handsome plant in a shallow container. It can be grown indoors in a cool location, but needs some sun. Bulbs can stay in the same pot for four or five years. It is a delicate plant and is sensitive to fertilizer.

Oxalis violacea grows wild from Maine to Florida. Flowers are rosy purple to white on 10-inch stems. It is rarely cultivated but could be used in rock gardens or borders.

Oxalis are easy to grow. They prefer a soil that is slightly acid with good drainage. Plant bulbs or rhizomes under 1 inch of soil in sun or light shade. *Oxalis* adapt well to hanging baskets. Many are grown as house plants in cold-winter areas.

Polianthes tuberosa
Tuberose

Family: Agavaceae.
Native to: Mexico.
Bulb type: True bulb with elongated base.
Bloom season & length: Late summer for 3 weeks.
Colors: White and orange-red.
Height: 18 to 48 inches.
Planting time: When weather warms in spring.
Planting depth: Tip of bulb at soil level.
Soil: A rich mixture with good drainage.
Water: Keep damp.
Fertilizer: Monthly with a complete fertilizer.
Spacing: 6 inches.
Exposure: Full sun and warmth.
Propagation: From offshoots around original bulb.
Pests & diseases: Few.
Storage: After foliage browns, dig and store in dry peat moss or vermiculite.

Polianthes tuberosa is valued for its unique, waxy white blossoms and sweet, heady fragrance. It is among the most strongly perfumed of all flowers. During the Victorian era, tuberoses were great favorites. Because they are native to tropical Mexico, where the growing season is long and warm, new bulbs were bought each year to ensure flowers. When the vogue ended, tuberoses disappeared except for those grown by dedicated gardeners.

A single-flowered form, 'Mexican Single', grows 3 to 4 feet high. A stockier, double form, 'The Pearl', grows to 2 feet. Clusters of flowers appear along the upper part of the stem. They are excellent and long lasting as cut flowers.

In Zones 9 and 10, tuberoses are left in the ground during winter. A long, 4-month growing period is required before they bloom. Florists force blooms in half that time. Gardeners in cold areas should start them indoors before last frost.

Tuberoses are fairly inexpensive and many gardeners plant new bulbs every spring to be certain of a yearly bloom. If left undisturbed in the ground, they may skip blooming for a year to build up strength for the next. This may be because they need the longer growing period, found in their native tropical Mexico, to build strength.

Polianthes tuberosa

Puschkinia scilloides

Family: Liliaceae.
Native to: Asia Minor.
Bulb type: True bulb.
Bloom season & length: Early spring for several weeks.
Colors: Blue and white.
Height: 4 to 8 inches.
Planting time: Fall.
Planting depth: 2 to 3 inches over bulb.
Soil: Loam with good drainage.
Water: Regular during the growing season.
Fertilizer: Not required.
Spacing: 2 to 3 inches.
Exposure: Full sun or part sun.
Propagation: Dig in summer and remove small bulbs.
Pests & diseases: Few.
Storage: Best left undisturbed.

Puschkinia scilloides can be found growing wild from Lebanon to Afghanistan. A 6-inch flower spike emerges in spring from the dark green, strap-shaped

Puschkinia scilloides

leaves. The spike holds 6 to 12, 1/2-inch, pale-blue flowers. When fully open they reveal a blue-green stripe in the center of each petal. A pure-white form sold as *P. scilloides* 'Libanotica' or as 'Alba' is also available.

It does well in colder areas such as Zones 3 to 8, thriving in full sun or filtered shade. It prefers gritty soil, so it is an excellent bulb for rock gardens or naturalizing.

Ranunculus asiaticus

Family: Ranunculaceae.
Native to: Asia Minor.
Bulb type: Tuberous root.
Bloom season & length: Spring for 6 to 8 weeks.
Colors: Red, pink, rose, white, yellow, gold or orange.
Height: 2 feet.
Planting time: Fall after soil is cool.
Planting depth: 1 to 2 inches of soil over bulb.
Soil: Sandy loam.
Water: During the growing season.
Fertilizer: Once a month while actively growing.
Spacing: 6 inches.
Exposure: Full sun.
Propagation: Tubers can be divided, but are brittle and must include a bud from the stem to grow. Usually propagated from seeds.
Pests & diseases: Few.
Storage: Must be kept dry during summer, which usually means digging and storing until cool weather returns.

Ranunculus asiaticus has an interesting history. In the Middle Ages, a high officer in the Persian government brought it to the attention of the sultan in Constantinople. He was delighted with the plant. The flower colors were varied, so he sent emissaries throughout Asia Minor searching for new colors. Returning crusaders brought roots to France. By the 15th century, *Ranunculus* grew in France in the garden of Blanche of Castille, mother of Louis IX. By Elizabethan times, *Ranunculus* had been carried across the Channel to England.

Ranunculus has had its ups and downs since its initial migrations. Today, after hybridizing and selection, it has regained its popularity. Besides being a beautiful garden plant, it is an excellent cut flower. Plants bloom for five to six weeks. The attractive flowers look like miniature double peonies.

The color range is wide, including shades of yellow, gold, orange, red, pink, rose and white. Those labeled 'Picotee' have various shades in the same flower. Individual flower colors as well as mixtures can be purchased. One of the best strains, Tecolote, is raised by the millions—42,000,000 were sold in 1980 and were shipped all over the world.

Ranunculus is ideally suited to areas with cool, rainy winters and dry summers. It does best with a long, cool, growing period. In mild-winter areas such as southern California, it is planted in November. Hot summer weather puts an end to flowering. In cold-winter areas, start *Ranunculus* indoors in 4-inch pots two months before the last frost. Plant outdoors after danger of heavy frost has past.

Plants require excellent drainage, especially when started indoors. Wet, warm conditions cause tubers to rot. Plant in damp soil. Wait until shoots appear before watering again, unless the soil will dry out completely.

Ranunculus Tecolote hybrid

Ranunculus Tecolote hybrid

Rhodohypoxis baurii

Family: Hypoxidaceae.
Native to: South Africa.
Bulb type: Cormlike rootstock.
Bloom season & length: Late spring to late summer.
Colors: Dark rose to white.
Height: 3 to 4 inches.
Planting time: Early spring.
Planting depth: 1/2 to 1 inch below soil surface.
Soil: Slightly acid sandy loam.
Water: During the growing season.
Fertilizer: Minimal amounts are required.
Spacing: 1 inch.
Exposure: Full sun to light shade.
Propagation: By division of rootstocks. Seeds.
Pests & diseases: Few.
Storage: Allow to dry in pot.

This small, attractive, South-African native, *Rhodohypoxis baurii,* was recently introduced to the bulb trade. It has many, star-shaped, 1-inch flowers held on stems just above ground level. Flowers appear in many shades from white to rose-pink. Foliage is hairy and grasslike.

Rhodohypoxis multiplies by offsets and self-sows its seeds. It is choice in rock gardens and between steppingstones. Try it as an eye-catcher in a small bonsai pot. Blooms in early summer.

Plant in sandy loam, 1/2 inch to 1 inch below the surface. It does well in Zones 9 and 10, but has not been tested in other areas.

Rhodohypoxis baurii

Sauromatum guttatum
Voodoo lily

Family: Araceae.
Native to: India.
Bulb type: Tuber.
Bloom season & length: Spring for a week. Also used as foliage plant.
Colors: Yellow, spotted.
Height: 2 to 3 feet.
Planting time: Spring after warm weather has arrived.
Planting depth: 1 inch over tuber.
Soil: Rich loam.
Water: Regular during the growing season.
Fertilizer: When flowers appear.
Spacing: 3 to 6 inches.
Exposure: Light shade.
Propagation: Offsets or seeds.
Pests & diseases: Few.
Storage: After foliage dies, dig and store dry until danger of frost has passed.

As the common name implies, this bulb is more of a curiosity than a traditional garden subject. *Sauromatum guttatum* forms a large, 5-inch bulb. Indoors, on a windowsill, it produces a flower that looks like a large, yellow-green calla dotted with dark-purple spots.

In mild climates, after bloom, plant bulb in the garden. It will soon produce leaves. The exotic-looking foliage is attractive, resembling a deeply cut, split-leaf philodendron with a squared-off end at the stem. Because of these distinctive leaves, it is an interesting container plant. Use a house-plant soil mix and keep soil damp while growing. Plants multiply from bulbs formed on top of the mother bulb near the soil surface.

Sauromatum guttatum

Schizostylis coccinea

Scilla peruviana

Schizostylis coccinea
Crimson flag, Kaffir lily

Family: Iridaceae.
Native to: South Africa.
Bulb type: Fibrous, fleshy roots.
Bloom season & length: Late fall for several weeks.
Colors: Scarlet and pink.
Height: 18 to 24 inches.
Planting time: Spring.
Planting depth: Cover with 1 to 2 inches of soil.
Soil: Garden soil improved with peat moss or leaf mold.
Water: Keep moist continually while in growth.
Fertilizer: Moderate amounts only.
Spacing: 9 inches.
Exposure: Full sun.
Propagation: Dig and divide clumps in spring.
Pests & diseases: Few.
Storage: Best not to disturb bulbs planted in the ground. Grow in containers if they need to be protected from cold.

Schizostylis illustrates the difficulty of identifying and using bulbs by their common names. It and *Clivia* are both called *Kaffir lily.* Both come from South Africa, have long leaves and many, scarlet flowers to a stem. Aside from these similarities, they are as different as you can imagine. See description of *Clivia,* page 78.

Schizostylis coccinea has numerous, 2-inch, scarlet flowers in a raceme on a 24-inch stem. The star-shaped flowers open flat near the stem. Cool temperatures prolong bloom. Swordlike foliage is reminiscent of *Gladiolus.* It is a good cut flower, lasting more than a week.

Schizostylis coccinea is grown in the ground in Zones 8 to 10. In nature, it grows in a peaty, damp soil along river banks where the rhizome is able to spread. To plant, cover the rhizome with 1/2 to 1 inch of soil. After flowering, allow plant to rest, giving occasional water until spring. If necessary, divide in spring into clusters of five or six shoots.

Scilla
Squill, Bluebell

Family: Liliaceae.
Native to: Africa, Europe and Asia.
Bulb type: True bulb.
Bloom season & length: Spring for several weeks. A few species bloom in fall.
Colors: Blue, white, pink and lavender.
Height: 6 to 12 inches.
Planting time: Fall.
Planting depth: Under 2 inches of soil.
Soil: Sandy loam.
Water: Keep moist during growing season.
Fertilizer: Not required.
Spacing: 6 to 8 inches.
Exposure: Filtered shade.
Propagation: Summer, from bulbs around mother bulb.
Pests & diseases: Few.
Storage: Can be left undisturbed, except for *S. peruviana,* which should be protected from freezing.

Scilla bifolia is a native of the lower slopes of central European mountains. It blooms early just as the snow recedes, producing 4 to 8, hyacinthlike flowers of intense blue. It prefers a cool or cold climate, and grows as far north as Canada. In mild areas such as Zones 9 and 10, it is difficult if not impossible to establish.

Scilla siberica is a related bulb with open, blue flowers. It is a little easier to grow, but also prefers a cold climate.

Scilla peruviana, from the Mediterranean region, is different. It is a large bulb, and does well only in Zones 9 and 10. Flowers are much showier. There may be 60 or more on a leafless stem that rises 1 foot high from a rosette of thick, green leaves. The purple-blue flowers have white anthers and form a cone shape. A white form is also available. In cold-winter areas, they can be grown as handsome container plants. They have the reputation of blooming every other year, but they multiply rapidly.

Cover *Scilla bifolia* and *S. siberica* with 2 to 3 inches of soil. Plant in sun or light shade. *S. peruviana* is tolerant of light shade. Cover with 2 to 3 inches of soil. All prefer loamy soil with good drainage.

See *Endymion,* page 91, for plants known as *Scilla campanulata* or *S. non-scripta.*

Sinningia and Smithiantha
Gloxinia, Temple bells

Family: Gesneriaceae.
Native to: Mexico and Brazil.
Bulb type: *Sinningia*—Tuber; *Smithiantha*—scaly rhizome.
Bloom season & length: *Sinningia*—summer for 5 weeks; *Smithiantha*—fall and winter.
Colors: *Sinningia*—red, white, pink, lavender and purple. *Smithiantha*—red, pink, orange, yellow and white.
Height: *Sinningia*—1 foot; *Smithiantha*—8 inches to 2 feet
Planting time: *Sinningia*—spring or summer; *Smithiantha*—summer
Planting depth: *Sinningia*—flush with soil surface; *Smithiantha*—cover with 1 inch soil.
Soil: Equal parts of leaf mold, peat moss and sand.
Water: Keep moist during the growing season.
Fertilizer: Monthly with house plant fertilizer.
Spacing: 1 foot.
Exposure: Bright shade, humidity.
Propagation: Leaf cuttings; *Sinningia*—division of tuber; *Smithiantha*—divide rhizome.
Pests & diseases: Mites.
Storage: Leave in pots.

Sinningia and *Smithiantha* are both gesneriads from the Western Hemisphere. They both grow under the same conditions. *Sinningia,* commonly called *Gloxinia,* is grown for its gorgeous flowers. It is usually considered a house plant, but it is easy to grow outdoors, much like a tuberous begonia. It normally does well in Zone 10 and the coastal areas of Zone 9. Compared to the relatively small stature of the plant, the bell-shaped flowers are huge—3 to 5 inches across.

Hybridization and improvements in cultivars continue, but the basic varieties of the 1890s remain the most popular: 'Blanche de Meru', rose with white throat; 'Emperor Frederick', scarlet with white border; 'Emperor William', violet with white border; 'Etoile de Feu', brilliant red; 'Mount Blanc', pure white and 'Hollywood', purple.

Buell's greenhouses in Connecticut grow and distribute some of the more unusual *Sinningias.* Some are shaped like slippers, with extra-large flowers. Others, referred to as *tigrinea,* are spotted or netted with blue, pink or red on a white background. The fuzzy leaves

Sinningia speciosa

Sparaxis hybrid

Streptanthera cuprea

are propagated the same as African violets. The stalk is inserted up to the base of the leaf in sandy compost. It is then placed in a warm, shady spot. After leaves root, they can be transplanted into individual pots.

Sinningias prefer a loose, fast-draining, house-plant soil mix. They are striking in a coastal rock garden where protected from wind and sun. The more light they receive, the better the flower quality.

Place only one tuber in a 6-inch pot. Plant so top of tuber is flush with the soil surface. Feed monthly or every other week with a diluted solution of liquid fertilizer. This produces lush foliage and large flowers. When blooming stops, withhold water and fertilizer for a couple of months to provide a rest period. Gloxinias can be brought into bloom any time of the year depending on when they are started.

Smithiantha, common name temple bells, has a spike of red to yellow, drooping, tubular flowers arranged on an 18-inch stem. Interesting, heart-shaped leaves form a cluster at the base. It is related to *Sinningia,* although it is not quite as spectacular. Culture is the same. Some varieties have dark foliage and showy scarlet flowers.

Sparaxis, Streptanthera and Tritonia

Family: Iridaceae.
Native to: South Africa.
Bulb type: Corm.
Bloom season & length: Spring for several weeks.
Colors: Red, yellow, orange, salmon, white and mauve.
Height: 12 to 18 inches.
Planting time: Fall.
Planting depth: 1 inch of soil over corm.
Soil: Sandy loam.
Water: Necessary only during the growing season.
Fertilizer: Moderate amounts only.
Spacing: 2 inches.
Exposure: Full sun.
Propagation: Often self-sows or by cormlets around base.
Pests & diseases: Few.
Storage: Keep on dry side during summer. Does not have to be dug or divided.

These three bulbs have been grouped together because all are about the same height, similar in appearance, have the same cultural requirements and originate in South Africa. They seem to differ primarily in the color of their flowers. All are charming bulbs deserving greater attention.

Sparaxis and *Streptanthera* species are so similar in appearance that only an expert could tell them apart. One clue is the fact that the anthers of *Streptanthera* are slightly twisted. The anthers of *Sparaxis* are straight. Flowers come in bright shades of orange, red, scarlet, white, yellow, copper, maroon and cerise. They often have black or purple centers, held on stems 9 to 12 inches high. Flowers are long lasting in the garden and make excellent cut flowers. Bulbs labeled as *Sparaxis* are most likely hybrids between the two. They hybridize easily.

Although similar, *Tritonia crocata* has an entirely different appearance due to the pastel colors of the flowers—shades of salmon, coral, peach, pink, orange and creamy yellow. Petals are often transparent near the center, which adds to their soft appearance.

All three bulbs are grown outdoors in Zones 9 and 10. They are especially well adapted to the dry summers of California and multiply easily. Plants are rugged and can compete with tree roots for space and nutrients as long as they receive sun. Plant 1 inch or more deep in soil with good drainage. Make sure bulbs receive plenty of water while actively growing.

All do well in pots. Plant a dozen or more bulbs in an 8-inch container. Use any soil with good drainage. After foliage dies down, place containers in a dry place for a summer rest. They multiply rapidly and can be separated the third year.

Sprekelia formosissima
Aztec lily

Family: Amaryllidaceae.
Native to: Mexico.
Bulb type: True bulb.
Bloom season & length: Late spring. Some cultivars are almost everblooming.
Colors: Bright red.
Height: 12 to 15 inches.
Planting time: Early spring after last frost.
Planting depth: Neck of bulb must be at soil surface.
Soil: Not fussy, but needs good drainage.
Water: Heavily during the growing season.
Fertilizer: Light applications of complete fertilizer.
Spacing: 6 inches.
Exposure: Full sun to half shade.
Propagation: From small bulbs that form around base.
Pests & disease: Snails and slugs. Mealybugs at base of leaves.
Storage: North of Zone 9, dig and store in dry location.

If you seek the unusual, try planting *Sprekelia formosissima.* The Aztec lily, native to Mexico, has bright red, 6-inch flowers that resemble a waxy orchid. Stems are usually short, but gradually become taller as the plants multiply—they have to reach above the foliage in search of sunlight. The strap-shaped leaves may be evergreen in mild climates.

Sprekelia is related to *Hippeastrum,* the Dutch amaryllis. Growth requirements are the same. You can encourage it to bloom more than once during the spring and summer. Plant it where it receives a half day to full day of sun. Allow a dry period after bloom, followed by regular watering.

Aztec lily is grown as far north as Zone 8, in areas where the temperature does not dip below 20F (−7C). Given the best conditions, it multiplies into a large group. It is content in a small container, and makes a dramatic pot plant. Fertilize lightly every month during the growing season. In cold areas, store plants in pots out of freezing temperatures.

Tritonia crocata

Sprekelia formosissima

Tigridia pavonia

Trillium grandiflorum

Tigridia
Tiger flower, Shell flower

Family: Iridaceae.
Native to: Mexico.
Bulb type: Bulb.
Bloom season & length: Summer for many weeks.
Colors: Yellow, orange, scarlet, pink, cream and lilac.
Height: 18 to 24 inches.
Planting time: Spring.
Planting depth: 1 to 3 inches of soil over top of bulb.
Soil: Sandy loam.
Water: During the growing season.
Fertilizer: Light applications only.
Spacing: 5 inches.
Exposure: Full sun.
Propagation: Small bulbs beside mother bulb. Seeds.
Pests & diseases: Snails, spider mites.
Storage: North of Zone 7, dig and store in dry peat moss or vermiculite.

Tigridia pavonia, commonly known as the *Mexican shell flower,* has three large petals spread out from the cup to form a flower 5 to 6 inches across. As a result of hybridization, many color variations are available, including white, yellow, orange, scarlet, crimson and rose. Many are bicolored. Those of the Immaculata strain are a single color without spots. The showy flowers last only one day but are replaced by others from buds along the stem. Leaves are sword-shaped and pleated.

Tigridias are grown outdoors, and can be left in the the ground as far north as Zone 5. They are more reliable from Zone 7 southward. They prefer rich, sandy soil and adequate moisture while growing. Cover corms with 1 to 3 inches of soil. In warm, arid regions, afternoon shade is beneficial. In these regions, they may also be attacked by red spider mites—pests easily controlled with a systemic insecticide such as Orthene. The bulbs multiply rapidly, but do not separate them until just before planting time. *Tigridias* are easy to grow from seeds and often bloom the first year if started early in the season.

Trillium grandiflorum
Wake robin

Family: Liliaceae.
Native to: North America and Asia.
Bulb type: Short, thick rootstock.
Bloom season & length: Spring for several weeks.
Colors: White, yellow, green, pink, purple and maroon.
Height: 6 to 18 inches.
Planting time: Summer.
Planting depth: 1 to 2 inches of soil over rootstock.
Soil: Moist and rich.
Water: Keep moist.
Fertilizer: In spring.
Spacing: 1 foot.
Exposure: Shade.
Propagation: By division and seeds.
Pests & diseases: Few.
Storage: Replant immediately.

Trillium grandiflorum, wake robin, is the most common species, growing wild from Quebec to North Carolina. This member of the lily family grows from a rhizomatous rootstock. In a wooded area it makes a delightful ground cover, increasing slowly year by year.

It bears three, broad, pale-green leaves, with a 3-inch white flower sitting in the center—all on a stem 1 foot high. The flower blooms at the end of spring. Other, rarer varieties of *Trillium* species are available in shades of greenish yellow and purple.

Bulbs need a cold winter to survive, so are not grown in Zones 9 and 10.

They grow best in a moist soil rich in compost, preferably in a shaded location. Plant in the fall and do not allow rhizomes to dry out while transplanting.

Tulbaghia
Society garlic

Family: Amaryllidaceae.
Native to: South Africa.
Bulb type: Rhizomatous rootstock.
Bloom season & length: *T. fragrans* winter to spring. *Tulbaghia violacea* in early spring to late fall.
Colors: Lavender.
Height: 12 to 18 inches.
Planting time: Any time.
Planting depth: 1 inch.
Soil: Sandy loam.
Water: Drought resistant, but tolerates regular watering.
Fertilizer: Not required.
Spacing: 1 foot.
Exposure: Full sun.
Propagation: From many offsets. Seeds.
Pests & diseases: None.
Storage: Plants are evergreen, so bring indoors in cold areas. Place in sunny window.

Tulbaghias originate in South Africa. They are easy to grow in Zones 9 and 10, and survive an occasional dip in temperatures to 20F($-$7C), rebounding when warm weather arrives. In other parts of the country, they make excellent container plants, and can be brought indoors during cold weather.

Two *Tulbaghia* species are commonly available. Winter-blooming *T. fragrans* has strap-shaped leaves and a 1-foot-high stem topped with an umbel of fragrant, lavender flowers. *T. violacea* is more graceful in appearance with a stem that grows up to 2 feet high. Its individual umbel of flowers is smaller but it makes up for it in quantity, blooming continuously from spring to fall.

Commonly called *society garlic,* new leaves of *Tulbaghia* are used as a substitute for chives. The edible flowers make a decorative addition to salads.

Plant tip of the bulb just under the soil surface in a spot where it will receive some sun. Plants are not fussy about soil and multiply rapidly. Separate planting when it becomes crowded to obtain new starts.

Tulbaghia violacea

Mixed border of *Tulipa* species.

Tulipa
Tulip

Family: Liliaceae.
Native to: Central Asia and Europe.
Bulb type: True bulb.
Bloom season & length: Spring for 6 weeks.
Colors: All except true blue.
Height: 4 to 30 inches.
Planting time: In fall after ground has cooled.
Planting depth: 4 to 8 inches of soil over bulb.
Soil: Sandy loam.
Water: During the growing season.
Fertilizer: Moderate amounts are beneficial.
Spacing: 3 to 6 inches.
Exposure: Full sun or light, filtered shade.
Propagation: Offsets when dug in summer.
Pests & diseases: Aphids, gophers, mice, bacterial rot, mosaic virus and botrytis.
Storage: After summer warmth has passed, which they need to form flowers. Store in cool area until planting.

The tulip is probably the best-known of all bulbs. It is grown all over the world, from the tropics to the arctic. Even where the tulip is not grown, it is known partly through legend and partly from pictures in books and magazines, having made a lasting impression with its brilliant spring display.

From the time the Austrian ambassador brought tulips from Constantinople in 1554, tulips have been exceedingly popular. The sultans of the Ottoman Empire coddled them, and the Dutch and other Europeans were frantic for tulips. At first, they were a hobby of royalty and the rich. Later, from 1634 to 1637, came the bonafide "tulipmania," when bulbs doubled in price from one day to the next. Everyone wanted to get in on this get-rich scheme. People traded horses, carriages, jewelry, loads of wheat and oxen for tulips. Eventually, promissory notes were traded for bulbs. Paper profits were bound to collapse, and did in 1637. However, the tulip has been famous ever since.

Hybridization between tulip species has made classification complicated. To sort out the many kinds of tulips, a classification system was devised jointly by the Royal Horticultural Society of England and the Royal Dutch Bulb Growers Society. This system catalogs descriptions and general use of tulips in shows. The system does not reflect botanical relationships. At present, there are 23 divisions. They are:

DucVanTol Tulips—Early flowering, with short stems and bright flowers. Although still available, they have largely been replaced by single early tulips.

Single Early Tulips—Often used for forcing but also valuable for outdoor planting. 'Couleur Cardinal' is a velvety crimson. 'General De Wet' is orange suffused with gold. 'Keizers Kroon' is a striking variety with bright-scarlet blooms edged in yellow.

Double Early Tulips—Flowers look like small peonies. 'Murillo' and 'Murillo Hybrid' are among the best.

Mendel Tulips—Developed by crossing Darwin tulips with early DucVanTol tulips. Seldom taller than 20 to 30 inches. They flower a little later than DucVantol tulips. 'Athleet' is pure white and a great subject for forcing.

Triumph Tulips—Derived from crossing Single Early Tulips with late-May flowering varieties. Generally,

Classic tulip display at Old Westbury Gardens, Long Island, New York. When viewed from a distance, the effect is spectacular.

Tulips in bloom are outstanding in contrast to lawn.

flowers have more substance and stems are stronger than Mendels. 'Olaf', with fire-engine-red flowers, and 'Aureola', yellow and orange flowers, are often used for forcing and massed in planting beds.

Darwin Tulips—Flowers are cup-shaped with tall stems. This is by far the most popular class. A wide range of colors—white, cream, yellow, deep gold, orange, scarlet, dark red, mauve, lilac, purple and shades of dark and light pink—is another reason why these tulips are so popular. New varieties are constantly replacing old varieties. This is why the tulip you admire this year might not be available next year.

Darwin Hybrid Tulips—This class is created by crossing Darwins with *Tulipa fosterana*. It increases in popularity every year. It includes some of the finest and largest flowers, the result of efforts by Lefeber and Van Tubergen, two of the most important tulip breeders of recent times.

From the Darwins, they get tall stems. From *T. fosterana* they get a large flower and a glowing, scarlet color. Their *T. fosterana* background also tends to make them slightly earlier than the regular Darwins. They are unsurpassed as bedding plants, but are not often used for forcing. The general color range is from scarlet-red to butter-yellow, nowhere near the color choice of regular Darwins, but what is available is magnificent. Fine reds include 'Apeldoorn', 'Franklin Roosevelt', 'General Eisenhower', 'London' and 'Parade'. 'Golden Parade' is a deep yellow with a black center. 'Gudoshnik' is a creamy yellow splashed and flecked with red in great variation.

Breeder Tulips—Characterized by oval flowers, often in bronzy, subdued colors such as brown, purple and violet, with some in terra-cotta and orange.

Lily-flowered Tulips—Distinguished by pointed petals that are often reflexed, bent outward, resulting in an upright, lily shape. Flowers are longer and narrower than Darwins. 'Mariette', bright pink, is a strong grower with long-lasting blooms. 'Queen of Sheba' is a glowing, rusty red with an orange edge. 'White Triumphitor' has an elegant white flower, but not quite as large as the others. 'West Point' is bright yellow with highly reflexed petals.

Cottage Tulips—Late flowering with egg-shaped blooms on long stems. Supposedly developed from tulips found growing in old cottage gardens in Ireland and elsewhere. Those called *viridiflora,* a subspecies, are favorites of flower arrangers, with green feathering on the petals. As with Darwins, new, improved varieties continually replace older ones.

Rembrandt Tulips—Darwin tulips with "broken" or variegated coloring. Because of their fancy markings and feathering, they are often depicted in old paintings. The "breaking" of tulips is believed to be caused by a virus inherited and transmitted to other varieties. Hence, do not plant them with regular tulips.

Bizarre Tulips—Broken breeder or cottage tulips. Striped or marked with brown, maroon, bronze or

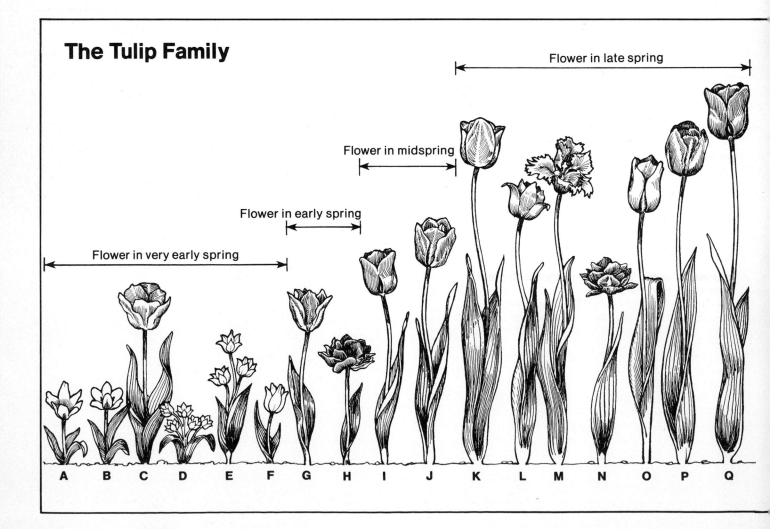

The Tulip Family

Flower in late spring

Flower in midspring

Flower in early spring

Flower in very early spring

A B C D E F G H I J K L M N O P Q

purple, usually on a yellow background.

Bybloemen Tulips—Broken breeder or cottage tulips. Striped or marked with rose, pink, violet or purple on a white background.

Parrot Tulips—Large, striking flowers with long, twisted and cut petals. Because of their large, unwieldy flowers, they are best grown in pots where they can be protected from the elements. A subgroup known as *fringed tulips* have a narrow edge of fringe on the edge of each petal. They do not have the green markings associated with parrots.

Double Late Tulips—An interesting novelty, flowers of some varieties look almost like small peonies.

The remaining divisions are devoted to species and hybrids of species. See page 152.

Growing tulips is not that difficult, but can be confusing because of the conflicting opinions as to the best method. All experts agree, however, that tulips are not fussy about soil as long as the drainage is good. Bulbs should be planted 6 to 8 inches deep. In Holland, tulips grown for cut flowers are planted in flats 4 or 5 inches deep with the tops of the bulbs showing at the surface. But planting deeply in the garden is beneficial. Planted too close to the surface, bulbs break up into many little bulbs that do not flower the next year.

Tulips are generally planted in a location where they have plenty of sun, yet this is not a hard and fast rule. At Keukenhof, the Dutch Bulb Growers Display Garden, they are planted under deciduous trees.

Unlike hyacinths, tulip bulbs do not contain all the nourishment required to grow for the following year. They cannot be grown in water alone. Tulips do not benefit from an early planting. The soil should be cool before planting, especially in areas with warm or mild climates. Do not plant tulips in southern California until after Thanksgiving. Planting can be delayed right up to February. Store bulbs in a cool place such as the vegetable bin of your refrigerator until time to plant. Don't allow bulbs to freeze.

When growing tulips in containers, keep them out of direct sunshine. The sun warms the container soil, which in effect signals bulbs that spring has arrived. Soon after, up go the flowers, but before an adequate root system has had time to develop. This is one of the most common reasons why container tulips flower poorly. The longer the soil can be kept cool, the better and more expansive the root system. Eventually, nature takes over and warms the soil. When the shoots appear, move pots to a place with light shade.

Tulips are favorites for forcing. A step-by-step guide to forcing is shown on page 36.

As soon as petals fall, remove flowerheads so strength from leaves and stems goes back to the bulb.

Tulips can be propagated from offsets, which require two to three years before blooming. Plant bulbs in sandy compost in fall. Do not allow them to dry out. Feed with a diluted, liquid fertilizer once a week to encourage them to reach blooming size.

A— *Tulipa greigii*
B— *Tulipa kaufmanniana*
C— *Tulipa fosterana*
D— *Tulipa tarda*
E— *Tulipa praestans*
F— *Tulipa eichleri*
G—Single Early. Hardy. Use in beds or borders.
H—Double Early. Similar to singles, but tends to bloom earlier. Not as graceful as singles.
I—Mendel. Hybrid of Darwin and early Dutch types.
J—Triumph. Hybrid of early singles and Darwin types.
K—Darwin Hybrid. Newest long-stem tulip. Large flowers are solid color.
L—Lily Flowered. Petals turn back, resembling lilies.
M—Parrot. Natural *sport*, mutation, of common garden varieties. Petals are fringed with green. Stems are often weak.
N—Double Late or Peony Flowered. Flowers resemble peonies. Actually a type of double triumph.
O—Cottage. Long, flexible stems. Flowers with long, pointed petals.
P—Breeder. Upright, stiff with stout stems. Cup-shaped flowers typically have artistic blending of bronzes and browns over brilliant solid colors.
Q—Darwin. First introduced in 1899. Strong stems, large flowers. Use for borders and arrangements.

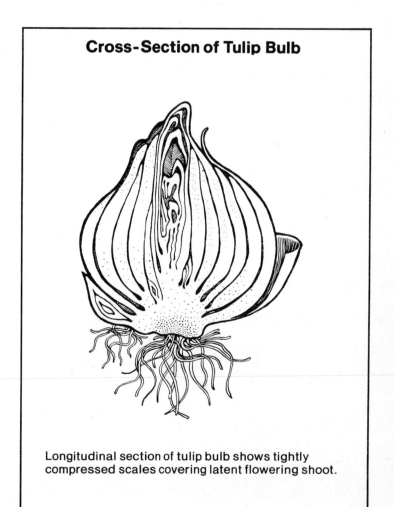

Cross-Section of Tulip Bulb

Longitudinal section of tulip bulb shows tightly compressed scales covering latent flowering shoot.

Gallery of Tulips

'Perry Como'

'Unsurpassable'

'Paul Richter'

'Golden Apeldoorn'

'Big Chief'

'Renown'

'Estella Rijnveld'

'Orange King'

'Golden Springtime'

'Sunkist'

'Mariette'

'Gudoshnik'

'Georgette'

'White Triumphetor'

'Aristocrat'

'Queen of Sheba'

'Jewel of Spring'

'Kurobegawa'

SPECIES TULIPS

Long-stemmed tulips such as the Darwin, lily-flowered and cottage varieties bring elegance and color to the spring garden. But *species tulips,* the tulips that grow naturally in Asia Minor and Europe, are just as eye-catching in a charming, informal way. Many of the wild tulips are small enough to use in a rock garden or between steppingstones. Some, such as *Tulipa clusiana,* the candy-stick tulip, may spread through the garden and bloom as if they were wildflowers. The biggest advantage of species tulips is that many, although not all, are more robust and dependable than hybrids. They return year after year, and sometimes multiply in the process.

There are many species of tulips. We cannot possibly do them justice here. Following are some of the more outstanding.

Tulipa acuminata is distinctly different from other tulips. It has long, narrow, slightly twisted petals of red and yellow. Some doubt exists as to whether it actually is a species tulip, but it is presently classified as such. It grows wild from the Pyrenees to the Levant, on the eastern Mediterranean, but it is not as rugged as some of the other species.

Tulipa batalinii is a small tulip on a 6-inch stem. Flowers are the most true yellow of all tulips, both outside and inside. 'Bright Gem' is a hybrid, crossed with *T. linifolia* to produce lovely, apricot-colored flowers.

Tulipa clusiana, 'Candy Stick' or 'Lady Tulip', is graceful, with a stem over 12 inches high. The star-shaped flowers are pink and white with a deep purple base. They make excellent cut flowers. Leaves are often bordered with a band of red. This makes them easy to identify when not in bloom. It prefers a hot, fairly dry summer. The small, 1/2-inch bulb can be planted 5 to 7 inches deep. *T. clusiana* sets few seeds but spreads rapidly by *droopers,* bulbs formed at the end of the root. Droopers take several years to bloom.

Tulipa clusiana chrysantha, sometimes listed as *Tulipa stellata* var. *chrysantha,* is from Afghanistan. It resembles *Tulipa clusiana,* but grows on an 8-inch stem. The inner petals are yellow and the outer petals are flushed with pink.

Tulipa eichleri is from southern Russia and Turkestan. Large, scarlet flowers with a yellow and black center appear on 12-inch stems. Gray-green leaves are waved at the margin. It is effective when planted in groups.

Tulipa fosterana from Iran is a striking tulip and a parent of many Darwin hybrids. The Fosterana Class includes many hybrids. 'Red Emperor' is the best known. 'Juan' matches the orange and yellow shades of a *Clivia miniata* exactly. They need a warm, dry summer to naturalize.

Tulipa greigii, noted for its variegated foliage, is also from Iran. It has a large flower for a species tulip, so it

Tulipa clusiana, candystick or lady tulip, naturalizes easily in mild-climate regions. It spreads by *droopers,* root ends that swell and develop into new bulbs.

Tulips, both species and hybrids, are well adapted to *forcing* in containers. See page 35.

is often used for hybridizing. The extremely large 'Oriental Splendor', with its red and yellow flowers, is a show-stopper at the Keukenhof gardens in Holland. Equally fine is the rich red 'Margaret Herbst', also named 'Royal Splendor'. Other named but smaller varieties in this class include: 'Cape Cod', yellow and bronze, 'Plaisir', vermillion with creamy yellow margins, and 'Red Riding Hood', a brilliant red.

Tulipa kaufmanniana is a low-growing variety with large flowers. It has been used a great deal in hybridizing. Many hybrids have names associated with music, such as 'Berlioz', clear yellow; 'Fritz Kreisler', light pink with yellow center; 'Johann Strauss', creamy white with red flush on the exterior; and 'Mendelssohn', large, creamy white with rose on the exterior. These bulbs can be left in the ground undisturbed for years. When they receive good soil drainage and summer warmth, they multiply by offsets.

Tulipa linifolia and *T. maximowiczii* are two similar species. *T. maximowiczii* blooms about two weeks earlier. Flowers are clear, waxy scarlet, held on 9-inch stems. It is excellent for rock gardens.

Tulipa praestans is outstanding, with each large bulb producing 4 to 6 flowers over a long period each spring. The best known is 'Fusilier', with intense scarlet flowers. It grows about 10 inches high and is showy in a flower bed or rock garden.

Tulipa saxatilis, from Crete, has distinctive, broad, glossy, light-green leaves. It often has more than 1 cup-shaped flower for each 7-inch stem. Flowers appear in shades of pink with butter-yellow at the center. Plant in a rock garden with good soil drainage in a sunny location. It multiplies by stolons.

Tulipa sprengeri is the last to bloom, often as late as June. It is unique in that it grows well in partial shade. Large, uniform, scarlet flowers appear on 12-inch stems. May naturalize in conditions similar to its original home, the wooded mountains of Turkey.

Tulipa sylvestris is a native of England and Iran. Yellow flowers appear on 15-inch stems. This species is well worth growing but don't plant it with daffodils. The flowers are the same color, and bloom at the same time, so the two bulbs blend together. The small bulb should be planted 7 inches deep. Left undisturbed, this species multiplies by stolons.

In order to produce flowers, species tulips need sun to warm the soil during the summer. Species tulips are adaptable to various soils, but they must have good drainage. They should also be planted deeply—more than twice the depth of the bulb. An extreme example is *Tulipa boeotica*. It is a small bulb that is planted 10 inches deep. Another advantage of deep planting, which is also true for daffodils, is that more energy is directed to the forming of individual bulbs. Shallow planting promotes development of little bulbs that produce fewer flowers.

Tulipa acuminata, horned tulip, is a novelty with its extremely long, thin petals.

Tulipa saxatilis is noted for its wide, attractive, apple-green leaves.

Urginea maritima

Urginea maritima

Urginea maritima
Sea onion

Family: Liliaceae.
Native to: North Africa, Mediterranean region, Europe and India.
Bulb type: True bulb.
Bloom season & length: Late summer for many weeks.
Colors: White.
Height: 4 to 6 feet.
Planting time: Summer.
Planting depth: Near soil surface.
Soil: Good drainage is required.
Water: Regular during the growing season.
Fertilizer: Not needed.
Spacing: 1 foot.
Exposure: Full sun.
Propagation: From offsets and seeds.
Pests & diseases: None.
Storage: Best left undisturbed.

This native of coastal North Africa grows among sand and rocks. For gardeners in warm areas that cannot grow *Eremurus,* foxtail lily, *Urginea* is a similar substitute.

It blooms in the late summer, starting with a leafless stalk, rising 4 to 6 feet high. Later, over half the stem is covered with white flowers striped in green. After the flowers are gone, rosettes of leaves appear. Commonly called *sea onion* or *sea squill,* the vapor from a cut bulb will bring tears to the eyes, just like an onion.

Handle the 6-inch-wide bulbs with care, preferably using gloves. In southern California, the bulbs work themselves up out of the soil so that half of the bulb is exposed. Zone recommendations are not defined, but it is commonly grown in southern England, planted 6 inches deep.

Vallota speciosa
Scarborough lily

Family: Amaryllidaceae.
Native to: South Africa.
Bulb type: True bulb.
Bloom season & length: Summer for several weeks.
Colors: Coral-red. A rare white form is also available.
Height: 15 inches.
Planting time: Spring.
Planting depth: Bury bulbs with tip at soil surface.
Soil: Sandy loam.
Water: Moist during growing season. Almost dry in winter.
Fertilizer: Feed monthly with complete fertilizer during growing season.
Spacing: 1 foot.
Exposure: Bright shade.
Propagation: Separation of offsets.
Pests & diseases: Narcissus fly.
Storage: Best not disturbed. Plants grow best when rootbound.

This genus has only one species— *Vallota speciosa,* the Scarborough lily. It is a popular house plant in England and Portugal. In the United States, it grows outdoors in Zones 9 and 10. Like its relative, *Hippeastrum,* it does well in small pots. In late summer or fall, it sends up 9- to 15-inch stems crowned with an umbel of funnel-shaped, coral-orange flowers. From 3 to 10 flowers are arranged on each stem. White and pink varieties are sometimes available. Foliage is an attractive glossy green.

As a house plant, give *Vallota speciosa* a small pot, allowing about 2 inches of space on either side of the bulb. Use a potting soil that drains well. The top and neck of the bulb should be left exposed. Apply diluted liquid fertilizer at weekly intervals after growth begins through June. Keep soil on the moist side from June to September, and barely damp from October to March.

Midsummer, before bulbs bloom, is the best time to remove the small bulblets that form around the mother bulb. Plant these in separate containers for new stock. Be careful when handling roots at planting time. In Zones 9 and 10, plant bulbs outdoors in a lightly shaded location as they become available.

Veltheimia

Family: Liliaceae.
Native to: South Africa.
Bulb type: True bulb.
Bloom season & length: Early spring for 3 to 4 weeks.
Colors: Usually pink, sometimes white or yellow. Height 15 inches.
Planting time: Fall.
Planting depth: 1 inch of soil over bulb.
Soil: Sandy loam.
Water: During the growing season.
Fertilizer: Lightly after bloom with a complete fertilizer.
Spacing: 1 foot.
Exposure: Light, filtered shade.
Propagation: By separation of small bulbs at base.
Pests & diseases: Few.
Storage: Best left undisturbed in pot.

Veltheimia is best planted in containers. The subtle colors of the flowers—pale pink, shaded with green at the edges—are almost lost in the outdoor garden. Wavy, dark-green, shiny leaves are attractive all year. By the end of January, 15-inch flower stems rise from the center. At the top, drooping flowers appear around the stem. Varieties with white and yellow flowers are available.

Veltheimia bracteata is from South Africa. It withstands a sudden temperature drop to 25F(−4C), but prolonged cold is damaging. It is a handsome house plant in leaf or flower, and makes an unusual, and attractive cut flower.

Plant bulbs in fall with the tip at the soil surface. They prefer a sandy loam that is rich in compost and well draining. Water sparingly until growth appears. Divide when plants become crowded. An unusual method of propagation is to take a leaf and insert it upright into a mixture composed of half sand and half peat. Increase the humidity around plants and mist leaves. In about 8 weeks, a small bulb forms at the base of the leaf. When the leaf dies back, the little bulb can be grown as an offset.

Vallota speciosa

Veltheimia viridifolia

Watsonia pyramidata

Watsonia

Family: Iridaceae.
Native to: South Africa.
Bulb type: Corm.
Bloom season & length: Late spring for several weeks.
Colors: Pink, red, white, salmon and lavender.
Height: 3 to 4 feet.
Planting time: Fall.
Planting depth: 3 to 4 inches of soil over corm.
Soil: Sandy loam is ideal but almost any soil is acceptable.
Water: During the growing season.
Fertilizer: Light applications only.
Spacing: 4 inches.
Exposure: Full or part sun.
Propagation: From cormels that form on base.
Pests & diseases: Few.
Storage: The same as for *Gladiolus*.

Watsonia species comprise a large group of South-African bulbs. They grow from corms and are closely related to *Gladiolus*. They are as good a cut flower as *Gladiolus*. Though not as showy, they are more graceful and less formal in appearance. 'Mrs. Bullard's White', a pure-white cultivar, is a favorite of flower arrangers.

Watsonias are well adapted to mild areas. Plantings eventually spread to form large clumps. Hybrids, which grow up to 3 feet tall, are available in white, pink, rose, lavender, orchid and mauve. Some of the evergreen species produce salmon, coral and orange flowers. Of the many wild species, *Watsonia beatricis* is perhaps most desirable. It is evergreen and grows 3 to 4 feet tall. Flowers are in various shades of orange and coral.

In Zones 8 to 10, corms can remain in the ground. They usually multiply. Upright foliage should be removed as it.turns brown. North of Zone 8, they are treated the same as *Gladiolus*. See page 99.

Zantedeschia
Calla lily

Family: Araceae.
Native to: South Africa.
Bulb type: Rhizome.
Bloom season & length: Spring and early summer for several months.
Colors: White, yellow and pink.
Height: 1 to 4 feet.
Planting time: Fall to spring.
Planting depth: 1 to 2 inches of soil over rhizome.
Soil: Sandy loam.
Water: *Z. aethiopica* will grow in wet soil. Others need good drainage.
Fertilizer: Occasional light applications.
Spacing: 1 foot.
Exposure: *Z. aethiopica* accepts shade. Others need sun.
Propagation: By dividing the rhizomes, fall through spring.
Pests & diseases: Few.
Storage: *Z. aethiopica* should not be out of ground any longer than necessary or bulbs dry out. Store in their pots in cold areas.

Commonly known as *calla lily, Zantedeschia* species are widely grown in mild-winter areas. Indoors, they are handsome potted plants. The white calla, *Z. aethiopica,* is an attractive and long-lasting cut flower and is the most adaptable. It grows with little water, or in moist soil at the edge of a pond. It blooms well in light shade or in full sun if the water supply is adequate. The white

Zantedeschia elliottiana

calla has attractive, evergreen foliage and makes a handsome landscape plant for large areas.

Zantedeschia aethiopica has many cultivars to choose from. Some grow only 6 inches high, others reach up to 4 feet high.

Zantedeschia elliottiana, yellow calla, has silver spots on the leaves. It is more fussy about soil and must have good drainage and full sun. It also needs a dry period after bloom when dormant. It grows about 2 feet high. *Z. albomaculata* is similar to yellow calla, but with white flowers.

Zantedeschia rehmannii, pink calla, is even shorter than yellow calla, with smaller flowers that show just above the leaves. It also goes dormant after blooming.

Hybrids between these species are available.

In Zones 8 to 10, callas remain in the ground throughout the year. Cover them with 1 to 2 inches of soil. Fertilizer, although not required, is beneficial. To grow as house plants, pot rhizomes of *Zantedeschia aethiopica* in fall. Keep barely damp until the first shoots appear. *Z. elliottiana, Z. albomaculata* and *Z. rehmannii* are available in stores in the spring. They need more light than *Z. aethiopica.*

Zephyranthes
Zephyr flower, Fairy lily

Family: Amaryllidaceae.
Native to: Warm areas of Western Hemisphere.
Bulb type: True bulb.
Bloom season & length: Summer and fall.
Colors: White, yellow, pink and rose.
Height: 5 to 8 inches.
Planting time: Spring.
Planting depth: 1 inch of soil over bulb.
Soil: Sandy loam.
Water: During the growing season.
Fertilizer: Not required.
Spacing: 2 inches.
Exposure: Full sun to half-day sun.
Propagation: By offsets, dug and separated in early spring.
Pests & diseases: Snails and narcissus fly.
Storage: Best left undisturbed, but can be dug and stored in dry peat moss or vermiculite during winter.

Zephyranthes is a charming member of the *Amaryllis* family. These low-growing plants resemble summer crocus, with only one small flower per stem. All species are natives of the Western Hemisphere and are closely related to *Habranthus* species. Many, such as *Z. candida,* have abundant leaves when in bloom. They have been hybridized so that varieties are available in shades of white, yellow, pink, rose and apricot. They are effective as edgings, in rock gardens and between steppingstones—anywhere a small plant is desired. Because of their size, they look best in groups.

Zephyranthes candida is the most common and most cold-hardy. Flowers are white with bright-yellow anthers above grasslike leaves.

Zephyranthes grandiflora has large, rosy pink flowers on a 1-foot stem.

Zephyranthes tubiflora, a deep-orange species from Peru. Flowers are 2 inches across.

Zephyranthes are grown outdoors from Zone 7 southward. They need at least a half-day of sun. Cover bulbs with 1 inch of soil. They are not particular as to soil quality. Bait for snails and slugs.

Zantedeschia rehmannii

Zephyranthes grandiflora

Glossary

Acid—A pH value below 7.0. The opposite of alkaline. Acid soil has a pH of 4.0 to 7.0. It is common where there is an abundance of peat, leaf mold and humus. See Alkaline and Neutral.

Alkaline—A pH value over 7.0. The opposite of acid. Alkaline soil has a pH of 7.0 to 9.0. Common in chalky or lime soils. Best for many bulbs.

Anther—The pollen-bearing end of the *stamen,* the male organ of a flower. The anther usually protrudes from the center of the flower. See Stamen.

Axil—The angle formed at the base of the leaf and stem.

Basal Plate—The lower, usually round surface of a bulb from which the roots grow.

Basal Rot—Rot of a bulb's basal plate. Most common in daffodils and lilies. It usually kills bulb.

Bulb—An underground, round, fleshy, storage organ, derived from the modified base of a stem. It consists of a basal plate, with modified, scalelike leaves and a bud in the center. This is the botanical true bulb. *Corms, tubers, tuberous roots* and *rhizomes* are also commonly called *bulbs.*

Bulbil—A small bulb that forms in the axil of a leaf on the stem of a bulbous plant.

Bulblet—A small, offset bulb, usually produced on the underground stem of the parent bulb.

Bulb Scale—One layer of a bulb.

Clone—Plants derived from division of an original bulb, duplicating it in all respects. For example, all 'King Alfred' daffodils originate from a single bulb.

Contractile Roots—Roots of some bulbs that contract to move the bulb slowly downward to the bulb's proper depth.

Corm—A hard, compressed piece of stemlike tissue bearing roots from below and a shoot above. Some have an outer covering like a true bulb, but corms do not have inner scales. Examples are *Crocus, Gladiolus* and *Freesia.*

Cormels or Cormlets—Small corms produced by a parent corm, usually around the base. They produce plants identical to the parent.

Cultivar—A plant produced by breeding, usually by man. A cultivar can also be created naturally. Example: *Narcissus* 'February Gold'.

Cup—A part of a flower. Example: a cup exists between the petals and stamens of daffodils.

Drainage—The movement of water downward through soil. If soil is saturated with water, air is forced out and roots perish from lack of oxygen.

Drift—A natural, free-form way to plant bulbs. Drifts imitate the look of bulbs growing in the wild.

Fall—The outer and lower perianth segments of an *Iris.*

Family—A group of plants with common characteristics. Example: The Amaryllidaceae family includes *Amaryllis, Narcissus, Hippeastrum, Clivia* and *Crinum.* See Genus.

Fungicide—A chemical used to prevent fungi from infecting plants.

Genus—A group of plant species that are structurally related. A genus is a subordinate member of a family. Example: *Tulipa.* See Family, Species.

Hybrid—The result of a cross of two parent plants, often two different species.

Inorganic Fertilizer—Simple mineral salts that furnish nutrients to plants. Example: sulfate of ammonia.

Leaf Mold—Decomposed leaves valuable for mulching and improving soil quality.

Loam—A soil high in organic matter. It is easy to work and has good drainage.

Neutral—Soil that is in the neutral range between acid and alkaline on the pH scale.

Offset—Small bulb that is produced from mature bulb. They can be separated and planted.

Organic Fertilizer—Nutrient-containing material originating from living matter, including animal manures and animal byproducts. Examples: blood meal, cottonseed meal and steer manure.

Ovary—The lower part of the pistil, female part of a flower, that contains the seeds.

Pedicel—The usually short stalk that supports a flower from the stem. Examples: *Agapanthus* and lilies.

Perianth—The outer, non-sexual parts of a flower, including the petals, or sepals or both. Used to attract pollinators such as bees.

Pistil—Female parts of the flower made up of *ovary, style* and *stigma.*

Pollen—Grains that are the transposable male elements of a flower.

Pollination—Placement of pollen on the receptive surface of the stigma. With nature, it is often done by insects. Pollination can be done under controlled situations to produce hybrids.

Reflexed—A flower petal that is bent outward or backward. Example: *Tigridia.*

Rhizome—A swollen, creeping underground stem.

Scale—A thin, membranous part of a bulb composed of modified leaves. Example: lily. Not to be confused with the insect pest *scale,* which has a hard shell and attaches itself to the stems and leaves of other plants.

Sepals—Leaflike structures that enclose the flower in bud stage. See Perianth.

Species—A group of plants having similar, distinctive characteristics. A species is a subordinate member of a genus. See Genus.

Stamen—The male organ of the flower, which bears pollen. It consists of a stalk—the *filament.*

Stigma—The top of the female organ of a flower. When sticky, it receives pollen from the anther.

Stolon—In bulbs, an underground, horizontal stem that bears additional or small bulbs or stems.

Strain—A group of hybrid plants producing offspring that are more or less true to their parents.

Style—A part of the pistil, the female organ of a flower. It is the elongated section upon which the stigma rests. See Stigma, Pistil.

Systemic—An insecticide or fungicide that penetrates into the inner tissues of a plant. It can be absorbed through roots or leaves. Its effects last longer than non-systemic sprays because it does not wash off.

Tuber—A fleshy, underground stem used for storing food for the plant and for propagation. Example: *Cyclamen.*

Tuberous Root—A fleshy root connected to a stem. To grow, a bud from the stem should be on the root. Example: *Dahlia.*

Tunic—The outer covering of a bulb or corm.

Umbel—A ball-like cluster at the top of a stem. Pedicels of flowers originate from the same point. Examples: *Clivia, Agapanthus.*

Variety—Variations in species that occur in nature. See Species.

Index

Names in italic type are botanical names according to *Hortus Third*, a horticultural reference book. Names in italics enclosed by parentheses are botanical synonyms. Names marked with an asterisk* are botanical synonyms preferred over the listing in *Hortus Third*. This book's organization also differs from *Hortus Third* in the case of the *Brodiaeas*. Rather than split these similar plants in three genera as *Hortus* recommends, they are grouped under their old names.

8.281 3-